THE SEXUAL LIFE OF ENGLISH

Next Wave: New Directions in Women's Studies

THE SEXUAL LIFE OF ENGLISH

Languages of Caste and Desire

in Colonial India

Shefali Chandra

DUKE UNIVERSITY PRESS

DURHAM & LONDON

2012

© 2012 Duke University Press
All rights reserved.

Designed by Katy Clove
Typeset in Dante by
Keystone Typesetting, Inc.
Library of Congress Cataloging-in-Publication Data
appear on the last printed page of this book.

For my Ai, Lilla Wagle Dhume
And as always, for Shailaja and Ramesh Chandra

CONTENTS

NOTE ON TRANSLITERATION AND SPELLING ix

PART ONE

1. LEARNING GENDER, KNOWING ENGLISH
An Introduction 3

2. "THE PRUDENT AND CAUTIOUS ENGRAFTING OF ENGLISH UPON OUR FEMALE POPULATION" Pedagogy and Performativity 29

3. "THE LANGUAGE OF THE BEDROOM"
Mimicry, Masculinity, and the Sexual Power of English 57

4. "A NEW GENERATION OF HIPLESS AND BREASTLESS WOMEN . . . TO THE FOREFRONT IN EUROPE AND AMERICA" Literature, Social Class, and the Wider World of English 83

PART TWO

5. "I SHALL READ PRETTY ENGLISH STORIES TO MY MOTHER AND TRANSLATE THEM INTO MARATHI FOR HER" Widowhood, Virtue, and the Secularization of Caste 117

6. "WHY HAD I EVER BEGUN TO LEARN ENGLISH?"
Desire, Labor, and the Transregional Orientation of Caste 137

7. DOSEBAI JESSAWALLA AND THE "MARCH OF ADVANCEMENT IN THE FACE OF OBLOQUY" 157

8. EPILOGUE: "I AM AN INDIAN. I HAVE NO LANGUAGE"
Parvatibai Athavale and the Limits to English 175

SALAAMS 191
NOTES 195
BIBLIOGRAPHY 245
INDEX 267

NOTE ON TRANSLITERATION
AND SPELLING

I have refrained from using any conventional style for transliteration of Marathi and Hindi words and phrases. Most names and words are easily recognizable in a simple, anglicized form. I have used identifiable English-language spellings for words from Marathi and other Indian languages that appear frequently, as well as for individuals, places, names, deities, and institutions.

The spelling of certain Marathi place names has increasingly become a matter for debate. For the time period covered in this book, a town will appear in Marathi-language sources as (for instance) Pune and in English-language sources from the same period as Poona. In my own writing, I have referred to the place as Poona, unless the contemporary print source refers to Pune. Similarly, I use Bombay and not Mumbai, unless stated otherwise in the source itself.

PART ONE

I

LEARNING GENDER, KNOWING ENGLISH

An Introduction

In 1995 the Marathi-language playwright and novelist Kiran Nagarkar penned *Ravan and Eddie*, an exhilarating satire on the class, caste, and communal politics of contemporary Bombay city. Nagarkar devoted an entire section of his novel to the mystique of the English language:

There are only two kinds of people in the world. Those who have English and those who don't . . . the haves and the have nots. . . . English is a mantra, a mahamantra. It is an "open sesame" that doesn't open mere doors, it opens up new worlds and allows you to cross over from one universe to another. English makes you tall. If you know English, you can wear a "suit boot," do an electrician's course or take a diploma in radio and refrigeration technology. . . . If you know English, you can ask a girl for a dance. You can lean Eileen Alva against the locked door of the terrace and press against her, squeeze her boobs and kiss her on the mouth, put your tongue inside it while slipping your hand under her dress.[1]

The versatile allure of English, its ability to signify and thus materialize mysterious resources of social mobility, comes alive in these lines. With a few deft strokes, Nagarkar illustrates how the power of English supersedes form or textual identifications, how it exceeds grammatical, linguistic, or literary definitions. It is more complicated than either its colonial past or its ability to ensure social mobility. Most striking, perhaps, is the narrator's reference to Eileen Alva, a signifier that, in the context of Bombay city, suggests the role of sexuality in carving distinctions between religiously marked communities: the Goan Christian girl next door, in the narrator's mind, is both sexually alluring and sexually available. A deliberately vague notion of English thus produces sexual power and is amplified through it. The language is, indeed, an "open sesame." It is a sign that has disciplinary, especially phallocentric, value. Nagarkar exposes the complicities between class and sexual power, between regional culture and religion, and he does so by stressing the centrality of "woman" in cohering otherwise disparate forms of desire. This is the selective, sexual, and symbolic axis upon which Indian English revolves. Himself a bilingual writer, Nagarkar recognizes that language can never be an unmediated mode of communication, or merely a collection of grammatical rules and lexical signs. Rather, he evokes the swirling *world* of English, a historically configured constellation of symbolic practices, expressions, possibilities, and prohibitions; an entire world manifested through social and sexual access and expressed immediately in local, communal terms. Assessments such as Nagarkar's go to the heart of the investigations I undertake here.

The Sexual Life of English traces the indigenization of the colonial language of power, the process by which English became an Indian language. My study breaks with commonsense assumptions that the prevalence of English in India marks the lasting success of British colonial culture, the inevitability of an Anglo-American globalization, or the rise to dominance of a pan-regional and cosmopolitan middle class. Instead, I argue that the English language was disciplined and materialized through the unfolding politics of a rigorously policed and sexualized modernity. No simple story of accelerating numbers, of widening social power, or of a mere rupture from a precolonial past, I argue that it was India's sexual politics that domesticated the authoritative power of English. This was accomplished by an array of social actors: colonial and "native," men, women, students, teachers, and writers alike.[2] They first brought the language to a select group of native women, and then they laid down new demarcations between indigenous and invading cultures, vernacular and English languages, normative and prohibitive sexuality, and the parameters of sexual desire itself. In the process, they universalized upper-caste strictures on knowledge and proliferated discourses on sexuality. The disciplinary power of English, its ability to stake differences between social groups and to produce the consenting Indian subject, was generated by the discourses of sex and gender. The ambition of some men to share the language of power with their women and the vociferous outrage that this provoked within native society consolidated existing social hierarchies and built fresh consensus on caste, sexuality, and knowledge. This magnified distinctions between English and vernacular languages. English became the means by which to convey the symbolic, social, and sexual parameters of native womanhood. In this way it was repeatedly unleashed to assert cultural difference not only from the "West," but from other Indians as well.

Women Make English an Indian Language

The Sexual Life of English emerges from a simple observation: far from widening the reach of English to those castes and classes historically excluded from learning, British India's English-educated subjects taught English to their own women. In doing so, they transformed the language. Bringing English to their wives and daughters, British India's English-educated men successfully secured the language of power within their class and caste location; they turned English toward consolidating, even fixing, the standards of caste, sexuality, and prohibition. The investment in gender enabled some Indians to stake early control over the symbolic power of the language. English and normative sexuality converged, in the process augmenting distinctions between indigenous and foreign, feminine and masculine, labor and knowledge. It was the normative Hindu and upper-class Parsi woman who anchored this selective modernity, and she did so by naturalizing the "regulatory fiction of heterosexuality."[3] This idealized female figure was key to the Indian elite's quest for cultural equivalence with Europe, its distinction from "other" Indians, and its ability to speak in the name of a national commonality. Despite its sexual potency and its bonds with the colonial project, English could and would be subsumed within the gender logic of upper-caste India to augment indigenous power. The history I track here thus demonstrates that far from characterizing the triumph of colonial culture, Indian English is a critical effect of native gender regimes.

Put simply, this book demonstrates how English became an Indian language. That English is fundamentally embedded in the history of modern Indian social stratification is no surprise; how it has become so requires greater scrutiny.[4] I deliberately break with those sociolinguistic theories that maintain the primacy of language in shaping and expressing human culture; rather, my contention is that social context determines the value, reach, and meaning of language. My analysis aligns with poststructuralist, anti-caste, and queer critiques of social power. Following Nagarkar, I maintain that languages are historically shaped signifying practices and not predetermined, transparent, or value-free forms of communication.⁵ "English" is a powerfully ambiguous sign that spans knowledge, literature, desire, fashion, virtue, labor, and sex. Rather than accepting that Indian English is entirely determined by its linguistic structure, or by its origin in colonial policies and literary texts, I pursue "English" to learn what people say it is and what it does.⁶ As becomes evident in the pages of this book, people were not primarily focused on the linguistic, literary, or grammatical nature of English. Instead, they deliberated in great measure on its power to change the parameters of Indian culture.⁷ Hence, I do not take its contemporary disciplinary location as evident, nor do I set out to rehearse its history through an examination of literary texts.⁸ I draw attention instead to the vexed process by which Indian English sprang from the fierce debates over Indian authenticity. How did native codes of gender and sexuality shape the history and symbolic power of English, and how, in turn, did English infuse conjugality, desire, and caste?⁹ The meaning of English was, I argue, produced through the proliferation of discourses over sexuality. English accrued traction through the nineteenth century and through an interest in fixing the parameters of normative sex.¹⁰ I am thus concerned less with how English operated as the colonial language of power; rather, I explicate its ability to take on a native phallogocentric power vis-à-vis so-called vernacular languages and native standards of gender.¹¹ The book exposes how some Indians symbolically and materially reinterpreted English through the vocabulary of gender in order to produce sexual difference, sexual desire, and thus new regimes of caste exclusivity.

The story takes place in the western Indian cities of Bombay and Poona between 1850 and 1940, urban locations characterized by the colonial economies of opium and cotton and by unprecedented higher-education facilities. From the work of a diverse range of historians we know how the colonial state and missionary agencies attempted to extend the reach of English studies, Christianity, and the Western education project.¹² Scholars of colonial discourse, on the other hand, have delved into the intricacies of English studies themselves, eliciting the symbolic power of English literary texts in strengthening the fiction of colonial power.¹³ More recently, literary scholars have examined the way that Indians used the language to shape transnational, spiritual conversations or how they reevaluated, even resignified, English literary texts.¹⁴ English operated in different registers for an array of constituencies; it could be a means for securing employment, a vehicle for Christianity, a route to humanist equivalence with

European power, or a break with upper-caste hegemony. Stepping back from a literary or form-bound definition of English, I investigate the contours of the English-education project when Indians gained the power to direct English studies for themselves. This approach has taken me to the terrain of education itself, the formation of schools, debates over the composition of the student body, and the determination of the curriculum. By tracking the relationship between a rather amorphous idea of English and the production of subjectivities, I reconstruct how English cohered over the course of ninety years through native attempts to discipline the normative sexual subject.

This book thus looks at the dynamic, changing history of Indian English in relation to pedagogic efforts on the one hand and the shaping of new subjectivities on the other. It details the formal, institutional efforts of some of these first English-educated native subjects to control English studies between 1850 and 1930. Through analyses of school reports and colonial education department files on native-managed English schools in Bombay and Poona, along with a close examination of debates in English and Marathi, popular cultural sources, newspapers, and plays, I track the convergence in debates over respectability, chastity, mimicry, liberalism, Hindu nationalism, and sexuality. These debates coalesced to keep English studies from moving beyond the caste and class location of the first native proponents of English education. What becomes most clear is that even in contestations on curricular content, English is referenced neither as a collection of literary texts nor as a mere language form, but as a sign that supervises behavior, sexual power, and caste. The early history of native pedagogic efforts reveals how English is managed by the modernity of Indian tradition, how historically contingent ideas on the relationship between sexuality and social power materialized the function and purpose of English.

The schools that I discuss in part I sought to disseminate English. But as chapter 2 discusses, through their curricula and ceremonies, the schools demonstrated that English would not disrupt caste power; in fact, it would educate its students to comply with caste strictures of monogamy, chastity, and the male monopoly over knowledge. I read this history critically, noting the performative power of English: its ability to operate as a sign that reinforces the very sexual norms that contain the language within upper-caste groups.[15] Chapter 3 turns to wider cultural debates that focused on the dangers of English, particularly on its ability to destabilize the relationship between women and sex, and between caste power and chastity. In the process of debating who should learn English, popular and literary sources reveal how anxieties over sexual difference were put in the service of protecting upper-caste power and how ideas of sexual difference served to inflate the distinctions between languages. The final chapter in part I shows how transnational debates over female sexuality were used as ammunition to redirect the caste project of Indian English toward managing sexual difference. Overall, part I exposes how upper-caste Indians invoked standards of gender to control the power of English, hence imbuing it with a native phallogocentric authority. They used sexual associations to establish hierarchies between languages, a process that I call sexual-citational grafting.[16] Together these revelations show the long history by which upper-caste power served to present itself as secular and undisputed.

By policing the "fact" of gender difference, a variety of subjects reinforced the exclusivity of Indian English. Part II tracks changes over the same locations and time period, 1850–1940, but looks to different sources and a different methodology. Here I turn away from a sociocultural study of school curricula and popular cultural debates to analyzing book-length studies—biographies, autobiographies, and novels—produced by a range of English-educated subjects. These works corroborate assertions in part I on the sexual power of language, the deployment of sexual associations to rank hierarchies between languages, and the way the investment in sexual normativity restricted English within upper-caste groups. By shifting my method in the second part of the book, I seek to destabilize any easy narrative of English and to reveal the complex way that English emerged amid a host of related sexual, sartorial, and affective formations. Part II thus elicits the "subject effect" or the networks between knowledge and subject formation, between English, liberal individuation, and caste, and between culture, consumption, and sexual desire.[17]

The chapters in part II reveal how caste strictures dovetailed with the seemingly willing turn to conjugality, how the engineering of sexual desire by the English-education project rendered caste power into something transparent, even secular. "Secularization" is widely characterized by the delinking of the religious from the political, although I use the term to indicate that upper-caste status was being delinked from religious ritual. Hence, in its alliance with English, caste was itself secularized, a process that served to normalize—even universalize—majoritarian power.[18]

Chapter 5 specifically illuminates how the virtuous woman appears to willingly tether English to the requirements of Hindu upper-caste culture. In chapter 6, I elucidate the careful, albeit ambivalent, engineering of desire within the marital bond so as to limit English to the new secular, upper-caste couple. Chapter 7 focuses on the tightening relationship between English and liberal cosmopolitanism at the turn of the century and the ways in which the secular subject operated in transnational registers. The final chapter tracks one woman's nationwide and multinational search for English. Although the quest ends with her self-declared failure to learn the language, the story corroborates the triumph of caste-specific gender requirements over English, and with that explicates how gender limits the disciplinary power of English.

Colonial Policy, Postcolonial Critique: "Mental Miscegenation" of the "Bastard Child"

Perhaps the most widely cited lines in the historiography of British India are those of Lord Thomas Babington Macaulay in his 1835 "Minute on Education," in which he made an impassioned plea to William Bentinck, governor general of India, for the anglicization of colonial education policy in India.[19] That British policy produced new, uneven, and restricted social hierarchies is no surprise. The study of English was enshrined as the central component in this policy, geared to generate desire for colonial culture and new intermediary class formations. Macaulay famously argued:

I feel with them that it is impossible for us, with our limited means, to attempt to educate the body of the people. We must at present do our best to form a class who may be interpreters between us and the millions whom we govern, a class of persons Indian in blood and colour, but English in tastes, in opinions, in morals and in intellect. To that class we may leave it to refine the vernacular dialects of the country, to enrich those dialects with terms of science borrowed from the Western nomenclature, and to render them by degrees fit vehicles for conveying knowledge to the great mass of the population.[20]

Macaulay has been interpreted for his invocation of racial difference, for using English to enshrine cultural distinctions between East and West, and thus for producing new social hierarchies.[21] Undeniably powerful, his words signaled a whole new way of administering India through the notion of cultural difference.[22] He was not operating in a vacuum. Possibly building on earlier, regionally oriented formulations, such as governor of the Bombay Presidency Lord Elphinstone's own "Minute on Education," Macaulay's words were reflected among contemporaries such as T. E. Trevelyan and, later, Arthur Mayhew,[23] all of whom propagated a particular brand of Whiggish liberalism and supported the need to craft new social hierarchies through the English education of select natives.[24] Macaulay's words had immediate effect; they served to usher in the three Presidency Universities in Bombay, Calcutta, and Madras, modeled on the constitution and curriculum of the University of London. Despite their origin in colonial policies, these universities were largely funded by native agencies.[25] The agreement between upwardly mobile natives and colonial education policymakers was cemented early on: Bombay University was significantly financed by natives participating in the new transnational economies of cotton and opium, specifically through the largesse of Premchund Roychund and Sir Cowasjee Jehangir.[26]

Historians have thoroughly documented the prominence of native elites—both vernacularists as well as Anglicists—in the overlapping histories of Western knowledge and English-language studies.[27] We are well aware of the role of the colonial state in sponsoring boys' education, of the English education schools set up to train school boys to take on petty clerical tasks in the administrative bureaucracy, and of the history of the Presidency Universities.[28] And we know how the native male interest in education and social reform elevated conjugality as a mark of social progress.[29] Bombay University recorded its first bachelor of arts graduates in 1858.[30] The first generation of English-educated men did indeed, as I elaborate, seize upon the pedagogic inclination of the civilizing mission. But by doing so, they performed a specific twist. They turned the demands of the social contract with colonial power toward the management of sexual difference, responding to allegations that they were inherently different from the West by citing "woman" as the next constituency in need of cultural pedagogy and then using their acquisition of English to manage new, internal hierarchies. This was how they domesticated English.

Posed as evidence of the native ability to close the civilizational gap between Europe and India, the move by native elites to educate their women in English repeated earlier histories whereby women of elite households were trained to become literate in the language of power.[31] But for those opposed to women's education, this nineteenth-century development was a hideous aberration in the logic of "native" social relations. Feminist historians have delineated the tremendous unrest spawned by the centering of women in the nineteenth-century contest between individual rights and native social relations, between ideas of Western and indigenous culture, and between social reform and caste patriarchy.[32] But a cultural history of English education reveals that the differences, in this case, were spurious. Instead, the debate on anglicization served the collected interests of a new class of upper-caste men, who through institutions such as The New English School for Boys (discussed in chapter 3) lamented the decline of the "golden" age of Hindu civilization in the face of "the Muslim invasion." The "danger" of effeminacy and nonconjugal female sexuality was invoked to secure upper-caste authority over English. Ultimately, the battle over native English education saw the ready amalgamation of liberalism with Hindu and upper-caste strictures and the growing acceptance that native men must mediate the transfer of English to Indian society. Sexuality was interjected into the history of English, a process that permitted some natives to seal their national, Indian status.

Surprisingly, extant scholarship has overlooked the symbolic role of gender in fueling the native history of English.[33] In general, social histories of English education and colonial education policy in India continue to be narrated through the historicist or the gender-free mode. Either muting the tendentious battle over gender and sexuality while relating an anodyne history of women's education, or providing gender-neutral accounts of English, the majority of historical work separates gender from the history of English. In all cases, woman and English appear as natural, self-evident categories. For instance, by studying collaboration between colonial and indigenous elites, scholars of the Cambridge School have noted that the English language was the most tangible marker of negotiation between British and Indian social groups.[34] There is, indeed, much to be learned from this body of scholarship, primarily its resolute interest in the local mechanics of caste and sociopolitical power. But the neglect of gender instigates other problems: the privileging of a rather archaic notion of the political and the elite, the separation of caste from sexual power, and the determination that English was fully formed prior to its introduction to India.

A significant shift in the scholarly analysis of English came in 1939 in Gauri Viswanathan's *Masks of Conquest*.[35] Viswanathan diverted the history of English studies away from social history accounts of collaboration between Indian and colonial elites. Specifically, she probed the relationship between power and knowledge and revealed the importance of literature in magnifying the cultural power of colonial English: "English literature appeared as a subject in the curriculum of the colonies long before it was institutionalized in the home country."[36] This elevation of English "literature" in British India was central to the "imperial mission of educating and civilizing colonial subjects . . . [which] in the long run strengthen[ed] western cultural hegemony."[37] Furthermore, "humanistic functions" were integral to English literary studies; these could be "taught" to colonial people while appearing to guide their progress toward civilization.[38] Viswanathan's research itself stops at colonial education policies and administrative debates, but her contribution dramatically shifted the debate over English studies, inspiring a host of important postcolonial analyses of the long life of English literature, both in the curriculum as well as in everyday reading practices.[39] Just as important, her work invigorated the postcolonial assessment of liberal humanism.[40] Significantly diverting from the focus on the inner workings of colonial power, Kumkum Sangari provides a a vivid picture of the re-narrativization of English literary texts in colonial India. With her signature focus on the primacy of gender, Sangari powerfully illuminates Indian efforts to translate and indigenize the English literary tradition, showing how native contests over community and identity recast English texts in an Indian context.[41]

But the history of literature is only one aspect in a complex story of change over time. Postcolonial scholars of English have largely been housed in English studies departments, which might explain why they privilege literature and literary productions in approaching English.[42] But this perspective does not always destabilize the primacy of colonial power. Recently, dwelling on the work that English performs in the contemporary Indian landscape, Rashmi Sadana even suggests that "Indian English literature has outgrown the line of critique and politics that casts English as the language of colonization."[43] For studies of the nineteenth century, however, the history of English continues to signal either literary study, public political negotiation, or the cultural conquest of the subcontinent. Colonial power is recentered often and predictably through the resolute deconstruction of Macaulay's "Minute." For my purposes, it is telling that the cultural conquest is itself most often characterized through psychosexual allusions. For instance, Benedict Anderson argues that Thomas Babington Macaulay intended "mental miscegenation" through his "Minute on Education."⁴⁴ Gauri Viswanathan says that the English literary text worked as a "surrogate Englishman."⁴⁵ And Homi Bhabha, who recalls Macaulay for spawning the "mimic men" of the Indo-British encounter, traces the "line of descent of the mimic man . . . through [the colonial educational directives of Charles Grant and T. B. Macaulay] to the works of Kipling, Forster, Orwell, Naipaul" in order to argue that the mimic man "is the effect of a flawed colonial mimesis, in which to be anglicized is emphatically not to be English."⁴⁶ In glossing over the *reproduction* of the mimic man, Bhabha suggests (even as he never explores) the politics of sexuality in controlling class and cultural change. Most recently, Sanjay Seth claims to speak as "one of Macaulay's misbegotten offspring" so as to celebrate the "pleasing irony in the thought that Macaulay's bastard children will have contributed to the critical appropriation of a knowledge that was once imposed on them."⁴⁷

Macaulay's "Minute" has received a fresh lease on life through the agenda of colonial discourse studies; for some, it indicates an entire mode of thinking about English literature, about liberalism, and about civilization. But my purpose is to look further, to probe more deeply within the spaces where English took root, to explain what happened to English in Indian society. Contrary to the picture of the nineteenth century disseminated by postcolonial studies, I argue that the social categories of Indian society shaped the history of English. Moreover, smooth references to sex that fuel the rhetorical style of some scholarship actually provide vital clues on the lingering, and largely unexplored, relationship between sexual power and the Indian history of English.

Language, Gender, and Knowledge in Western India

By directing their studies on specific, regional locations, historians have foregrounded an appreciation for historically contingent social categories. For western India, Veena Naregal has highlighted the "indigenous" class and caste interests nurtured by the extension of colonial education in western India.⁴⁸ Resisting a primary focus on colonial education policies, Naregal turns instead to a social history of print culture and the emergence of native Marathi-English bilingualism. By looking beyond English literature, Naregal demonstrates instead the class-caste relationship between English and Marathi linguistic practice, the rise of the "new colonial" Brahmans and Parsis of western India, and the determination among the first generation of Western-educated "natives" to claim a dedicated intermediary position ultimately supportive of colonial knowledge.[49] Significantly, Naregal argues that the new knowledge economy of western India was characterized by "laicization," or the necessary restriction of knowledge at the very moment of its dissemination. As she demonstrates, the rise of upper-class Parsi and Brahman power came at the expense of widening the base for modern education—a development immediately yoked to the ability of newly anglicized, bilingual social groups to claim the right to speak for indigenous interests.

The caste-stratified relationship between knowledge and power in western India reinforced the dominance of literate Marathi-speaking Brahmans in the colonial nineteenth century.[50] The standard British dismissal that native society possessed no literature, and hence no history, immediately provided new routes for the expression of caste power. An important example is the nineteenth-century nationalist historian's desire to establish the antiquity and continuity of the Marathi language.[51] This tradition identified all written productions from the precolonial period as "Marathi" and forged the consensus that Marathi and its literary-religious texts formed a recognizable corpus by the thirteenth century.[52] But Muzaffar Alam's important research has firmly established that throughout the medieval and Mughal periods, scholarly and secular-bureaucratic work was conducted and codified in Persian.[53] Alam's assertion is corroborated by Stewart Gordon, who demonstrates that, in the case of western India, court records of the Bahmani kingdom were preserved in Persian by upper-class Hindus who held scribal positions.[54] Marathi rose to prominence only with the institutionalization of the Peshwa court in Poona in the second half of the eighteenth century.[55]

Such a dynamic relationship between linguistic form and political power, between Marathi, Sanskrit, and Persian, underwent a further twist in the early nineteenth century.[56] Once again, it came about at the expense of Persian. New patronage of Sanskrit was encouraged during the governorship of Mountstuart Elphinstone, specifically through the inauguration of the Poona Sanskrit College (later Deccan College) in 1821.[57] The new institution aimed to nurture Sanskritic texts and produce linguistic knowledge for the benefit of the East India Company. It also served to further accelerate the literary dominance of Marathi-speaking, new colonial Brahmans. The Peshwa court had never initiated such an exclusive policy toward Sanskrit. Elphinstone's efforts, therefore, worked to marginalize Persian, not Marathi; they rewarded a group of upper-caste men for referencing Sanskritic antiquity and the claim to represent the masses. The nineteenth-century emergence of Marathi as the iconic regional language of the Bombay-Poona area was borne on the wings of Sanskritization, Brahmanism, Hindu majoritarianism, and, as Naregal has demonstrated, English. This was a multilingual upper-caste formation, actively supported by the colonial state's educational policies.

What, then, are we to make of the native conviction that the British conquest of the Deccan deliberately initiated the marginalization of Marathi? There is no question that high-ranking colonial officials regularly explored the possibility of introducing English as the lingua franca for the entire country, going much further than Macaulay's desire to selectively anglicize an elite group of native men. The tenure of Sir Erskine Perry, president of the Bombay Board of Education from 1848 to 1852, was undoubtedly marked by a deliberate policy of anglicization.[58] But Perry argued that English, as a classical language, be made to replace Persian and not Marathi.[59] Despite that, a new group of Marathi nationalists reinterpreted colonial linguistic desires as a mounting threat to Marathi culture. Richard Cashman has identified the Chitpavan Brahman sub-caste as the leaders of this new strategy of beleaguered nationalism.[60] Prominent Marathi nationalists deliberately opposed any possibility of social change for members of other communities and famously agitated against the reservation of free scholarships in the Deccan and Fergusson Colleges for Muslims and "backward" Hindu castes. It is no coincidence that one of the leaders of this group, Vishnushastri Chiplunkar (discussed in chapter 3), portrayed Marathi as a vernacular under threat from English and closer to so-called real native political desires. Chiplunkar simultaneously quashed the anti-caste critique of Jotiba Phule when the latter drew attention to the rise of Brahmanic control over language and power.[61]

The role of education in consolidating the power of the Brahman caste cannot be separated from the systematic efforts made by some upper-caste men to negate attempts made by members of the Muslim community and the lower castes to gain access to the same facilities. In its partnership with the upper class of the commercially successful Parsis, this very same new colonial intelligentsia argued that the educational activities of the colonial state were surreptitiously anglicizing and eroding the vernacular. This was despite the fact that Marathi was undoubtedly ascendant. The Hindu nationalist and alarmist machinations of Chiplunkar's

Chitpavan-caste colleague, Bal Gangadhar Tilak, are well known in terms of his invention of the Ganapati festival, invocation of a beleaguered Marathi culture, and mobilization against Muharram.[62] But Tilak's writings were, as I discuss in chapter 3, also at the helm of the new debates that forged fresh associations between normative sexuality, English, and caste.

I explore this history of language to demonstrate how the discourse of linguistic decline was relentlessly gendered. New sexual standards bolstered assertions that the Marathi language was under threat. The logic of sexual difference popularized the cause of the "mother" tongue, even as this very logic served to further exacerbate caste-based social hierarchies and the Brahmanization of Indian culture. The perception that the spread of English devalued the vernacular continues in the present day; but in reality, as I stress, Marathi was never replaced by English, either socially or materially. Instead, by the 1880s, as evident from the writings of R. G. Bhandarkar and B. G. Tilak, the hegemonic class of elite, anglicized Brahmans had completely embraced Marathi, a relationship that included the elevation of Sanskrit and English.[63]

Just as Macaulay's posturing cannot stand in for the fraught, contradictory, and miserly realities of colonial education policies, nor should our reading of the projections of colonial policy be allowed to erase the historically produced contingencies of language, knowledge, caste, and sexual power. In 1901 Marathi was officially recognized as an academic subject for the entrance examination to the Bombay University. In 1909 the language was made compulsory for the statewide matriculation examination. Both developments were lauded by the writings of the native elite in English- and Marathi-language publications. But potent expressions regarding the humiliation of the Marathi language by the encroaching power of English continued and even accelerated. For instance, writing on the occasion of the public examination of matriculated school boys, Tilak's English-language paper, *The Mahratta*, cautioned against the "absurdity and tyranny" of the present educational system, deploring "the unnatural phenomenon of a student being deplorably ignorant of his Mother Tongue and its Literature. . . . The root cause of all these phenomena is what we may call the tyranny of the Dominant Language—English—over the vernaculars of the subject races." The article first blamed "the British administrators [who] invested their own language with undue and unnecessary importance and predominance in all the Government Departments and Secondary Schools," and then went on to make the following claim: "The result of this policy has been so disastrous that a boy of eight years, before he is scarcely well acquainted with his mother tongue is weaned away from it, and is not only forced to learn a foreign language, but is also soon compelled to learn all other subjects through that foreign language as if it were his mother tongue."[64]

English, as is so evident in this editorial, was a sign that gained traction through culturally specific discourses of sex. It was separated and differentiated from Marathi through an investment in the inevitability of maternal and reproductive functions. Heteronormative expectations rendered both languages as volatile signifiers, competing for cultural space. Polarities between the indigenous and foreign, as well as the vernacular and English, were bolstered through the use of gendered imagery: English encroaching on the mother language. Anxieties about the decay and decline of this feminized culture spurred the call to protect national culture. Sexualcitational grafting, the association of sexual signs with languages, brought Marathi into the center of political and cultural history. Despite the growing recognition of Marathi in educational institutions and through printed forms such as newspapers and magazines, upper-caste discourse maintained that English was supplanting her rightful position.[65] The sexualization of language took place through an evocative discourse of decline and effacement, at the very moment that standardized Marathi (in its Devanagari script) rose above the history of Persian and other regional dialects.

Sexual Normativity and Caste Power

Warning against the decline of Marathi was a potent rhetorical strategy, with wide-ranging social consequences. But the subject most captured by this discourse of decline and degeneration was that of woman. Elevating or reforming the condition of women brought together otherwise competing social groups and provided the field for a new kind of class and caste homosociality.[66] Nineteenth-century records certainly corroborate that Chitpavan Brahmans and commercially successful Parsis concurred on the value of using English to redirect "native" social relations once English was brought to native females. But if we concede that gender is being produced at the moment of its invocation, then a more complex picture emerges. Ideas of sexual difference were directed upon English. As chapter 2 describes, successive school reports testified glowingly on the amagamation of English with native culture, an amalgamation performed by native women at parades and recitations held at annual functions for the interested gaze of colonial and native audiences. Gender performativities enabled some social groups to claim exclusive control over English. The battle over women's education, over anglicization and indigeneity, thus disguised a wider development, the ability of upper-caste patriarchy to restrict the dissemination of knowledge through the performance of normative sexuality.

Feminist scholars have illuminated the socially conservative role played by the concept of woman in the battles over social power throughout the nineteenth century.[67] Fixing, or reforming, the relationship between woman and sexuality actually served to consolidate anticolonial nationalism with caste interests.[68] Of course, the expectation of female obedience, chastity, conjugality, and the ritualizing of sexual difference did not emerge purely through the colonial encounter; rather, the ritualization of restrictions over female sexuality had long historical roots in India. In western India, the power of normative sexuality in thwarting change was firmly entrenched in the caste-based logic of the area. Before colonial rule, upper-caste power had systematically articulated its exclusivity through the performance of female chastity. For those castes seeking state sanction for upward mobility, the demonstration of inviolable sexual strictures of monogamy and chastity was essential.[69] This compounded over time and was exacerbated by the selective union with Victorian sexual mores. Susan Bayly identifies the nineteenth century as the period in which marriage became "the paramount social act [whereby] people whose so-called caste life styles permit divorce and the remarriage of widows have been seen as distinct from the more refined populations who regard these practices as low and uncivilized. . . . For people claiming exalted caste status . . . the greatest merit accru[es] to those who display the most elaborate and restrictive kinship rules."[70]

By the nineteenth century, marriage was essential to caste exclusivity and hence caste status. Uma Chakravarti has illustrated how the strictures against nonconjugal female sexuality multiplied with the caste ambitions of a social group.[71] The rituals of social mobility necessarily proliferated the discourses of sex. Enforced, punitive widowhood was the most visible means of claiming and maintaining upper-caste status. Simultaneously, those women uncontainable by marriage were immediately marked as outside of caste and hence society itself.[72] Rosalind O'Hanlon has corroborated the centrality of marriage in enshrining caste ambitions, noting how upper-caste women who failed or rejected the institution of marriage were repressed and sexually punished. In the nineteenth century, as she reveals, the "Marathi terms for widows and prostitutes were in many contexts interchangeable."[73] The debates over normative sexuality significantly amplified transregional Brahmanical power, "both sati and restrictions on remarriage helped to disseminate and reinforce models for female self-abnegation and deference to a much wider audience of Indians than were ever directly affected by either."[74] The wife-prostitute binary was central to caste power, with the ostracized widow functioning as the necessary supplement.[75] The demonstration of lifelong devotion to the marital bond was exemplified in the regulatory example of widowhood. It elevated the normative married woman as the a/sexual symbol of the nation and projected the exclusivity of the Brahman caste.

The significance of this sexual-symbolic formation was not lost on western Indian women themselves.[76] They voiced their critiques of the nexus between knowledge and sexuality through a range of modes. Many scholars are familiar with the satirical diatribe penned by Tarabai Shinde in 1882,[77] the assessment of the *shastras* by Pandita Ramabai,[78] and the active challenge to the law courts by Dr. Rakhmabai.[79] Pandita Ramabai's life, indeed, exemplifies the tightly engineered bond between English and the normative woman. As Meera Kosambi has related, Ramabai's father once witnessed a Peshwa's wife speaking Sanskrit. Deeply impressed by her ability to recite sacred texts in a language otherwise forbidden to women, he took it upon himself to educate his wife similarly. But for this he was sharply ostracized by his fellow Brahmans. While it was possible for women of royal families to learn the language of power, it was not permissible for a poor Brahman woman to learn Sanskrit. The entire family was forced to retreat to a life of peripatetic wandering and itinerant income. Despite the punishment, the young Ramabai was taught Sanskrit by her mother. Perhaps as a result of her father's ostracism, Ramabai was never subject to the expectations of an early marriage usually imposed upon young Brahman women. Her father's desire to educate his wife in the language of power sparked off a host of economic, sexual, and intellectual changes in the daughter's life.

With time, Ramabai's knowledge of Sanskrit produced social currency, enabling her to engage in transregional debates over the scriptures with Brahman men in Calcutta and earning her the title of "Pandita," great scholar. Her first published work, *Stri Dharma Niti* (Morals for women), was written in Marathi and was a gender-conservative prolegomena. Sales of the text funded her trip to Britain to study for a medical degree.[80] She strongly advised the Parliamentary Committee on Education (the Hunter Commission) in 1882 that native women must learn English.[81] Once in England, she tried to learn English in return for teaching Sanskrit to British men, but her plans were dismissed by her sponsors.[82] It is indeed significant that she never learned English while in India, as English-language facilities did exist for upper-caste women in the Bombay Presidency. Despite her personal intellectual privileges and her relative disengagement from normative institutions, Ramabai could not acquire the language.[83] In my assessment, it was precisely the absence of a male mediator—an upper-caste husband or father figure—that rendered her sexually illegible, if not disruptive, and for that reason thwarted her early ability to learn the language. In other words, her gender identity was not mediated by marriage; hence, the new markers of caste exclusivity remained beyond her reach.[84] But unlike the later story of another Brahman widow, Parvati Athavale, Ramabai did not fail entirely. Instead and over time, she went on to write and publish extensively in English, addressing a liberal, reform-oriented Euro-American public, challenging the patriarchal interests of Brahmanism and becoming increasingly ostracized by upper-caste men. Critiques of her work further entrenched the parameters of religion, education, and sexuality.[85]

Ramabai's life, in many ways, encompassed the sexual trajectory of the English language in the nineteenth century. It was over exactly the same years that western India saw another theoretically and institutionally innovative critique of the nexus between knowledge, gender, and caste. Mahatma Jotiba Phule (1827–1890) worked to demystify the relationship between gender, the Brahman-bureaucratic state, English knowledge, and new forms of caste ascendancies.[86] Phule and his wife Savitribai were of the lower castes, specifically the agricultural *mali* caste. Phule's ideals derived from a post-Enlightenment idealization of rationality and humanism, which he had learned, along with the English language, from Western missionaries.[87] In his writings, he discussed the need to change the very principles of social hierarchy rather than merely producing additive outcomes or simply widening access to the very facilities that cemented elite privilege.[88] Rosalind O'Hanlon has written of the time that Phule employed a Brahman widow, at a very high pay rate, to take care of his home. It was a symbolic move with wide ramifications: it repudiated those Brahman households that first ostracized and then forced Brahman widows to perform domestic labor for no compensation; it drew attention to the potential of payment to subvert the affective bonds that maintained caste patriarchy.

Phule started both the first lower-caste and first native-organized effort to educate female students in western India. He opened his first such school in 1850, with his wife, Savitribai (1831–97), as a teacher.[89] Their school taught reading, arithmetic, grammar, and some English.[90] Savitribai, Jotiba, and the others with whom they worked were not simply setting out to modernize women or members of the lower castes or to support Brahman power.[91] Rather, their work exposed the complex logic of Brahmanism: the ritualization of sexual difference so as to restrict other castes from accessing knowledge.[92] Immediately, orthodox Brahmans protested Phule's attempt to introduce education to lower-caste women, arguing that "knowledge and learning was seeking shelter in shudra homes."[93]

The Phules' pedagogic and artistic work on English was firmly connected to the battle over signification. According to Gail Omvedt, Savitribai determined that "shudras and ati-shudras [Dalits] . . . have the right to education, and through English, casteism can be destroyed and Brahmanical teaching can be hurled away."[94] Savitribai was a published poet and writer, and she wrote her literary works for an audience of lower-caste people. She drew on the poetic form to disrupt normative categories, turning contemporary symbolism on its head when she wrote that "Peshwa rule has been vanquished, Our Mother English is here."[95] Contrary to the debates being played out in *The Mahratta*, Savitribai Phule maintained that British rule had liberated some from the Brahmanical period of Peshwa rule and instead ushered in English as the mother of culture. She inverted the nationalist celebration of the indigenous-maternal and, with that, transgressed the hallowed sanctity of the "mother."[96] The invocation of "our mother English" in Savitribai's poems, intentionally operating within the heteronormative nationalist gender regimes of the time, indicates the symbolic, gendered battle being waged between competing audiences in the nineteenth-century English ecumene.[97] It marks a radical disidentification, a redirection of dominant symbolism, and it is an indication that her strategy was aimed at multiple audiences.[98] Most significant, it boldly appropriates the normative "native" woman to expose the role of sexuality in staging upper-caste exclusivity. Rejecting the Hindu nationalist claim that the precolonial period of Brahman-Peshwa rule generated desirable cultural standards, Savitribai deployed gender as a signifying practice that imbued English.

Some eighty years later, Dr. B. R. Ambedkar (1891–1956) made even more pointed observations on the role of sexuality in securing the intellectual monopoly of the Brahman caste.[99] Ambedkar recognized that there could be no caste without Brahmanism, and the primary power of knowledge in shaping Brahmanical exclusivity infected even those who might not be Hindus. This was ensured through a complex system of restriction and denial, as "India is the only country where the intellectual class, namely, the Brahmans, not only made education their monopoly, but declared acquisition of education by the lower classes a crime, punishable."[100] Significantly, Ambedkar recognized that language is knowledge, for it is in India that "it is an offence for a member of the Untouchable community to speak a cultured language."[101] And furthermore, he exposed the alliance between sexuality and caste, "the status of a caste in the Hindu society varies directly with the extent of the observance of the customs of sati, enforced widowhood and girl marriage."[102] Brahmanism was secured through crafting hierarchies between languages and by requiring the symbolic performance of the woman's compliance with the permanence of the marriage arrangement.[103] The rituals adhered to by upper-caste women rendered Brahmanical power as exceptional: desirable and prohibited. Hence it is that "duplication and exclusion are essential to caste."[104]

The significance of Ambedkar's insights is compounded afresh through the caste-specific history of English. Those of the Brahman caste actively restricted non-Brahmans from learning, but they did so by conceding a selective form of this privilege to those held responsible for reproducing upper-caste citizens and upper-caste culture: their wives, their daughters, and even their widows. Ideas of chastity, virtue, and marital devotion redirected the charismatic power of English. And then they could proclaim that English-educated women would comply with the sexual regimes of caste; the power of English would be disciplined by caste-specific behavior. The disciplinary power of English, its ability to shape the consenting sexual subject, emerges from the caste-based struggle over knowledge and sexual normativity. This is why the English language had to filter through some women to engender distinctions from "other" Indians, essentially marking new, "indigenous" social hierarchies. The English-education project, whereby upper-caste and upper-class men mediated the dissemination of English, maintained and in fact ritualized bifurcations between intellectual power and sexual labor. The chaste, virtuous, English-educated upper-caste woman projected the continuation of Brahmanism's exclusive relationship to knowledge, this as she demonstrated her compliance with sexual and domestic labor. Upwardly mobile caste and class groups magnified, even normalized, upper-caste patriarchal power, and they did so by deploying English to occlude battles over sexuality and to distinguish between labor and intellect.[105]

Rituals of power were supported by the "structuring definitional leverage" of terms—wife, widow, woman—that marked certain ascribed sexual positions as deviant under the sign of normativity.[106] As Afsaneh Najmabadi, a historian of Iran, has so lucidly described, the "heteronormalization of eros and sex" was widely waged through symbolic means, a process itself integral to the project of "achieving modernity."[107] Indeed, the concerted heterosexualization of society under the watchful eye of Brahmanism served to redirect the project of English education. Here my debt to the organizing precepts of some queer theories should be evident,[108] specifically those that study how expectations of normative sexuality organize power and resources.[109] After all, as Rosemary Hennessey has argued, "if the hegemonic heterosexual norm is over-determined, this over determination entails relations of labor as well as gender and sexuality.... All are in various complex ways involved in the reproduction of capitalism."[110] Thus the prospect of heterosexuality works to naturalize distinctions between labor, sex, and knowledge; this is how it systematically obscures manifestations of power. The normative gendered subject, in other words, is produced in a crucible of caste-based desires that provide coherence to the English-education project. Less a language form, or a collection of texts, English is materialized in assemblages, "techniques, intensities, authorities, apparatuses."[111] The multiplication of sexual anxieties produces the disciplinary power of English, its ability to shape the consenting Indian subject.

Labor and Liberalism in Colonial Modernity

Historians of gender in colonial modernity have long impressed upon us the primary power of "woman" to thwart, stabilize, and accelerate consensus across otherwise disparate political positions and, with that, to obscure new manifestations of power. Tani Barlow has alerted scholars to look for the world-historical "advent of women" to reveal how "the process of becoming invested in the historical event of women is . . . part of the colonial, semi-colonial and modern colonial developmental processes."[112] Barlow stresses that scholars must look beyond the West as the point of departure for "modernity" or even for its critiques. Specifically for India, Brahmanical power invoked woman to naturalize distinctions, even binaries of intellect and labor, wife and non-wife, conjugal versus aberrant sexuality, upper-caste practice and prostitution.[113] This did not always produce easy oppositions between colonial and native interests. Instead, the binary was essential to cementing new caste and homosocial solidarities. The reproductive and conjugal figure of woman masked battles over caste mobility and cohered a range of positions between colonial and native interests.

Still, some historians remain invested in hard distinctions between colonial and native; they disregard the interests served by the making of this normative gendered subject. Famously celebrating the "refusal of nationalism to make the woman question an issue of political negotiation with the colonial state," so that questions of female emancipation were disappeared from the "public agenda of nationalist agitation in the late nineteenth century,"[114] Partha Chatterjee, for example, conflates the worldview of a select group of upper-caste Bengali nationalists with the creative, anticolonial power of "India."[115] His understanding is that nationalists infused ideas of indigenous culture with prescriptions on feminine deportment and spirituality; this served as resistant alterity against Western modernity. Strikingly disinterested in the longer social history whereby the normative sexual subject was deployed to consolidate upper-caste interests, he then goes on to dismiss the history of English: "Much of the content of the modern school education was seen as important for the 'new' woman, but to administer it in the English language was difficult in practical terms, irrelevant because the central place of the educated woman was still at home, and threatening because it might devalue and displace that central site where the social position of women was located."[116]

Chatterjee's work has drawn critique from an array of scholars: for its "modular" recentering of the history of colonial Bengal; its empirical shortcomings; its investment in enshrining Hindu nationalist patriarchy as anticolonial response; and its ability to concede to "Europe" the entire battle over equal rights.[117] Despite that, his formulation continues to be referenced by a range of scholars, even by those who work on neither Bengal nor India.[118] Chatterjee's argument is most visible in the work of those scholars who critically reexamine the tenets of European liberalism, science, "Western education," or the Enlightenment itself.[119] Leading stalwarts of South Asian histories have extended Chatterjee's valorization of nativist cultural reactions, arguing that "colonized subjects" successfully exposed the hypocrisy of European claims to universalism by redirecting European intellectual traditions through ideas of spiritual, "indigenous," and female culture.[120] But the generative power of "Europe" remains in place, even as upper-caste rituals are celebrated as resistance.

Moving from the prescriptive to the descriptive, Chatterjee portrays his female subjects as entirely derived from male desires, simply imbibing and parroting the male ambivalence over colonialism's modernity. He reads active conflicts over caste and labor as evidencing nationalist sentiment on gender. He does not question *why*—in positing their consenting conjugal companions as the foil against colonial power—upper-caste men felt empowered to speak in the name of the Indian nation. And why did they feel justified in repressing the woman question? Chatterjee overlooks the exigencies of caste, the role of the normative woman in sanctioning the exclusivity of upper-caste power. Instead, the control over gender, for him, obscures the production of caste. By treating sexual difference as fixed and by assuming that the voluminous writings of the nineteenth century were aimed solely at a European audience, Chatterjee silences obvious battles over authority, whereby caste-mobile groups idealized female sexuality to claim an elevated social standing vis-à-vis other Indians. The connection between sexuality and caste mobility—so powerfully documented by feminist historians—is ignored, so much so that Partha Chatterjee maintains that the silence over sexuality in his sources further testifies to nationalism's critique of Europe's logocentric liberal modernity.[121]

What are the real politics of these silences, and why do some Indian historians defer to colonial power as the point of origin while rendering caste heterosexuality as natural, inevitable, and anticolonial?[122] Charu Gupta's path-breaking *Women, Muslims and the Public Sphere* presents an alternative analysis: the debates of the period were rife with contestations over sexuality. Upper-caste Hindu men deployed the trope of sexual excess to mark differences from "other" communities, particularly Muslims. As she demonstrates, "Hindu publicists were able to compound and conflate images of Hindu masculinity, alleged abductions of Hindu women by lustful Muslim men, and victimized and heroic Hindu women."[123] The purported anxiety over sexuality served to mark other Indian communities as violent, antisocial, and foreign. And Ratna Kapur has conclusively demonstrated that the contests of the nineteenth century were not only between social reformers, political nationalists, and the colonial state, but "over the power and authority to define Hindu culture and traditions."[124] Most crucially, she writes that "private sex is thus only immunized if it is legitimate private sex, i.e. sex within marriage, familiar and culturally grounded."[125] Kapur's use of cultural and feminist studies modes of analysis recognizes the "nationalist resolution of the woman's question" for its caste and communitarian interests. It is the heteronormative Hindu upper-caste community that has enjoyed the privilege of projecting sexuality as simultaneously private, domestic, and anticolonial—when it strives to secure its distinctions from "other" Indians. To return to Chatterjee, I argue that the silence over sexuality speaks to the complacency of the upper-caste contract with Victorian codes, and to the way historical work on gender blithely disregards the engineering of sexuality.[126]

Explaining how the upper-caste woman was idealized requires that we work to interrupt the expectation of heterosexuality, and to account for the secularization or universalizing of upper-caste power through heteronormative presumptions. Even as the normative upper-caste woman was configured to mark distinctions from other communities, her sexual, affective, and domestic labor was silently put in the service of the newly secularized joint family. Gendered relations of labor were determined in the process of fixing upper-caste power, itself reliant on the monopoly over knowledge. The chains of control crafted by colonial pedagogic imperatives did not end with the English education of the compliant native man; on the contrary, those very men deployed a naturalized discourse of sexual difference to restrict English within their caste location, mapping the colonial-native, parent-child relationship upon the marital bond. The success of colonial mimicry lay in how English-educated Indians deployed sexual difference to contain English within their caste and class locations, turning colonial desire for the native male mimic into a revitalized Indian hetero-nationalism.

The chapters that follow track how a range of native men and women deployed gender to discipline the English language, and how English was redirected and materialized through the sexual exigencies of modern India. Much like gender, English too was under constant redefinition. It was a culturally contingent repository for the discourses that universalized upper-caste norms. English was not the adversary of any inner, spiritual, feminine essence. In fact, Indian English emerged out of the competition between sexuality, politics, and power. It was coeval with the discourses of desire, gendered performance, and sexual difference. The investment in gender and the struggle over sex, sexual function, and erotic power shaped the history of Indian English. Deploying gender to sanction their caste hegemony, the new English-educated, nationalist elite colluded actively with the colonial state. Indian English thus prospered through the ritualization of sexual difference, which preserved the class and caste interests of a minority. The idealized woman provided the semantic glue, legitimizing the caste-based claims to national power in the nineteenth century and guiding the truth claims of gradual reform, paternalism, and liberal humanism as they became incorporated into the caste-based logic of the twentieth century. English as a linguistic structure, a cultural sign, and a metaphor was domesticated through the crafting of sexuality, desire, and class and caste power. This is how English was rendered an Indian language, a critical effect of native gender regimes.

2

"THE PRUDENT AND CAUTIOUS ENGRAFTING OF ENGLISH UPON OUR FEMALE POPULATION"

Pedagogy and Performativity

Following the East India Company's takeover of Peshwa territory in 1818, Mountstuart Elphinstone, the first governor of the Bombay Presidency and president of the Bombay Education Society, immediately sought continuity with the previous administration's institutions. Elphinstone noted in no uncertain terms the sensitivity of the "circumstance of our having lately succeeded to a Brahman Government."[1] The previous Chitpavan Brahman–dominated Peshwa administration had actually composed a loosely connected confederacy of scattered Maratha states but was considered to have posed the very last state-organized threat to the territorial expansion of the company. Even as he pensioned off the house of the Peshwa, Elphinstone recognized the necessity of working with the bureaucratic intermediaries who had served the previous government. For this purpose, he crafted new institutional means to cultivate native participation in his administration. While his policies appeared to follow his predecessors, in reality they transformed the language of administration and the very linguistic identity of the area.

Elphinstone first drew on the Dakshina Fund, an existing scholarship fund that the Peshwa had granted to some literate Brahman men in recognition for their knowledge of Marathi.[2] While continuing to sponsor this fund, Elphinstone actually produced transformative changes. Historians of western Indian colonial education policies have noted how, under Elphinstone, the Dakshina Fund initially encouraged Sanskrit learning and then was redirected toward elevating English in the intellectual repertoire of a select group of the new educated natives.[3] By emphasizing Sanskrit and then English, colonial education policies actively marginalized Persian as the original language of bureaucratic record-keeping. In 1821, Elphinstone inaugurated the Poona Sanskrit College (later renamed Deccan College), and in 1823 he started the first English-language schools for native boys in Bombay city. But the colonial state was hesitant to be involved in girls' education over the first half of the nineteenth century. At that time girls' education was for the most part directed by missionary activities and served lower-class students by providing translated Marathi-language texts for their schooling.[4]

Simultaneously, during Elphinstone's rule, the language of liberalism—discourses of individual progress toward freedom from social coercion—rose in the political rhetoric of governance.[5] Yet the ideals were immediately refracted through a conviction in gradualism, paternalism, and education. Liberal pundits ensconced in Europe believed Indians were not yet ready to govern themselves. They therefore had to be carefully and selectively educated to develop an appreciation for rationality and enlightened modes of thought. As the historian Prachi Deshpande has discussed, Elphinstone was an especially firm advocate of the possibility of the gradual evolution of human societies.[6] Deeply appreciative of the Orientalist scholarship being produced in Calcutta, he was instrumental in encouraging similar ventures in Bombay, especially the Bombay Branch of the Asiatic Society of Bengal and the Bombay Literary Society. Within two decades, his government's education policies had contributed to the sharp rise of a new colonial Brahman class that was intellectually produced through institutions such as the Dakshina Fund, the Poona Sanskrit College, and the schools of the Bombay Native Education Society and the Asiatic Society. Ideologically, this class of native men was influenced by the language of liberalism and its tenets of gradual and controlled amelioration of custom.

This first generation of English-educated natives in the Bombay Presidency reacted surprisingly quickly to the supposedly civilizing mission of English studies. Veena Naregal has presented the "new colonial Brahman" as a class identity expressed through an investment in bilingualism, a commitment to the Marathi language, and the marginalization of traditional Sanskritic Brahmans from the knowledge economy.[7] As the first generation of English-educated native intermediaries arose, so did fresh recommendations from the British Parliament on the matter of Indian education. These suggestions, contained in the Wood's India Despatch of 1854, advocated additional English-language education where demand was expressed, a wider role for the state in guiding female education, the nurturing of student-teachers through teacher-training "normal" schools, and new public-private partnerships and "grants-in-aid" between the state and private agencies in fostering native education.[8] The interplay between colonial policies and the intermediary role of the new colonial Brahmans provides the backdrop for the native interest in English education by the second half of the nineteenth century.

In this chapter I turn to the first native-directed educational efforts in the Bombay Presidency. My interest lies in the immediacy with which this intermediary class, through its zeal for institution building and pedagogy, entered into and diverted the language and codes of colonial power. Using the records of the first native-directed schools, I draw attention to the way native men activated the supposed fact of sexual difference to control the reach of English education. The restricted, or laicized, nature of Indian English emerged through the definition of a particular ideal of woman. English was defined through an upper-caste desire for female chastity, passivity, and tradition; this, in turn, served to further deepen modes of caste differentiation. While an influential group of historians has argued that nationalist ideas of female spirituality were crafted to restrain European cultural power, I argue for a deeper appreciation. Statements on (or performances of) native female sexuality enabled some natives to gain control over English studies. Sexual difference was produced to restrict English within the class and caste location of the new colonial Brahmans.

The history of the three schools that I discuss here reveals how the production of gender subjectivities and performativities defined the reach of Indian English. As the records from the Alexandra Native Girls' English Institution, the schools of the Students' Literary and Scientific Society, and the Female Normal Schools reveal, a particular kind of woman and a specific constellation of affective expressions consolidated caste power, along with intellectual and commercial interests, within native society. We know from the work of Uma Chakravarti and Rosalind O'Hanlon how the process of universalizing upper-caste ideals of female sexuality served to craft differences between castes. The school reports I analyze here reveal how that very process shaped the cultural power of English while it also marked differences between languages and their speakers. New, upper-caste standards of female sexuality buttressed the hierarchy between English and vernacular languages. Female sexuality strengthened the power of English by restricting it to certain social groups. Furthermore, this process saw the gendering of languages themselves. Sexual ideals were projected upon English and Marathi, endowing these languages with sexual identities and power. The colonial state was certainly not absent from these developments. Working under the guise of liberalism, the state would ensure certain sexual standards, devalue nonconjugal ones, and in the process enshrine companionate marriage as the hallmark of civilizational progress. With that, the state would also supervise the wider process by which English became infused with native, upper-caste ideals of sex and sexuality.

Liberalism, Acculturation, and the Meeting of the Races

In 1842, soon after returning from touring England and other parts of Europe, Manockjee Cursetjee Shroff, a Parsi judge at the Court of Small Causes in Bombay city, embarked on another, far more complicated journey: introducing his daughter Kooverbai to a "thoroughly English education."[9] Many years later he recalled the source of his inspiration. While visiting the house of his British friend Captain Moresby, Cursetjee heard the "thrilling notes of music resounding from the upstairs." On learning that the sounds had been produced by Moresby's daughter, Cursetjee found himself longing for "that happy day when such music will be heard in our native households!" He resolved to personally introduce a similar kind of intellectual and cultural education to his daughter, an education that he defined as consisting of "English and Music."[10] Unlike other efforts at home education prevalent at this time, Manockjee Cursetjee hired an English governess to teach his daughter.[11]

A little while later, another prominent member of the upper-class Parsi community, Sir Jamsetjee Jeejeebhoy (1783–1859), introduced his daughter to this novel experiment.[12] But it soon became apparent to Cursetjee that native society's "pet idol—the monster custom,"[13] would conspire to thwart his efforts; Jamsetjee Jeejeebhoy withdrew his daughter from Cursetjee's home tutoring classes and, according to the latter, began to actively work to hinder this educational experiment. But Cursetjee was not deterred. In 1849 he sent his youngest daughters, Aimai and Serenbai, to an English school conducted by two Irish women in Bombay. Simultaneously, he wrote to J. E. D. Bethune in Calcutta to ascertain whether high-class Bengalis sent their daughters to school, the cost of maintaining such a school, and the possibility of employing an English governess to teach there.[14]

Conversing through a series of letters, Cursetjee informed Bethune that "Marathee and the Guzrathee... abound with more impure and unchaste terms... denoting the mental degeneration of the people."[15] Conscious of the new efforts to standardize the vernacular, of "converting it from its defective state and dilapidation, into a language of literature (divesting the same of the unchastity of thoughts and ideas),' Cursetjee pointedly asked Bethune "whether the English or the vernacular should be the language through... which to impart to the plastic minds of the girls here the knowledge of Europe."[16]

Cursetjee was convinced of the superior literary and intellectual power of English. He argued that only "English [was] complete in all its useful and entertaining elements, and adequately expressive of individual thoughts, feelings, and wants." He envisaged a relationship between English and the liberal individual who could voice his or her wants and desires.[17] Even more crucially, he signified a hierarchy and distance between English and the vernacular by relating the values of "unchastity and impurity" to the latter and individual self-consciousness to the former. Cursetjee's concern over the difference between English and the vernacular echoed contemporary social reform rhetoric on moral and sexual improvement, which itself elevated masculine authority while targeting a select group of native women.[18] English, already associated with a modern, literary, and enlightened Europe, was juxtaposed with the impure and defective vernacular. English provided the model while the vernacular was the object of reform. The two languages were culled from the structure of signification that differentiated agency and passivity, originality and impurity, male and female.

Linguistic histories of precolonial South Asia have demonstrated that languages have always existed in symbiotic relations with one another, evidence of deep multilingual realities.[19] Languages derived their identity from associations to power and access, not merely from physical, linguistic structure. The relationship between languages was characterized by symbolic power; status was determined by the association of each to a set of attributes and privileges. This representational space, which somewhat uneasily maintained the relationship between high and low classes, was vigorously interrogated in the 1700s. In the case of western India, new competition between social elites over access to the Peshwa court had disrupted the relative power encoded in the Persian, Sanskrit, and Marathi languages.[20] Cursetjee's interest in determining the relative worth of English and the vernacular Gujarati thus followed a well-established history of fixing the symbolic value of specific languages. What was strikingly novel, however, was how he culled this relationship. His multiply coded references to gender indicate the increasing importance of sexual difference in determining cultures of power for an emerging nationally oriented identity. Through a process of sexual-citational grafting,[21] Cursetjee produced the differences between English and the vernacular.

The rhetorical field was saturated with gendered associations, and ideas of sexual difference were directed toward fixing the comparative value of languages. In writing about the feminization of languages in modernity, Sumathi Ramaswamy has argued that the rise of Tamil as the "mother tongue" reveals why South Asian languages cannot be folded into the modular, and predictable, history of vernacular language formations in modernity.[22] Instead, the structures of devotion that turned languages into objects of worship in the late nineteenth-century Tamil ecumene interrupt any easy conception that national-linguistic culture emanated from Europe to the world.[23] Ramaswamy argues that feminization involves the rendering of Tamil as wife, mother, and goddess and her larger point on the feminization of all languages in modernity is tremendously useful here for understanding the relationship between English and Marathi. But Cursetjee's letters suggest that gendering might go beyond just invoking female figures, to actually establishing class parameters through the gendered vocabulary of purity and chastity. I propose, therefore, that gendering is also a significatory strategy that need not index biologically differentiated bodies. Instead, the gendering of Indian languages as expressed by Cursetjee suggests the forced, even awkward, correspondence between bodies and genders; the female is not the only lever for gender. Second, the uneven, symbiotic relationship of English to the vernacular reveals too that not all languages were being gendered in the same way. By aligning with male control, by being put to the task of disciplining the vernacular, and by posing as the resolute example, English hailed both a vernacular and desirable native femininity into being. It, too, was gendered, although it was not necessarily feminized. The project of gendering languages revolved around new discourses of sexuality. English had the power to determine the femininity of vernacular languages, but it also had the power to determine the native male's desire to define female behavior. Cursetjee's desire to attribute independent agency to English and unchastity and impurity to the vernacular-in-the-making reveals how commonsense notions of gender were deployed to fill the cultural space between English and non-English languages.

Bethune's reply never addressed Cursetjee's query about language. Rather, he declared that "it is of far more consequence to have the principle admitted that girls ought to be educated than to determine precisely what that education should consist of."[24] Over the following decade, Cursetjee worked to materialize his own vision. In 1860, this former government clerk opened a girls' school in his own house, Villa Byculla. He hired a "competent English woman," one Mrs. Smith, on a salary of RS. 200 per month, to supervise the school, assisted by Cursetjee's now competently English-educated daughters. Three years later this school became the Alexandra Native Girls' English Institution, formally inaugurated on September 1, 1863, and so named to commemorate the wedding of the Prince of Wales (later King Edward VII) to Princess Alexandra.

Once inaugurated, the school expressly stated that "none but girls and ladies of the most respectable families, or of those otherwise distinguished for their intellectual and moral worth, and being well recommended, be admitted into the Institute."[25] Cursetjee's efforts, which appeared to encourage gender equity in learning, actually deepened the association between social privilege and English education, nurturing through exclusion the class interests of an upwardly mobile English-educated intelligentsia. Emphatically bringing together the anglicized, the domestic, and the celebration of a selectively shaped indigenous culture, the school's first printed report (for the year 1863) described the first ceremony to mark the new school. The report approvingly noted the students' deportment, hair styles, and "dress, which though blazing with jewels or gold spangles, had still some similarity to the dress of an English girl."[26] Native women had to show not just their intellectual achievements, but also their attainment of the markers of indigenous and Western culture. The education that Manockjee Cursetjee had in mind for the girls of his English school was not only about the English language, even though language was at the heart of this pedagogic endeavor. Cursetjee envisioned the progressive westernization of these girls as a necessary ideal that would influence other aspects of social and cultural life.

The Wood's Despatch mentioned earlier had proposed that the colonial state monitor native efforts to educate others, which would then inform its decision on the level of financial support needed by these native-run pedagogic efforts. In that vein, the colonial state took an interest in the

Alexandra School from the very start. The chief guest at the 1863 function was the governor of the Bombay Presidency, Sir Bartle Frere, who proceeded to congratulate Cursetjee for bridging the gap between Indian men and women through his pedagogic work; increased sociability was now possible because of the English education of Indian women. Frere maintained that Indian men who traveled to England were often struck by the fact that they were, "in education and attainments, fully able to understand, and feel on a par with educated gentlemen in England," but they were unfortunately aware that "they could not venture to bring their wives and daughters into society with any hope of feeling that, in intellectual attainments, they were on a par with the ladies they would meet."[27] The governor thus applauded Cursetjee for facilitating increased interactions between men and women, as well as between Europeans and Indians in the city.

Records from the school reveal that the students had to perform the trappings of Victorian gender norms alongside the academic knowledge they attained; both were demonstrated at Annual Ceremonies, such as the one described in the first Annual Report. This report included excerpts from an article published in the European-owned *Times of India* newspaper, which reported glowingly on the level of intellect displayed at this occasion: "We cannot conceal from ourselves the fact that native young ladies are quite equal, if not superior in point of intelligence, to their English sisters of a similar age. We question whether we could easily find at an English boarding school a girl of thirteen who could recite an extract from Moliere or Goethe, with such fine modulation of tone and accuracy of pronunciation as a young Parsee lady did some English pieces."[28] The students' accents and appearances signaled the success of Cursetjee's experiment. The school continued to examine its students on the standards of the English language and culture. Two years later, the school's Annual Report recorded that the Reverend Fletcher tested the students on some points in English history: "One young lady could tell who conquered the Saxons, another what was the name of the Norman king who led the victorious host, a third was able to tell how many wives Henry VIII had. . . . In spelling, one spelt 'stick' without the 'c' and though Pitman might have declared it phonetically correct, it did not satisfy the orthological acumen of one of the pupils, who at once supplied the truant letter. . . . *We should add that the examination was conducted entirely in English.*"[29]

In 1868, five years after having formally inaugurated the Girls' English school, Cursetjee wrote to the education department of the Bombay Presidency to request financial assistance (a grant-in-aid) for the school.[30] First recalling his energetic attempts toward English education, Cursetjee recalled that it had been his "constant aim and unremitting endeavour, for upwards of a quarter of a century, to found or see founded an Institution . . . for the introduction of the English education among our female population."[31] The purpose of this "prudent and cautious engrafting" would "diminish native prejudice and dislike to European civilisation, and at length . . . take root and become acclimatised" among the native population. Native women provided the means through which "European civilisation" could be instilled in native society; they were the conduits for cultural change. Cursetjee then went on to describe the seething opposition to his efforts, the "prejudice, difficulties, calumny, and even insults" that he endured in enacting his ideals.[32]

Cursetjee conspicuously posed himself as less subjected to (if at all) the hierarchies of colonial racism and far more to the cultural nationalism of native vernacularists. Jim Masselos has noted that Manockjee Cursetjee was involved—over exactly these years—in disputing the "revivalist and puritanical" efforts of the Parsi Panchayat.[33] Masselos has drawn attention to the dense caste- and class-based conflict between social groups in Bombay city at the time. Indeed, Cursetjee emphasized the urgency of his mission by invoking the opposition of other natives. In writing to the colonial state, he deployed the agenda of gender reform, through English education, as a way to distance himself from other native social groups. Cursetjee's desire to educate native women in English was aimed at securing power over women and English; in the process, it served to establish a privileged distance from the constituencies of "native prejudices."

In general, colonial officials were hesitant about directly administering women's education. But the speeches that officials made demonstrate that the administration was delighted to advise the English-educated native male elite on how to shape such an acculturation. Over a decade after its inauguration, the school's annual day ceremony saw the governor of the Presidency, Sir Richard Temple, address the audience of students, their parents, and prominent members of other philanthropic societies in the city. Speaking of the "highest and most superior kind of education" imparted at this institution, Temple highlighted English. He conceded that although the education was not "perhaps exactly the same as that which is given to English ladies [it was nevertheless] an education on the same principle and on the same model, and mainly through the medium of the English language."³⁴ Immediately approving the performativity of gender, he noted how the young girls had been trained to publicly demonstrate their acquisition of culture, behavior, and comportment. He recalled how "we saw from the graceful way in which [the students] were so good to defile [sic] . . . before the ladies and gentlemen present, that they are being instructed exactly in the same graceful address and manners as those we hope distinguish, and will ever distinguish, the English young ladies."³⁵

Native girls were being educated to resemble "English young ladies." It was a selective semblance and it had to be performed for the interested gaze of an elite native and European audience.³⁶ These performances were then accentuated and repeated in the statements that described them. School reports, annual day speeches, and newspaper accounts all furthered the production of gender through English.³⁷ The ceremonies did not merely celebrate the acquisition of English by certain people; rather, through the display of a certain kind of femininity, English was deemed appropriate for natives. Class-specific ideas of gender hailed English into being. In Temple's enthusiastic assessment of the "defiling" students, a specific idea of upper-class English acculturation and docile behavior rendered English desirable for young native girls. This standard was renewed at every annual function, presenting English as universal and all-powerful. Suggesting that English education managed cultural acquisition, the idealization would always portray native girls as being in need of controlled refinement.

Temple continued his speech by dwelling on the relation between class, liberal progress, and the state's investment in marriage. Cautioning his audience that while native men were being educated in the "arts, the sciences, the poetry, the literature, the politics, the history of Europe [and were] accustomed to liv[ing] in houses constructed upon and furnished in the English style," their women were yet to feel the power of these cultural benefits.³⁸ The cultural deficiency of a selective group of Indian women thus betrayed the mission of universal anglicization. Ultimately, however, Temple believed that native men would "seek the companionship of women educated somewhat in the same manner, women who are able to appreciate and understand all those pursuits, studies and sciences."³⁹ Further conceding the "remarkable progress and proficiency" attained by native youth, Temple felt compelled to caution that "at present the women of India are very much below, intellectually, the women of

Europe . . . the circumstance that the women are so well educated in Europe is one great reason why households are well managed, and why children are well trained."[40]

The governor was convinced that the education introduced to Bombay's new male elite would create new wants and desires, and new habits. But these would be meaningless unless native women were also trained to appreciate the same refinements: "Your houses are closed to us. . . . It is quite hopeless for our people to learn your ways, the only chance of a meeting between the two races is this, that you should learn our ways, that your ladies should acquire our language, should study our literature, should be accustomed to our manners. . . . I do not know anything that would please us better . . . than to see many of the native ladies of Bombay coming out and mingling in our society. . . . Undertaking to educate your native young ladies . . . will conduce to your happiness in life, to your national progress, and to your attachment to British rule."[41] The governor implied that educating native women in English would produce closer bonds between native and English men, and thus secure the national attachment to British rule. Invoking the desire for mutual understanding "between the races," he rendered transparent the homosocial, class interests of the beneficiaries of English education. The state's interest in engineering affective bonds around English was portrayed as generosity. And the governor redirected the native desire for self-recognition and cultural equivalence onto that group's ability to participate in controlling and mediating gender. Condoning racialized, colonial power by blaming the cultural deficiency of the native woman, he challenged native men to reconcile cultural difference, as indexed by gender, through language. The non-English-speaking native woman marked the radical impermeability of tradition. Class and caste differences were smoothly erased and new affinities were crafted between English studies and the intermediary status of English-educated Indian men. Because, as the governor suggested, Europeans would never be either willing or able to learn about native languages or customs, the burden of linguistic and cultural translation was, by this stage in history, firmly on the native population.

English and Sexual Danger

Colonial education policies had enshrined the English language as a prize of classical stature, attainable only after other forms of "modern" language had been secured. Elphinstone advocated "schools for the purpose of teaching English to those disposed to pursue it as a classical language and as a means of acquiring knowledge of European discoveries."[42] Divesting the execution of these policies on the Bombay Education Society,[43] Elphinstone had decreed in 1863 that English be developed as "a reward of merit in other studies . . . which might tend to render it an object of ambition."[44] First placed beyond universal reach and then reintroduced as a reward for acquiescing to the colonial hierarchy of knowledge, the study of the language was thus deliberately crafted to cast its intended—and excluded—students as culturally lacking and inferior. Indeed, by 1860 English education significantly "rewrote not just the lives of those with access to colonial schools and an English education. . . . The majority encountered English as a condition that denied them knowledge and power."[45] Altogether, the experience of *lack* was integral to the psychic project of English studies.

Educated natives, mainly upper-class Parsis and Brahmans of the Chitpavan sub-caste—took to this new structure with gusto. New associations were formed around the pursuit of English. For instance, records from the Bombay Native Education Society show that it moved quickly to forge collaborative links with the European administration, but it did so by deploying the language of egalitarianism-in-education so as to erase earlier privileges accruing to vernacular-based, lower-class, and Sanskritic education. In 1834 the Society advocated for the foundation of the Elphinstone School, the first public institution for native boys to offer an English-language education. Among the first students of the Elphinstone School was the noted nationalist leader and social reformist Mahadev Govind Ranade. Students from this school went on to enter the new Bombay University, which graduated its first students—including Ranade and the Orientalist scholar R. G. Bhandarkar—in 1858.

Ellen McDonald has described how colonial education policies ushered in the urge to cultural mediation. Her work illuminates how the desire to negotiate between colonial and native was immediately transferred upon the reform of native society.[46] While McDonald is concerned with a slightly later period (one I turn to in the following chapter), it is important to note the connection between English education and the rise of liberal social reform institutions in the Bombay area. Records from the Students' Literary and Scientific Society (SLSS), a pioneering organization for intellectual and social interaction between Indians and the British, help us understand the class formation of the new bilingual intermediaries. The SLSS was set up in 1848 by the students of Bombay's Elphinstone College in collaboration with their European professors. Initially intended to provide a forum for the discussion of literary and scientific topics, the speeches and essays of these male intellectuals invariably and consistently turned to discussions on the need for social reform through the intellectual and moral development of the natives of Bombay which was in turn recognized as being best initiated through the education of women. The lofty idealism of the SLSS was well reflected in its tireless introspection and practical reformist zeal; the faculty and professors of Elphinstone College actively encouraged the students to develop and express ideals of reform and the improvement of native society. Prominent among the group's earliest members were Dadabhai Naoroji and Viswanath Narayan Mandlik. A few years later, they were joined by Bal Mangesh Wagle, Narayan G. Chandavarkar, and K. T. Telang.[47]

The members of the SLSS may well have been among the first English-educated colonial subjects of the second British Empire.[48] They were definitely the first ones to benefit from the new schools and colleges inaugurated under the auspices of the British government in western India. In the Society's earliest recorded session, held in August 1849, Dadabhai Naoroji read an essay on "The Duties of a Teacher." Naoroji is remembered today for his potent economic critique of the "drain of wealth" from India to Britain and as a founding member of the Indian National Congress; his role in women's education must be read alongside an awareness of his "moderate" nationalism.[49] Another paper presented at the session was by Behramji Khursedji Gandhi on "Female education." B. K. Gandhi expressed the fervent desire to "do some thing," and advised "every student here present [to] use his influence with the members of his own family to get one [female] pupil at least."[50] The plea was received with wide approval among the audience. The implicit suggestion was that these students reach out urgently to the women of their own families and thereby enliven Macaulay's directive on reaching out to the native vernacular masses.

As in the case of the Alexandra School, here too class and caste restrictions were instituted from the start. In 1853, membership of the SLSS was officially extended to all educated persons, and not just students of the

Elphinstone College. But it was withheld from *shetia* (trading) castes and other castes oriented toward business and commerce.[51] The Society grew in membership from 24 (18 were students) to 106 in 1852. Almost immediately, the Society procured rent-free classrooms and (male) voluntary teachers for its project of educating girls. Separate boys' schools were also inaugurated. On October 21, 1849, three schools opened for 24 Marathi Hindu girls, while 44 Parsi girls entered the Parsi school. Classes at these schools were conducted entirely in Marathi.[52] However, the boys' schools supervised by the SLSS were teaching English and one vernacular language to its students. Reports indicate that the boys were being trained to enter the Elphinstone College, whereas moral education was the most prominent and consistent aspect of the teachings in the girls' schools.

At first the girls' schools did not excite much opposition, but that changed dramatically in 1852. At the annual ceremony for the girls' schools that year, Sir Erskine Perry, the president of the Board of Education for the Bombay Presidency (1848–1852) and the chief justice of the Supreme Court, recommended the need for a particular class of lady teachers for the female students. Perry's wider interest lay in the systematic anglicization of India; in 1853, he published a scholarly report on the method and purpose of introducing English as the lingua franca of the country.[53] Moreover, in official records, he had openly insisted that only Indians of the higher classes and castes be educated in colonial schools, so as to create a class of Indians "qualified by their habits and acquirements to take a larger share, and occupy higher situations, in the civil administration of the country than has hitherto been the practice."[54]

In his speech at one of the SLSS girls' schools, Perry advocated the formation of a "Ladies Committee" staffed by European women. The suggestion was immediately hailed by the members of the SLSS, who emphasized that they "knew and felt that women of superior culture could alone have any proper perception as to what might be most suitable and becoming for young persons of their own sex to learn."[55] Though Perry did not mention English language or literature in his speech, some Gujarati journals interpreted the involvement of European ladies in the education and cultural training of Indian girls as an indicator that the English language would be introduced into the girls' school curriculum.[56] Outrage ensued. The most evocative diatribe against Perry's proposal was presented in the Gujarati-language paper, the *Chabuk* (Whip, or Satirist). This paper was controlled by the very Parsi *shetia* (trader) caste that was barred from membership in the SLSS. The *Chabuk* printed a cartoon depicting Perry presiding at the Supreme Court, "expecting, with ill concealed malignity, the arrival of the luckless husband, whose termagant spouse, vociferating in terrible English, 'Knowledge is Power!' triumphantly hurries into Court to answer her claim for separate maintenance."[57]

It is uncanny how perfectly the criticism invoked by Perry's speech preceded the famous case of Dr. Rakhmabai by more than thirty years.[58] The outburst in the *Chabuk* shows the already entrenched fear that educated women would have the power to invoke legal procedures to shun their husbands' authority and initiate separation; educated women would repudiate the marital bond. The paper went on to express its disapproval that the SLSS broke "with the custom of our forefathers" precisely by breaching the expectation that "English learning and English manners would not be introduced." Writing about the annual examination of schools, the critic noted:

[It was evident] how much show was made and how much of English manners *and English liberty* was allowed to be introduced. . . . What need is there of teaching English morality and English manners and customs in these schools? Simple Gujarati is quite enough. Why then should we have the superintendence of European *Christian* ladies? . . . These girls, instead of living quietly with their husbands, will desire to *make slaves of them*. If they cannot succeed in this, they will drag them into Courts of Justice, to make a display of their talents, their civilisation, and the "power" they shall have acquired by their "knowledge!"[59]

The determination to police appropriate female behavior elevated the power of "English" over its linguistic features. The debate over sending girls outside the home indicates that the upper-caste ideas of family and home were being shaped through the expectation of a consistent availability of female domestic and reproductive labor. Furthermore, the critique in the *Chabuk* evidences a deep discomfort with European ladies being the mediators in this process of linguistic education. Finally, invoking girls as the locus for sexual difference, this passage also establishes the centrality of familial relations in securing normative gender.

The female students of these schools were the wives, daughters, or close relatives of the members of the Students' Society. Even though the *Chabuk* criticized the agenda of women's English education, the wording reveals widening consent on the coalition between the heterosexual family, class and caste mobility, and the English language. Any cultural change introduced to women would immediately reverberate through the family and hence society at large. Upper-caste women were the lightning rods for this dreaded possibility. Women educated in English would not fulfill their reproductive responsibilities within the heterosexual family structure. English emanated sexual power. Whether they supported, or criticized, the English education of native women, all participants in the debate concurred over the alliances between caste, conjugality, and English, and second, that the power of sexuality heightened the symbolic value of English over its linguistic structure.

In his social history of urban western India, Jim Masselos has recorded that the Gujarati-language *Chabuk* voiced the interests of the *shetia*, the trader caste, and it represented the rising power of Gujarati commercial interests in Bombay city. Formerly the *Mumbai Vartman* (Mumbai News), it was considered by colonial observers to be the "most liberal and independent: at times the most scurrilous" of native newspapers.[60] The editorial must be read in terms of the wider contest over caste participation and class mobility enacted over membership within the SLSS. At its inauguration in 1849, the SLSS had restricted membership from this caste of natives. But this changed as the SLSS increasingly needed greater financial support; it could no longer deny membership to the trading castes. The organization was forced to turn to the leading *shetia*, Jagonath Sunkersett [Shankerseth], for monetary support; in fact, by the 1880s, one of the girls' schools was named for his largesse.

The effect of *Chabuk*'s diatribe was immediate: no further move was made toward any sort of "Ladies Committee."[61] The English language reached beyond its form, emanating culturally specific meanings. Repeatedly bringing class and conjugal partnership into alliance, the debate simultaneously contended with the question of *who* was authorized to guide native women through their education. Cautioned by the *Chabuk*, the SLSS nevertheless continued to grapple with the issue of language and social power. In 1854 the SLSS began publishing a monthly Marathi magazine, *Sumitra*, for girls who had received a basic Marathi-language education.[62] The first page of the first issue printed an *Abhang* (a devotional song) in praise of female education.[63] Other articles argued that a girl should be educated in her own language in the early stages of her schooling, and only after having studied her own language should she attempt to learn English. The bulk of the articles presented simple sewing patterns in Marathi and short, moralistic stories that extolled the virtues of religious belief and

Hindu tradition. The magazine repeatedly explained why the more malleable and compassionate nature of a woman should be molded to complement that of a man's, with the woman organizing all the activities within the household.[64] A comparative study on the learning of British and Indian children highlighted the laziness and tardiness of Indian students.[65]

One regular feature printed in the magazine was a fictional, Marathi-language conversation between an uneducated mother, Parvatibai, and her school-going daughter, Saguna.[66] The daughter would patiently explain to her skeptical and illiterate mother all the details of what she had learned in school, from innovations in sewing to empirical facts that established that the earth was not flat. In one encounter, Saguna painstakingly disabused her mother of the mythological belief that the earth was carried on the hood of the serpent god, Sheshya. Parvatibai expressed her hostility to this information by dismissing it as unnecessary and "English" knowledge. The mention of a term or concept that was new or alien to Parvati (and most were) caused her to reject its veracity or utility. Her daughter would then patiently explain that the knowledge was not English but adaptations of little-known Sanskrit terms,[67] or just plain common sense.[68]

The mother's suspicion of English parodied the mistrust of the language among the uneducated or those who might associate it with anything unfamiliar, from science to the blasphemous. Building consent among an imagined community of new and female readers of Marathi, the piece highlighted Parvatibai's laughable reactions, proving that an aversion to English was antithetical to reason and resulted from a lack of knowledge. On the other hand, Saguna's patient reasoning worked against the allegation that English would override a practical domesticity. In fact, the daughter's role in the debate was to perform, with scripted dedication, how the education she received was highly practical for the womanly world of native domesticity and that it was irrational to characterize that education as an English one. It is significant that *Sumitra* was published for the caste-specific schools of the SLSS. It indicates that the native elite readily adopted missionary and colonial discourses on the cultural backwardness of native society and the possibility of controlled amelioration through women's social reform. Moreover, the symbolism of the mother-daughter exchange disguised certain forms of knowledge within the depiction of normative gender roles.

Representatives of the colonial state continued to attend ceremonies at the school, and to pontificate on the issues of language, femininity, and native culture. Speaking to the same group of SLSS members in the 1860s, the governor of Bombay, Sir Bartle Frere, commended the students for the "purity of their motive, [their] single hearted desire to extend to the daughters of their race the same advantages of education which they themselves had enjoyed and so highly valued."[69] The speech was favorably received in the Girls' Schools' Annual Reports. Frere sanctioned native men to transfer the advantages of liberal education to their women. He applauded their desire to extend the pedagogic nature of the colonial relationship with India, specifically through the prism of gender.[70] The form of knowledge referenced by Frere encoded cultural judgments; this was evident in his description of the ideal education system, which, he asserted, should entail "not merely reading [and] writing . . . but that the woman should be as completely educated as the man . . . the fit companions of the educated men." So important was the equitable companionate ideal to the pedagogic enterprise that "Europe would always distrust the highest pretensions to civilisation, in which this one distinctive mark was wanting."[71]

For Frere, the cultural codes that determined native sexual difference (between women and men) undermined claims for cultural advancement being proposed by the native male subjects to whom he was speaking. In other words, "pretensions" to civilization on the part of male English-educated natives were immediately thwarted by what he saw as the absence of companionate and equitable modes of communication. Frere's sermon provides important clues on the role gender as difference played in staging claims to human universalism. Citing companionate conjugality as the ultimate reward of an equal, and hence English, education, the governor challenged the native male elite to recognize the route to progress and civilization. For all concerned, woman was always and already in the service of the reproductive family. But here she was also to produce affective resources for the conjugal bond. Proceeding then to speak on behalf of his wife, Lady Frere, the governor went on to remind his audience that she "hoped on her return from Europe, that some of the young ladies in these schools would be able to converse with her in English," although the reality of the situation caused him to fear that "it would be liable now that Her Most Gracious Majesty the Queen would have difficulty in finding, among her Bombay subjects any one Hindu lady of rank, who would be able to converse with Her Majesty in her own language."[72]

The backwardness of all "Bombay subjects" was located in an appraisal of native women, positioned by their access, or lack thereof, to English education. Despite Frere's challenge to native men to alter matters and, with that, claim equality with "Europe," fears such as those raised by the *Parsi Chabuk* editorial reminded all concerned that women's English education could disrupt the foundational logic of social organization. The conflict over the control of capital in Bombay city, immediately reflected in the ownership and audience of newspapers like the *Times of India* and the *Chabuk*, provides important information on the stakes of the debate. At least at this moment, the majority of Hindu trading groups remained alienated from education and print ventures, while Hindu Brahman castes did not control capital resources.[73] In general, most of the print ventures of the 1850s were in the hands of the Parsi trading classes.

The following year, SLSS reports recorded the exchange between Rao Saheb Vishwanath Mandlik, a member of the SLSS, and Governor Frere.[74] Mandlik argued that there were two conflicting positions on the question of language in women's education: those "who look down on education through the Vernacular" and those "inimical to English education."[75] Mandlik cautioned against either stand, advocating instead "properly conducted English schools for such girls as were well grounded in their own Vernaculars, and whose parents could afford the luxury as it at present is."[76] Advocating a hierarchy between languages, Mandlik might also have been supporting a controlled bilingualism for native women. The governor concurred, propounding on the interrelatedness and interdependency of the vernacular to English in the case of gender. Frere maintained that since the Society specifically aimed to "educate the mothers of future generations . . . a correct knowledge [of] the mother tongue of the pupils, ought to be the first object." The governor continued, stating that the "mother tongue," which really was "the shell of the building," could not be the only credential acquired by the educated women, for just "as a house with bare walls, floor and roof might contain all that was necessary for existence but still be a very incommodious residence," neither could an education be "complete without a knowledge of English or some equally rich and complete foreign language."[77] Then directly addressing the issue of "vernacular English education," the governor thus made the two languages mutually supportive, so much so that the cultural effect of one would balance that of the other. This symbiotic relationship was essential to women's education.

The reference to the non-English language as mother tongue emerged early in western India; in fact, it might have been first invoked in the case of upper-class women's education.[78] This exchange in 1864 between Mandlik and the governor is one of the earliest references to the term "mother tongue" in the Bombay Presidency. Not only produced through negotiations between colonial and native, the term also indicates the contest over caste-specific interests.

The question of whether to introduce English remained a volatile one, and the SLSS was hesitant to institute any English-language education in its girls' schools.[79] It would not be until 1883 that the prohibition on teaching girls over twelve years of age was reconsidered and two more classes (standards V and VI) were added to the Jagonath Shankerseth School in 1884. But legislating on an expansion of the curriculum to incorporate English was not enough. The pressing concern, by 1884, was who should teach these girls. The society would have preferred to have the class taught by a female, although the few women who would have been equipped to perform this function were hesitant or unwilling. Native social opinion maintained that only women with disreputable morals or motives would learn English or take on "employment," that is, work outside the home. Finally, Mr. Bal Mangesh Wagle, the Society's officiating secretary and one of the four first graduates of Bombay University, appointed his daughter-in-law, Sitabai, as an honorary teacher and the Jagonath Shankerseth School's manager. This step, in 1883, proved an ideal one to "inspire confidence in the minds of the parents of the girls."[80]

The early history of the SLSS provides a glimpse into the intertwined history of liberal ideas of progress, class, and the control over female sexuality. Native men responded, albeit cautiously, to Frere's challenge of human universalism. While Frere decreed that their cultural equality with Europe would remain in question until they educated their women equally, the men of the SLSS remained burdened by the logic put forth in the *Parsi Chabuk*. Their awareness was that the cultural equivalence promised by English could only be attained through a vigorous disruption of the caste and gender balance of native society.

Class and Conjugality

The SLSS girls' school experimented with including English in its curriculum, but cautiously. Caught between the desire for cultural equivalence and the coded conflict over capital and caste formation, the SLSS voiced the claims of overlapping social groups, claims to new forms of bicultural and elite authority. As the history of the SLSS demonstrated, one barrier to increasing female access to English lay in the absence of suitable teachers. For this reason, the members of the SLSS collaborated with the British philanthropist and antislavery social activist Mary Carpenter, who visited western India in 1867 to train female teachers, institute prison reform, and introduce technical education. She had already suggested and implemented similar reform ventures in Britain, impressing influential sections of British society on aspects of liberal reform as she saw them. Carpenter had been fascinated with India from the time she first met Raja Ramohan Roy during his 1833 visit to Britain. She immediately garnered the strong support of the educated Indian male elite.[81] Upon returning to Britain, she wrote to the secretary of state for India, the Right Honourable Sir Stafford Northcot, M.P., outlining her plan for Female Normal (teacher-training) schools for western India.[82] There was little doubt in her mind that the gender-sequestered social conventions of India, and hence the social condition of Indian women in general, discouraged them from considering teaching as a profession in the near future. The most effective way to surmount this difficulty was to set up female teacher-training schools staffed by "European or other Christian teachers who have themselves been trained.... It is necessary to bring them in the commencement from England."[83]

Most significant was Carpenter's conviction that the native women she hoped to educate would be drawn to teacher training because it would result in salaried jobs. Further breaking with the agenda of the Alexandra School or the schools of the SLSS, the curriculum and purpose of Carpenter's teacher-training schools would not be determined by native men, nor by their conjugal interests. Rather, the students would be taught by European ladies and eventually they would become teachers for other native women. In contrast to the education of native men, which made scarce reference to the cultural incompetency of British teachers, Carpenter acknowledged that European teachers would have to be specially trained for their work; they would have to learn languages other than English and "study the wants and habits of the [native] children."[84] Carpenter followed English education standards: the students of the Normal school would be deliberately feminized, attaining skills such as needlework, singing, and music. They would also have to learn the English language and other subjects in the Western education curriculum.

Carpenter's suggestions were closely heeded. In 1868, the government of the Bombay Presidency sanctioned one Normal School for Bombay and another for Ahmedabad. The school in Bombay would teach the three lowest Anglo-vernacular standards.[85] Classes would be taught in English and Gujarati so that once the students completed their studies, they could teach those languages along with arithmetic, history, geography, needlework, and music.[86] The government would contribute an amount of RS. 15,520 per annum to the entire endeavor if the native community matched that amount. On Mary Carpenter's personal recommendation, one Miss Richmond was appointed as the supervisor of the girls' school in Bombay. In July 1869, the school was formally placed under a committee of native gentlemen who were to advise its efforts, collect funds, and select candidates. There were twenty-four applications for stipends in 1869; of these, nine were selected for monetary assistance.

The developments did not go unnoticed in the native press. The colonial state closely followed debates in the papers, which were then translated and recorded in the monthly *Report of Native Newspapers* (RNN).[87] According to the RNN, *The Suryadoya* of November 23, while praising Carpenter's ambitions, predicted that she would be ultimately disappointed, for "the idea of a native female school managed by a European lady will only excite derision." And there would be little utility in "native females" learning the skills of "sewing, playing on stringed instruments, dancing, cooking, embroidery . . . which go to form an accomplished English lady."[88] Initial support for the school from the native elite soon diverted toward a shrill outcry against its agenda. New statements calling for restricting English to members of the "respectable" classes sparked allegations on the morality of the teachers and students in the teacher-training school. For instance, *The Bombay Samachar* noted that the Bombay Female School had only two Parsi girls and about fifteen or seventeen Hindu girls, none of whom belonged to the upper or middle classes but to the lower ones. As a result, it was "doubtful whether they will come to the school respectably dressed."[89]

The matter of European instructors teaching the students of this school became an obsession in the native press.[90] Discussing the suitability of the European lady appointed as headmistress of the Ahmedabad Female Normal School, one newspaper declared, "She does not know Gujarati, and as long as she remains ignorant of that language; her services can be of little use to the school." Further, the paper noted that the teacher was "of a hot temper," often threatening to "beat her pupils." Most curious were "her ways of teaching," for "she attempts to teach the terrestrial globe to girls who have not mastered even the Gujarati primer."[91]

Opposition to Carpenter's agenda mounted rapidly. Extensive arguments among Carpenter, the officials of the Education Department, and sections of the native community arose almost immediately over the content of the curriculum in the Normal School. Keen to maintain the government's sensitivity to "indigenous" cultural sentiments, perceived in this case to be exemplified by regional difference, the director of public instruction for the Bombay presidency, Alexander Grant, wrote to C. Gonne, secretary to the Bombay government, noting that in "Bombay it was thought that all the normal pupils must be required to learn English." However, in the case of Ahmedabad, "it was feared that this . . . might have the effect of alarming the people" as a result of which, in the latter case, "it would be better to . . . provide vernacular female teachers for the two thousand girls now under instruction."[92] Language was the most sensitive issue, although it came entwined with the wider problem of cultural mores. As the director noted,

[Carpenter] appeared by no means likely to be satisfied with aiming at a merely intellectual improvement of the women of this country, she would not be satisfied with teaching a large number of them to read, write, keep accounts, and understand something of the Geography and History of the world. She appeared to me to under rate all this in comparison with influences to be produced on their character and manners; she wanted them taught to modulate their voices, to sit in an upright and energetic attitude, to adopt the cheerful music of England, to practice plain sewing, and if possible, to give up wearing bangles.[93]

In striking distinction to Frere's advocacy of English cultural and linguistic standards, the director was aware of the potent threat posed by "English" education when it came to the question of these particular students. His opinions framed the official curriculum for both schools in the Bombay Presidency: it was now decided that the pupils in Bombay would learn "some" English, although their instruction would be predominantly in Gujarati or Marathi. In Ahmedabad, on the other hand, the learning of English was made entirely voluntary.[94]

The argument between Carpenter, the officials of the education department, and native male opinion, as expressed in the native press, was over the social reach of English—over deciding to whom English would be made available. They also argued over what constituted English. Class-making dovetailed with English; both were materialized in the performativity of gender. According to the government, only "those classes who have participated in the advantages of superior English education" would want English to be taught to native women.[95] The expectation was that an English education—extending as it did over various aspects of culture, morality, and behavior—would expand its students' intellect, as well as their tastes, desires, and familial relations. However, were it introduced to classes unfamiliar with English, it would upset existing sentiments and habits and "place the domestic relations of every family on a new footing; and break up existing social habits and tradition."[96]

The first official inspection of the Normal schools at Bombay and Ahmedabad was carried out by the Board of Education in 1870. The school in Ahmedabad, with its voluntary level of English, was considered to be performing well. But the school in Bombay was not up to the mark. All students were examined under the Anglo-Vernacular standard III, but only some of the scholars in Bombay passed in English, arithmetic, history, and geography. The director of education noted "fair progress . . . in most of the branches of an English education," but it was now a matter of grave concern that "in their own vernacular their attainments are so limited that I am quite unable to give them certificates of qualification as teachers, or to recommend their employment."[97]

So serious was the failure of the students at the Bombay Normal School that the educational inspector swiftly decreed that the government's association with the school be discontinued and that the institution be moved to Poona. The school in Bombay was to continue under Miss Richmond but solely for the purpose of providing Gujarati teachers. The move from Bombay to Poona appeared entirely motored by the students' inability to acquaint themselves with their "own" vernaculars. The colonial state's power of intervention in this case is no less than remarkable. The decision, heavy-handed and largely counterintuitive, provoked intriguing reactions from the students themselves. Immediately invoking the original contract of admission, the students of the Bombay Normal School petitioned the government with feelings of "deep regret and mortification." Deploying the discourse of individuated desire and the form of the written petition, the female students argued that the government had required the candidates to bind themselves to a contract of study but had itself shown no such permanence in its own actions.⁹⁸ More crucially, these women wrote in English, of their own aspirations:

> In consequence of the peculiar customs, observances, and prejudices of their respective castes, your Memorialists had to encounter difficulties of a very serious nature in procuring the consent of their relatives and friends to their joining the Female Normal School. . . . In doing so they unhappily not only alienated the sympathy of those relatives and friends. . . . Being desirous of deriving the benefits of an English education, some of your Memorialists declined offers of marriage. . . . [Hence] fram[ing] for their conduct of life plans widely differ[s] from those commonly followed by the females of the communities to which they belong; thus bringing themselves to the notice of the people in a manner most unpleasant and hurtful to their feelings.⁹⁹

The 1870 statement from the students is one of the earliest instances I have found of female students asserting their own aspirations. They state in no uncertain terms that their personal ambition to learn English thoroughly conflicted with familial relationships, especially those sedimented through marriage. That the repercussions conflicted so strongly with social requirements raises urgent questions as to why exactly the women students remained so steadfastly committed to an English education. The students already knew they had challenged the mores of their communities in their independent pursuit of an English education. They posed social constraint —the expectations of custom and family—as antithetical to the realization of their independent desires, which were borne by English.¹⁰⁰

The colonial state remained immune to the vocabulary of liberal redress in this case. Despite all his professed sympathy for the native desire to deploy English in order to dismantle sexual "tradition," the director of public instruction responded to the petitioners' plea with special callousness: "If they have already distanced themselves from their families, then they will not have such an issue moving to Poona to continue their studies."¹⁰¹ Sections of the local press did support the students of the Female Normal School. The strongest statement supporting the Memorialists came from the Parsi paper *Rast Goftar*, which voiced deep concern that the fifty-three girls who had joined the school in Bombay had been pushed to leave.¹⁰² Mentioning that the students "came to the school with the sole and great desire to learn English" but had been forced to discontinue for want of facilities, the paper recorded its "great regret" that "such a large number of Parsi girls [who] have shown great eagerness to learn the English language . . . be disappointed."[103]

The Normal School in Bombay was moved to Poona and the English language was purged from the syllabus. The students' lack of command over "their own" languages and the presence of the English language in the curriculum led to the closure of the original school in Bombay. But unpublished files later record the eruption of another controversy: the unsuitability and gross negligence of the school's supervisor, Miss Richmond, and the grievous immorality of the students in the Bombay school. Writing confidentially to the Chief Secretary of the Government of Bombay on March 14, 1873, the Secretary to the Government of India marked his deep opposition to the "perilous nature of . . . prematurely placing Indian women in a position of independence beyond that which the opinion or practice of their own class and country would assign to them." Even more urgently, he noted, "some serious scandal has recently been caused by the discovery, in a normal school for the training of native school mistresses, that the women admitted to the institution have been leading lives of gross immorality, and that their way of life had been notorious in the town long before it was ascertained by English officers at the same place."[104]

Resonating with the outburst in the *Parsi Chabuk* from the 1850s, this was certainly not the first time that an indirect, though potent, connection was made between English and morality.[105] But what is especially striking in this case is how women were being referenced. The absence of conjugal or kin-connected male mediators overdetermined the proclivity of some women toward "immorality." The suggestion that women's sexuality was nonconjugal spawned a chain of connotations. Non-normative, antisocial, and therefore disguised beyond the state's purview: a series of references that, as I discuss in the next chapter, further strengthened the connection between chastity and caste. Accounts such as this one were never publicized, although the connection between the students of this school, their education, their ability to earn money, and their moral vices were forged continually.[106] In the process, a particular definition of respectable conjugality protected English from certain social groups. Whatever the social class, the logic of gender served to obfuscate the contingencies of history as well as to determine the reach of English.

By 1878 the Education Department reiterated that the students at the Poona school were making gradual, yet most satisfactory, progress. The

European women teaching at this school were also learning Marathi. It was noted that because most advanced students had achieved the highest vernacular standard, the idea of starting an elementary English class could now be considered.[107] A few years later, a newspaper report on the Education Commission of 1882 quoted Mrs. Mitchell restating that Marathi was the chief medium for instruction. Thirty-four students had completed the course of study in that period. The only improvement she suggested was that "a few of the more promising students should have English as a foreign language added to the above standards."[108] In the case of staffing paid posts, "English as a foreign language" could be taught to the more accomplished students, but only after they demonstrated their acquisition of a vernacular-language education. The policy closely echoed Elphinstone's 1823 directive that English be made a 'reward for merit in other studies."[109] But the social context was rapidly changing. As I discuss in the next chapter, by the 1880s, Hindu upper castes gained control over the print and capital resources of Bombay city. Simultaneously, English was filtered through gender and then put to the task of containing critiques of Brahmanic authority. Knowledge and sexuality remained central to the social upheaval of the period, essential in shoring up new caste formations. It is to the role of gender in naturalizing, even secularizing, Brahmanical power over English that we now turn: the way sexuality shaped the hierarchy between English and non-English languages, the de-ritualization of caste-specific exigencies of female sexuality, and a shifting conception of native masculinity.

3

"THE LANGUAGE OF THE BEDROOM"

Mimicry, Masculinity, and the Sexual Power of English

July 19, 1884, saw a large and influential gathering of Poona's native and colonial elite in the Hirabaug Town Hall. It had been raining incessantly and the especially heavy downpour was well documented in newspaper accounts from the time. The meeting had been convened to discuss plans for the Poona Native Girls' High School (PNHS). It was followed, a few weeks later, by a deputation from the "People of Poona" to the governor of the Bombay Presidency to urge the immediate inauguration of the school, which would teach its students the English language in a standard Western education curriculum. The proposed school would be the first native-managed institution to teach girls and women to the level of the matriculation examination.[1] Newspaper accounts from the period note that the women's forum, the Arya Mahila Samaj (AMS), started by Pandita Ramabai (1858–1922), had already met to discuss these plans.[2] According to one such report, Pandita Ramabai was herself in England, where she had gone to pursue an education, but the women of the group—nearly one hundred in number—had met and reached a resolution, which they entrusted to M. G. Ranade.[3] Now presiding over the public meeting, Ranade emphasized that the resolution, written in Marathi, evidenced that it was native women themselves who most urgently expressed their desire for a high level of education. Categorically stating that the benefits of male education would be "multiplied a hundredfold" if women had similar opportunities, Ranade reiterated that the AMS supported the effort "to start a high class school for teaching the higher standards in vernacular languages along with English and Sanskrit studies."[4] Ranade stressed that native women had expressed these sentiments independently.

But had they? As Ranade's wife would later recall in her memoirs, educated Indian men regularly guided and supervised the AMS.⁵ The statement from the AMS projected the authority of a certain class of English-educated men who served as mediators between the desires of indigenous women and the mission of colonial modernity. As school reports from 1850 to 1880 show, access to English was subtly ritualized through gender by a process that also sealed knowledge and caste with sexuality. Those years also saw a shift in the ownership of the "native" press, from Parsi and merchant interests toward Anglo-Marathi and Brahman interests.⁶ This chapter focuses in greater detail on the role of gender in coding and decoding meaning, in producing the symbolic connotations of English.⁷ The history I track here reveals how a new class of English-educated native men augmented their power by controlling the English education of native women. In the process, ideas of sexual difference and standards of desirable femininity were grafted onto English. The language and culture were domesticated by the sexual standards of a newly hegemonic class coalition. Simultaneously, as I demonstrate, English was deployed to control female sexuality and, with that, caste power. In this chapter, I continue to trace the strong overlap in the rhetorical strategies deployed by opposing camps as they debated the relationship between English, the vernacular, and women. The gendering of meaning between English and non-English languages marked each as hermetically sealed against the other. In turn, English was deployed to determine the parameters of sexuality, but not just for women. Seething tensions over native masculinity and male homosociality were deflected, even contained, by building consent over the power of English to direct subjectivity, power, and desire. While opponents of English studies pilloried native men for their emasculate and effeminate ways, and their desire to ape the cultural trappings of the Englishman, native men countered those charges by reinscribing the phallogocentric power of English. Conflicts over native masculinity and allegations of cultural mimicry were subdued by linking English with the correct socialization of native women.

English, in other words, rapidly surpassed linguistic purpose and became a tool of both feminine and masculine gender control. As Indian English became aligned with masculine authority, it rapidly gained the power to manage caste status as well as normative desire; to regulate gender difference against allegations of cultural deficiency; and to deflect otherwise wide-ranging allegations of effeminacy and cultural mimicry. In turn, some Indians heightened their indigenous, class, caste, and nationalist power by extending the authority of Indian English into sexually differentiated spaces; in other words, by deploying English to bolster a new and self-consciously "native" identity.

The Milk of the Tigress

The sexualization of language is the process by which sexuality came to infuse the comparative value of language. Particularly informative here is the example of the Marathi-language writer Vishnushastri Chiplunkar (1850–1882). Chiplunkar's short life, characterized by fervent literary productions, exemplified the ability of a new generation of indigenous linguistic nationalists to shape receptive audiences and creatively redeploy colonial concern with native gender relations. He was the son of the noted Sanskrit and Marathi scholar Krishnashastri Chiplunkar, who in his capacity as Reporter of the Vernacular Press in the Department of Translation would have supervised the Report of Native Newspapers and performed other cultural gate-keeping duties. For instance, Veena Naregal has pointed out that Krishnashatri Chiplunkar was "probably associated with the Dakshina Prize Committee when [the radical anti-caste intellectual] Jyotirao Phule's manuscript was rejected in 1855."[8] For his part, Vishnushastri Chiplunkar aggressively condemned Phule's evaluation of Brahmanical hegemony, characterizing Phule as "shamelessly bark[ing] away at Brahmans, and [vying] for crumbs that might be thrown at them according to the convenience of those in power."[9]

Vishnushastri Chiplunkar studied in English schools in Poona and graduated with a BA in English, history, and Sanskrit from Deccan College (formerly Poona Sanskrit College). He initially embarked on a teaching career in the state-funded Poona High School, but then broke with the strictures of colonial-funded educational policies as well as existing native publishing ventures.[10] First creating the Marathi literary magazine *Nibandhmala* (Garland of Essays) in 1874, he went on to establish the Chitrashala Press in 1877 and the Aryabhushan Press in 1880. Both sought to print works of cultural and political import, bringing an array of publications within the reach of the Marathi-reading, middle-class public. The *Nibandhmala* particularly embodied the bilingual prowess of the new colonial Brahmans; it claimed, by virtue of being published in Marathi, the right to speak for the masses while actually arguing for the maintenance of anglicized, Brahman leadership over native society.[11]

Chiplunkar's writings establish the widening practice of engendering meaning between English and the vernacular. Increasingly, Chiplunkar began to collaborate with the Hindu nationalist leader Bal Gangadhar Tilak and the social reformer Gopal Ganesh Agarkar. Seamlessly rendering their own Brahmanical investments as invisible and universal, the three men would go on to determine the very parameters of cultural nationalism. Reflecting the philosophical histories once favored by Mountstuart Elphinstone, Chiplunkar, too, advocated for the complete history of the Maharashtrian people, narrated, as Prachi Deshpande has discussed, through the "establishment of political and military power."[12] In clear distinction to contemporary writers such as Jyotirao Phule, "Chiplunkar argued for a modern Marathi idiom squarely based on its Sanskrit roots" and that only "by anchoring themselves to their heritage of Sanskrit conventions, grammar, and vocabulary . . . could Marathi writers survive and absorb English knowledge without being asphyxiated by it."[13] Hence, even as he sought to "classicise Marathi expression, he also passionately argued for a greater absorption of modern English forms such as history into its modern prose repertoire."[14]

In addition to founding the widely circulating Marathi- and English-language newspapers published at the Aryabhushan Press—*Kesari* and *Mahratta*—Chiplunkar, Tilak, and Agarkar also founded the New English School for Boys in Poona in 1880.[15] Amalgamating English education with a critique of missionary and colonial schools, the school stated its intention as imparting a revitalized Hindu patriotism. Carefully crafting a connection between the English language and a nationally oriented and desiring subject, the school's first superintendent, V. S. Apte, took care to align the school with the master narrative of British supremacy, drawing attention to the "benign rule of the present rulers, who unlike the former conquerors of India that were only territorial conquerors, have won the hearts of the people by showering on them innumerable blessings of which Education is the greatest."[16] The school opened with 19 students on the rolls; that number rose rapidly within months, and by 1883 there were 732 enrollments.

In tracking the reciprocal relationship between English and Marathi in western India, Veena Naregal has discussed how the new colonial and bilingual Brahmans of western India sought privileged control over Anglo-Marathi literary productions by "internalising liberal discourses . . . [so much so that] Indian modernity internalised the tensions between liberal egalitarian norms and the divisive and hierarchical effects of a bilingual education policy."¹⁷ In 1881, Vishnushastri Chiplunkar wrote a series of critical articles for *Kesari*, edited at the time by G. G. Agarkar. Prominent among these were his pieces on the Hindu proclivity to imitate their rulers, first the Muslims and later the English. Chiplunkar's concern with the mimicry of English cultural practices was cleverly expressed by invoking subtly gendered codes. He expressed deep contempt for those Indians who drank alcohol and those who used glasses, gloves, or socks; the latter, he maintained, could be used by women but not by men. Certain patterns of consumption and dress indicated the stability of cultural and gender difference. He expressed strong regard for the British reliance on "punctuality, efficiency, spirit of adventure, patriotism, sense of unity and solidarity," he advocated that Indians should indeed imitate those British qualities.¹⁸ And it was in *Nibandhmala* that Chiplunkar worked assiduously to forge a modern literary style for the Marathi language. While convinced of the relative autonomy of Marathi, he also conveyed to his Marathi reading audience his admiration for English literature and state formation. He sought to build community both around "high" literary Marathi discourse and a selective knowledge of English literary and historical developments.¹⁹

Chiplunkar was interested in shaping a cultural identity for Marathi. For this purpose, he first produced cultural analogies for both English and Marathi and then grafted the one upon the other. His discussions of Marathi regularly referenced English and vice versa, thereby entering into the wider rhetorical exercise by which English and Marathi were being endowed with new cultural qualities. Both by virtue of his writings, which were self-consciously in Marathi, as well as by his dedication to inscribing Maharashtrian Brahmanical power within a network of the "new colonial Brahmans," Chiplunkar's activities reveal too that the gendering of language was by no means restricted to the pro-colonial, anglicized elite, as represented by Manockjee Cursetjee and the members of the SLSS. Despite being passionately committed to securing the ascendancy of Marathi, Chiplunkar simultaneously drew sustenance from the power of English, specifically its sexual power. It was in his best-known essays, published shortly before his death, that he elaborated on the associations between mimicry, masculinity, and English. In eight issues of *Nibandhmala*—a searing collection on nationalist sentiment, knowledge, and religion—he dealt with "the condition/plight of our country" (*Aamchya deshachi sthithhi*) and pronounced that "English knowledge is like a tigress. He who has thrived on her milk will never turn out to be irresolute."[20] Native masculinity, he maintained, could fortify itself by imbibing the most powerful aspect of the female—her life-giving and reproductive ability. Soon after he wrote about "eastern languages," likening them to "cow's milk: sweet and pure."[21]

The tiger has deep cultural significance in the history of Maharashtrian Hindu identity formation. Regularly referenced in folk and Hindu nationalist histories is the fable that the Maratha king Shivaji triumphed over his (Mughal) adversary, Afzal Khan, through the use of a concealed tiger claw. Contemporaneously, the tiger is the electoral symbol of the right-wing Hindu nationalist party, the Shiv Sena. And it was exactly at this time in history, the nineteenth century, that the cow was referenced in debates on the protection of "Hindu" culture; calling for the ban on cow slaughter ignited the politics of a range of regional revivalist organizations across British India.[22]

Chiplunkar's writings corroborate the increasing importance of sexuality in signifying cultures of power for an emerging nationally oriented identity. Chiplunkar was not staking out simple binaries between the masculine and the feminine. He referenced gender codes differently from those invoked in European or Anglo-Indian discussions.[23] It is important to recall here Chiplunkar's close partnership with Bal Gangadhar Tilak, who resurrected military and masculinist symbols in expanding Brahman power over a new Maharashtrian cultural collectivity.[24] Chiplunkar's commentaries on English cultural change and his strident views on language instantly made references to female power, indigenous masculinity, and cultural mimicry.[25] His writings suggest the importance of female sexual power in enabling the selective appropriation of culture. Language had to be redirected, in fact "reproduced," to augment its power; female sexuality was integral to this agenda. Chiplunkar did not carve out exclusionary differences between "Western" and "Eastern" culture; consequently he did not stake polarities between masculine and feminine. Instead, he advocated an active incorporation of the feminine into the masculine.[26] In itself, this critical absorption of the feminine to augment native masculine power was an interesting disavowal of the charges of native effeminacy extended by the colonial state and in British cultural productions.[27] Chiplunkar's purpose was double-headed. He refuted colonial allegations of upper-caste effeminacy, and he invoked the power of female reproductive sexuality to shape the meaning of English. The "spread" of English would draw upon sexual difference, even as it contained female power within its execution.

Learning Gender, Knowing English: Shaping the Curriculum

Less than a month after the initial meeting at the Town Hall, mentioned at the start of this chapter, the plans for the girls' high school were formalized. The school would comprise students "of all respectable parents, of whatever caste and creed, and whose fathers and husbands or other guardians will not object to their learning English and Sanskrit . . . to become useful helpmates and equal companions to their male relations."[28] The meeting resulted in a deputation of the aforementioned "People of Poona," a group that visited the governor of the Bombay Presidency on August 9, 1884, and put English at the top of the proposed school's agenda. Speaking at the ceremony, the Rao Bahadur Chhotalal of Ahmedabad emphasized that "an acquaintance with English is essentially necessary to enlighten women on the practical questions of the day, and to enable them to take an intelligent interest in the pursuits and aspirations of their husbands and to encourage the growth of vernacular female education in general."[29]

The presence of the Rao Bahadur, a colonial-supported dignitary, from Ahmedabad at this ceremony signals the broader regional interests served by the new school and the English-education agenda. In stressing that respectable women represented a vital constituency of vernacular speakers, the Rao Bahadur promised that the girls' school would bring to fruition the central tenet of the colonial state's linguistic trickle-down policies. His expectation was that this act of linguistic and cultural ventriloquism would forge new, complementary relationships between English and the vernacular, and between some husbands, their wives, and daughters. English-educated women would nurture the vernacular and, in doing so, would bring progressive ideals of domesticity and companionate love to fruition.

The Poona Native Girls' High School was inaugurated soon after by the governor of the Presidency, Sir James Fergusson, on September 29, 1884. It was the first native-managed school across British India to administer education to girls at the level of the matriculation examination, imparting English language, literature, history, geography, and other elements of the

"Western education" curriculum to its students.[30] While the superintendent was an English woman, the managerial structure of the school remained in the hands of Indian men. At the end of the first year, the school's official report mentioned that the girls' knowledge of "their vernaculars" was barely up to the mark and needed to be improved.[31] Similar to statements about the Female Normal Schools discussed in the previous chapter, here, too, the state education department concurred that students aspiring to enter the school, as well as its higher English classes, must first be tested in Marathi or Gujarati, as the "girls were not well grounded in their vernaculars."[32] The statement signals the growing centrality of a written and formal structure in determining the standards of language, even so-called vernacular language.

The school retained the patronage of the native and colonial male elite over the years, a group that—much in the manner of the SLSS—forged favorable connections between the English language and companionate domesticity. At its annual function in 1891, the governor of the Bombay Presidency, Lord Harris, noted that women's education should train a woman to communicate with the men of the household on all matters and subjects. Further eliciting the connection between language and domesticity, the noted Orientalist scholar R. G. Bhandarkar (1837–1925) emphasized:[33]

It is in consequence of our contact with England and Englishmen and Englishwomen that conception[s] of higher social and moral ideals have dawned in our minds.... We do not propose in this institution to make our women learned and teach them to neglect their household duties and take to books. What we intend to do is to make them more fit to discharge those duties, and to open a window in the prison house of our social system through which they may look into the modern world. That window is the knowledge of the English language—the language of modern civilisation and of healthy human progress.[34]

Recalling the ideals espoused by the members of the SLSS, Bhandarkar, too, maintained that femininity entailed the performance of certain tasks that institutionalized the domestic and conjugal as modern. English would itself be performed in a way that superseded linguistic features and in that way embody a combination of traits, behaviors, and presentations. In the process, a gender order characterized by the primacy of the heterosexual couple and an affective partnership between husband and wife would arise. Far from maintaining rigid divides between the "spiritual" and the "modern" or between the feminine and masculine, English would thrive on complementary sexual standards. Bhandarkar's words evidence the centrality of Indian men to this transfer. English had already been established in colonial discourse as the language of a superior civilization. Now it was refashioned by colonial subjects as the conduit through which to introduce some native women to the apparently advanced gender order of the modern world, but only if native men directed this act of cultural and linguistic ventriloquism.

A few weeks before the opening of the PNHS a lengthy and impassioned debate occurred in *The Mahratta* and *Kesari*. The former was a widely read English-language newspaper edited by Bal Gangadhar Tilak, while *Kesari*, the most prominent Marathi-language newspaper of the time, was edited by the social reformer Gopal Ganesh Agarkar.[35] Agarkar was among the moderate contingent and he, too, espoused complete equality in the curriculum for men and women. In fact, he believed that separate schools for women should themselves be eradicated. Tilak and Agarkar parted ways over political differences, a legendary splitting after which the latter went on to found and edit the Marathi newspaper *Sudharak*. In this, Agarkar argued that separate spheres of existence, as exemplified in rigidly differentiated curricula, only made women synonymous with social ornaments and reduced them to objects of desire, bordering on titillation.[36]

The larger dispute between Tilak and Agarkar, which is more conventionally dated to the mid-1890s, was actually rehearsed almost a decade earlier in the context of women's English education.[37] Initiating the debate, *The Mahratta* commented on the course of studies to be adopted in the school, remarking that English may be studied as a luxury and not as the medium of instruction: "We are already aware how the knowledge of matriculated boys is superficial [because] English [is] their medium for learning everything."[38] But the same issue of *The Mahratta* printed a letter signed by "Will-O'-The-Wisp," who argued against Marathi-language education for the girls of the new English school. Insisting that the pleasures of reading in general and literature in particular could at present be secured only by one who had knowledge of English, this writer believed that the Marathi-reading girl would have a very poor set of resources to satisfy her thirst for knowledge. Most significant, the writer rejected any possibility of English and non-English languages coexisting in the curriculum and in the life of an educated woman.

The debate was immediately picked up by the Marathi-language newspaper *Kesari* and rapidly turned into heated exchanges between, and within, both papers. *Kesari* described the antagonism against the new educational system and noted that popular opinion considered the English language to be *vittalshi*.[39] Dictionaries from the early twentieth century define the term as "impurity, pollution" and "menstrual discharge."[40] Female sexuality and impure social status were indicated by the same word. Connoting English as ritually impure, the statement actually indicates the centrality of the purity/pollution worldview, or the upper-caste patriarchal interests of the intended audience. The role of sexuality in supporting caste difference is evident; once more, the underlying charge was that social access to English would negate the specificity of Brahmanical culture and hierarchy. Similarly invoking an indigenous structure of sentiment, another writer, identified simply as G.B.L., wrote on the same subject to *The Mahratta*. The writer argued that were Indian women to learn English, then, "under the powerful, magical influence of such a language, poor Marathi, already crippled, will soon be discarded as the dialect of the illiterate Kunbi."[41]

The history of linguistic change evoked sharp anxieties over caste and rural-urban boundaries, establishing the longer, status-centric politics of language in South Asia. In this case the fear was that English would encroach on Marathi, that upper-caste women who spoke English would annihilate both the Marathi language as well as all organic ties to indigenous culture, history, and tradition. With that, they would relegate Marathi to being the language of the rural antimodern peasant. The overarching implication was that the status of Marathi was dependent on its use by upper-caste women. It was these women who had to perform their knowledge of Marathi so as to ensure that caste culture remained organically indigenous and resistant.

The power of normative upper-caste women lay in their ability to signify and thus maintain cultural parameters. Gendered subjects could situate the relative status between English and Marathi. Were women to learn English, then the language would exceed linguistic form. If incorrectly schooled, native women could permit both the irresistible cultural ascendancy of English and destroy the existence of the vernacular. Continuing in this vein, G.B.L. stated that "the ambition of every woman . . . will be to blubber in a tongue whose force will be soon overpowering."[42] Not only would English encroach on Marathi, but the two languages simply could not coexist; the presence of one in the curriculum in the girls' school signified the eradication of the other.

In arguing that English could provide an intellectual example to Marathi, G.B.L. expressed views that resonated with Cursetjee and Chiplunkar. If works were translated from English, then the "most choice pieces of poetry, of thought, of philosophy" would be introduced into Marathi; the vernaculars could be reformed through infusions from English.[43] G.B.L., a self-identified native writing in one of the most prominent English-language newspapers of the time, voiced the conviction of colonial education policies: that the existence and quality of literary works established the superiority of the corresponding culture. In addition, G.B.L.'s views marked an emerging consent over the relation between languages and the symbolic use of the culturally compliant woman in universalizing caste power. While the vernacular might have been relatively barren—in terms of literary content and its ability to encode sophisticated thoughts and feelings—it was also malleable and open to transfusion. This was how the physical structure of Marathi could be improved, though not violated, by the example of the other language.

"Women" had the power to maintain the boundary between English and non-English languages. Of course, these were a particular class of native women. Writing to *The Mahratta* the following week, a "correspondent" further elaborated on this point. If English were taught to "our" women,

It will be our Lingua Franca and it will efface every trace of the old Vernaculars. English will be the language of the streets, the market, the kitchen and the bedroom. Whatever be the excellences or special qualifications of the English language, we are not at all prepared to leave our mother tongue in its favour, for everybody knows the affection which he feels for every thing that he can call his own. . . . I say that we are not prepared to lose our nationality in the loss of our language. Sad and mournful will be the day when a Hindu child will say to his mother Mamma, I am hungry; Get me the moon, Mamma!! This will be the ultimate fate of India if the medium of educating females be made the English language.[44]

When native mothers learned English they would immediately and irrevocably surrender the vernacular, initiate its demise, and disrupt the culturally permissible boundaries of gender difference. Then English would permeate the public and the private, disrupting commercial transactions as well as public order. And most outrageously, it would infiltrate the site for the production and reproduction of national subjects and the foundation of the bourgeois domestic-private space: the bedroom. Implying that female sexuality had no location or purpose outside the inner recesses of the bourgeois-nationalist home, the words fanned the fear of sexual excess. Implicitly, they voiced distress over the possibility of non-reproductive female sexuality.

Invoking the "mother tongue" further elicited loyalty, affection, and the expectation of a sacred domestic culture. The associations were essential for the sentimental response that the writer hoped to extract from the public at large. Successfully manipulating the multiple possibilities encoded in references to the mother, the correspondent exhorted "every champion of the Marathi language [to] whet his sword and be ready to enter the lists. Courage is necessary as the affairs are critical!!"[45] The slide between domesticity, the mother tongue, Marathi, and the mother, all besieged by a crusading foreign culture, amplified the urgency of preventing women from learning English. Simultaneously, it anticipated a militant, and male, response.

Between the Burkha and the Ballroom

The energetic exchange between G.B.L. and Will-O'-The-Wisp continued through the following weeks, eventually turning to contest the ability of women to produce literature. The debates illustrated only superficially contradictory opinions. Ultimately, discussions on the anglicization of India revealed the tightening consensus over the parameters of Hindu caste power. Seemingly insurmountable differences between indigenous and foreign were increasingly amplified through polarities between Islamic and modern culture. These binaries were, in turn, brought into alliance with the assumption that conjugality signaled civilizational progress, and that English would ally with caste power to discipline non-normative female sexuality.

In the evolving debate, Will-O'-The-Wisp cited the case of several Parsi girls who had translated English books into Gujarati and thus enriched the "vernacular." For this reason, Will-O'-The-Wisp argued in favor of an English education.[46] G.B.L. replied the following week, first questioning the very existence of these Parsi girls, and then arguing that "even in

England ... literature has ... been an occupation with the male section of the community. I know of very few female names who have added perceptibly to the stock of human knowledge."[47] Further noting that the numbers of women in India who may have contributed through translation were minuscule, if not negligible, G.B.L. declared that the lessons of history and the examples from Europe together proved that women could not be original writers. Women could be *taught* literature, but it was unlikely that they would *produce* it. Literature became the means by which to assimilate language and woman to one another. In fact, it defined the power as well as the parameters of language. Having argued two weeks prior that the vernacular should be a passive receptacle for literary infusions from English, G.B.L. could now state that women remain merely receptive to the masculine and literary productions of the time. Hence, literature could reinforce sexual difference to dictate a suitable education for women; literature was produced by men and directed upon women.

The debates were not restricted to the newspaper columns; they appeared almost immediately in conversations over the curriculum. One year after the PNHS had been inaugurated, the Gaekwad of Baroda[48] argued at its first Prize Distribution Ceremony that through English literature the education of girls and women must complement the education provided to men. Maintaining "very strongly" that India was going through a period of "transition" that entailed the adoption of "Western modes of thought," the Gaekwad first distinguished between "rudimentary vernacular instruction" and "Western education," and then emphasized:

If our women were trained, if their intelligence were awakened and their imagination directed to take in the beauties of art and poetry, the minds of our men would expand likewise. ... As all the useful knowledge of the present comes from the West and owing to the poverty of our vernacular literature comes to us through the medium of English, let ladies of the upper ranks, at any rate those who have the leisure for it, acquire a knowledge of English. Let not the minds of our men be active abroad and stagnant at home owing to the absence of sympathy in their helpmates.[49]

The civilizing, conjugal power of English could be harnessed to the particular needs of upper-class society. Whether in agreement (or not) with the agenda of anglicization, modernity and companionate love were coupled and structural agreements were forged within the new class of the English educated.

"THE LANGUAGE OF THE BEDROOM"

But these arguments did not subdue critiques of the new Poona Native Girls' High School. Critics evoked the threat of excessive and non-normative female sexuality. Entwined with the assumption of insurmountable cultural difference, these developments ultimately secured the authority of a select group of native men to legislate on the parameters of culture. One of the most controversial of diatribes against the Poona Native Girls' High School appeared in the Marathi *Poona Vaibhav* of August 24, 1884. The article, entitled "Stri Shikshan" (women's education), claimed that its objective was to compare the prostitutes "amongst us" and the females of other religions. But, the article argued, as females of those other religions would be attending the new school (the PNHS) and would be offended by a criticism of their domestic habits, the writer would content himself with comparing "the manners and customs of English people, after whose model [people of other religions] have shaped their [manners], with those of prostitutes among us."[50]

The paper described in excruciating and lascivious detail the relationship between a European prostitute and her master, the English method of taking a bath, and the customs enacted in ballroom dances. The writer particularly specified that European women liked to bedeck themselves and "colour their faces" when "going out" in public. The sensual perusal of "fruit, wines, [and] flesh" in European social situations and the customary dress which "keeps the ladies' hands and chest entirely uncovered" in ballroom gatherings were detailed. The method of taking a bath received special attention: "They rub and shake their bodies again and again and [when] their bathing is over . . . the lady addresses her boy . . . he is only to be called a boy, but he is a grown man with beard and moustaches. . . . He fills the pot with water, the lady being all this while naked. . . . Sometimes she goes so far as to point to a part of her body [to] ask [the] boy, do you see any dirt here?" The article drew to a close, thunderously asking "our young and promising people whether this action would not put our prostitutes to shame?"[51]

Practices such as bathing, eating, and dancing were laden with disciplinary, caste-specific associations. Each of these rituals indicated upper-caste boundaries. Most provocative was the juxtaposition between the female prostitute and the wife. Kunal Parker's important work on this period has illuminated how the yoking of Victorian norms with colonial law and the elevation of Brahman texts as scripture successfully produced prostitution as a category outside of Hinduism itself.[52] Female "prostitution" was the necessary "other" to a notion of "Hindu" society. The latter was policed through idealized expectations of lifelong domestic labor and unquestioning devotion of the wife to male sexual control. Nonconjugal sexuality was the crucial trope; it implicitly served to index upper-caste culture.

The "Stri Shikshan" article elevated the reproductive, ritual-abiding betrothed to a sacred standard against which to condemn or judge English culture and, hence, the issue of anglicization. The colonial state immediately unleashed its power. The allegation that the bodily activities of white women exceeded the limits of the reproductive unit could not go unchallenged. The administration instantly demanded that the editor of the *Vaibhav* be prosecuted under the Criminal Practice Code. Since he was a member of the highly reputed (native) Sarvajanik Sabha, the state additionally demanded that other members of the group issue a strong public apology for the article. And, indeed, a letter signed by V. Mudliar, R. G. Bhandarkar, M. G. Ranade, Shanker Pandurang Pandit, and other upper-caste native leaders was presented to the government, apologizing for the crude and misdirected images construed in the offensive article.[53]

The quick response might have mollified the colonial authorities, but it also indicated the rising authority of one section of the native elite. Here, as in the statements and speeches over the Alexandra and SLSS schools, it becomes apparent that the colonial state worked with educated natives to control social mobility. Women's education, in short, permitted the colonial state to sponsor and regulate the leadership of some "native gentlemen." The symbiotic relationship between English and bourgeois conjugality eased the patriarchal ascendancy of "the natural leaders of native society."[54] Standards of "respectability" were central to the coalition between colonial and native: the Education Department decreed in 1886 that "native gentlemen" must maintain control over the screening of applicants to the girls' school, so as to judge their propriety and background. This was because "there is an undoubted demand for Anglo-vernacular education among a class of females who require it for illicit purposes. . . . Even admission of one of a doubtful character will give a handle to the opposition of all natives who look with horror upon what they consider female emancipation."[55]

Over 1886, *Kesari* published a series of articles mulling over the curriculum of the Poona Native Girls' High School. The paper first reiterated that native women must relearn their vernaculars to prevent the unnatural crusade of English and English values. It then questioned the purpose in teaching native women to be proficient in a foreign language, asking why the school taught women "English language and culture, English songs, to read English, [and] to play English musical instruments? What use is this to our *Hindu* ladies? The school equips them to participate in balls with men, to play the piano, which will fill them with an attraction for another world and detract them from performing their familial duties."[56] Differentiating between literary texts and the cultural power of English, the article attacked the PNHS "for teaching secular subjects and housing high class girls as well as low class girls."[57] Of course the writer was in error here, for the PNHS took care to cater only to upper-caste and Parsi women and, in fact, spilled much ink in denying allegations that the school had ever admitted "non-respectable" women.[58]

It is difficult to ascertain who the authors of these articles were, but there is little doubt that Bal Gangadhar Tilak played a significant role in shaping *Kesari*'s debate. In 1887 he took over from G. G. Agarkar as the editor of *Kesari*. Paramila Rao has revealed that Tilak's entry into the debate over the school was primarily motivated by his desire to quash the move to grant women the right to vote on resolutions within the Indian National Congress (INC). The INC was characterized by native pro-English moderates, men such as G. K. Gokhale, Vishnu Moreshwar Bhide, and H. N. Apte. In fact, Vishnu Moreshwar Bhide's daughter was the first student to enroll in the PNHS.[59] A minimum standard of education was already required for determining voting qualifications within the INC. Educated women, as the student body of the PNHS evidences, would largely have been the wives and daughters of this very group. Thus, agitating to extend the vote to women would have doubled the power of moderate, English-educated Brahmans in claiming leadership over the Congress. Tilak's own politics were stridently "pro-Marathi," populist, and Hindu extremist. He first ridiculed the idea of English women claiming the right to vote for members of the Parliament and to sit in the House of Commons.[60] But Tilak's words signal much more than a resistance to liberal education; they indicate the role of conjugality in securing class mobility and in marking caste through reference to "Hindu" culture. Eventually Tilak's agitation forced the moderate group to abandon their proposal in 1895. He continued, however, his own contract with upper-caste Hindu nationalism. In 1903 he advocated that native schools should teach *Dharmashastras*, texts that were forbidden to women and non-Brahmans, a suggestion that would have had the effect of discouraging all non-Brahmans from attending school altogether.⁶¹ His opinions were undeniably powerful and, as Rao argues, his opposition to the PNHS was so severe that no new school for the English education of women would be established for decades.

Kesari's harangue continued the following week, combining references to religious difference with a mounting class anxiety. Railing against the new school for keeping its curriculum in a "burkha," the paper argued that drastic changes in customs, laws, religion, and family arrangements in native society had thoroughly impoverished the middle class.⁶² In the midst of these changes, "English educated, piano playing, singing and dancing women, Grace Darlings and Elizabeths" were threatening to usurp the once-sacred position of Ahilyabai and Sita.⁶³ This critique referenced not only Western women but (a reified idea of) Islam, Christianity, Hinduism, and the permissibility of leisured domesticity. English, argued the writer, was useless to the hard-working and impoverished Hindu middle classes. While it might suit underprivileged or *anaath* women who sought employment, it could never benefit middle-class women, for their purpose was to serve their families. As with the developments in the Female Normal Schools discussed in the previous chapter, here, too, women who sought employment were seen as lacking male protection. By arguing that English was somehow antithetical to the duties and functions of those Indian women who benefited from the security of the heterosexual contract, these debates materialized a cultural field that brought Indian culture into conflict with other communities, and English into conflict with normative family relations.

Kesari wrote more directly against the curriculum adopted in the school, asserting that its embrace of modern ways could potentially create or nurture vices and ill habits. To this, Venubai Panse, the school's official biographer, wrote some forty years later, "We have no idea what he [Tilak] meant by a defiled vice or ill habit. By that token, drinking sodawater and travelling by train could be considered licentious, and all of Maharashtra would be defiled. Did he say that because we were taught by European ladies?"⁶⁴ Panse indicates here a ready awareness that Marathi, English, and the concept of woman were loaded signifiers in the nineteenth century; she was well aware of the inseparability of language from cultural power. Her rebuttal took the form of parodying Brahmanical caste logic. Framed forty years later, she could refute Tilak, evenly exposing his allegation that physical association with non-caste members was contaminating. For its part, *Kesari* continued with its harangue, predicting that the girls studying in this school would, by virtue of learning English, take to wearing "bootstockings," playing the piano, and going to watch dances. The article continued in this vein, vividly arguing that women's education was itself not new to "our" culture; what was new and foreign was the presence of English. Dismissing the superficiality of the English educated for their *vibhushit* or artificial behavior, the writer claimed that people were rightfully afraid that English-educated people would dilute centuries-old traditions. If the education was alien for men, then it was twice so for women.[65]

An English education, foreign and therefore unacceptable, forced licentious cultural practices. It was the opposite of the activities and beliefs that a well-socialized native woman was expected to possess. Decadent and culturally polluting, it was opposed to the strictures of upper-caste patriarchy. The constellation of terms that contrasted the immorality and cultural decadence ushered in by English included references to "Hindu culture and tradition," the middle class, and the *desh*. Women's education enabled bourgeois conjugality to stand in for the middle-class aspirations of Hindu Indians, which in turn were being invoked as indicative of the needs of all Indians.[66]

Kesari next went on to praise Narayan B. Kanitkar for having revealed the complexities of the school through his play *Taruni Shikshan Natika* (1886).[67] Prachi Deshpande has recorded that Kanitkar was a prolific playwright; he assembled a total of twelve plays that supported Tilak's cultural nationalism and conservative gender politics.[68] *Taruni Shikshan Natika* was itself followed by a similar venture, *A Drama in Four Acts, Directed against the Modern High-Class System of Female Education* (1898).[69] Deshpande stresses the connection between Kanitkar's other, more historically oriented plays, and his unambiguous portrayal of deep hostilities between Hindus and Muslims. Her analysis of the historical plays reveals the gradually cohering relationship between Brahman caste anxiety and Hindu majoritarianism. But in addition, while focusing primarily on the gender politics of English, *Taruni Shikshan Natika* dwelled in striking detail on the matter of female sexuality out of wedlock. First published in 1886, its printed version went into several editions and was staged every week in Marathi theaters around the city of Poona, where it was viewed by "both the educated and the uneducated Hindus of Poona."[70]

"THE LANGUAGE OF THE BEDROOM"

Primarily, the play set out to lambaste the promiscuity of the PNHS female students who were learning English. It opened by quoting an opponent of the new women's education, saying that he did not think that "women should be imprisoned at home in a *burkha*, but nor should they be allowed to participate in balls."[71] The play depicted the lives of a number of female students in the new institution, describing them both at school and at home. Central and recurring themes were the flirtatious and sexually motivated behavior of the native female students, their enactment of European dances and mannerisms, and their mercenary inclinations. The women were driven by their desire for an English education, and the play described how their single-minded pursuit of an English education drove them to prostitution and extra-marital affairs. English was repeatedly invoked to signify the very opposite of normative culture, motherhood, and femininity. For instance, a central scene in the play described Chimni, one of the English-educated female characters, dressed in "bootstockings," sitting in a room furnished with chairs and tables, a mosquito net, and piano, attempting a geography lesson in English. Viewing an illustration from the *Ramayan*, she expressed longing for Ram's physique and then repugnance for her husband's appearance. In an obvious reference to the recently concluded and heavily publicized case for the restitution of conjugal rights (the case of Dr. Rakhmabai), Chimni stated aloud that her education was far more desirable to her and she had decided that she would not accompany her husband to his new home away from Poona. The play then depicted her flirting with her male English teacher

Kanitkar's play portrayed English as diverting women from the core of womanhood: marriage, domesticity, and motherhood. The play wove its way through feminist rants, threats of divorces and elopements, and ended with the central character turning to prostitution to earn a living. Its most striking feature was how it sexualized English-educated women. Earlier representations (such as in the school reports from the 1870s discussed above) had framed the agenda for women's English education differently: celebrating English-educated women who presented, performed, and preserved Hindu tradition, domestic values, or their maternal responsibilities. Gender presentation determined gender identity. But *Taruni Shikshan Natika* vividly represented womanhood through an impressionable sexuality that was undesirably compromised because of the female characters' desire for English. Women who desired English were not recognizable as women; the sexual desire for English would separate Indians from their gender identity. In other words, desiring women could disrupt the otherwise inviolable relationship between the female gender and the female sex. English unleashed gender trouble.

The play was quite obviously penned in response to Rakhmabai's legal case. As mentioned in the previous chapter, anxieties that English-educated women would repudiate their husband's sexual rights had overdetermined the outcome of the Rakhmabai case. Just as crucially, the case reveals new alliances between caste ascendancy and virtue. Here it is helpful to invoke Gayle Rubin, who argues that discourses of "sexual morality have more in common with ideologies of racism than with true ethics . . . [because they] grant virtue to already dominant groups."[72] Rakhmabai herself was not a Brahman and her caste had not enacted the restriction against widow remarriage or female inheritance, as was the practice among Brahmans.[73] But the (upper-caste) press consistently judged her actions through Brahmanical standards: the expectation of sexual monogamy and the notion that the conjugal contract survived the husband's death. These were standards that up until that point only Brahmans and a small section of caste-mobile groups had claimed.

The amplification of upper-caste morality in Kanitkar's play reveals how the concept of woman was re-signified for caste power. The play clearly signaled the upheaval of the contract between caste, knowledge, *and* sexuality. In analyzing a similar development among eighteenth-century European thinkers, Linda Zirelli has argued that the trope of the transgressive woman suggests that the gendered referent was being diversified and re-signified for conservative outcomes. Eighteenth-century canonical (Western) political theorists "*produce[d]* woman as transgressive to service [a] larger argument about the crisis in political meaning. The trope of the disorderly woman is used . . . to tame the unnameable abject . . . also to make sense of social, cultural, and political change. Woman as the bearer of chaos is the . . . figure invoked to symbolize the larger social, economic, and political forces that appear . . . increasingly outside the realm of human control and to threaten specific configurations of gender and class."[74] The transgressive women of *Taruni Shikshan Natika* point to the shadow cast by the Rakhmabai case, and a wider anxiety over fixing indigenous culture, specifically the relationship between the Hindu and the Brahmanical. And in addition, the play suggested another eruption. Boldly introducing the tendentious issue of the object of desire, the play suggested that women who learned English were defined primarily by sexual desire.[75] Because of that, they might fall outside the parameters of gender altogether. Such repeated and disturbing portrayals of the excessive sexuality of the English-educated woman effectively established that the phallocentric power of English would be compounded because of gender disorder. And then, desire and sexual passion would erode the fundamental, though vulnerable, connections between woman and gender.

Almost forty years after the first publication of *Taruni Shikshan Natika*, another Marathi author, Vithal Vaaman Haddap, created an equally resounding sensation with a similar depiction of Indian womanhood corrupted by English education. Entitled *Bahekleli Taruni* (literally, the blundering or corrupted young girl), the 1924 publication repeated all the tropes and anxieties aired in Kanitkar's play.[76] The protagonist studied in the same Poona Native Girls' High School and, like the sexually uncontrollable Chimni, rapidly took to prostitution because of the ideas and cultural mannerisms that she absorbed in the school. Most significant was the yoking of prostitution to English education, a structural connection that drove the plot of the novel in much the same way it did in Kanitkar's play. Prostitution marked the limits of caste for both writers; in both cases English had the power to push upper-caste women over the edge of respectability. The similarities did not end there. Like Kanitkar, Haddap was better known for his historical plays detailing the military exploits of Shivaji, and Haddap also posed Shivaji's vigor as evidence of a deep-rooted mastery over Muslims.[77]

Of Mimicry and Woman

Taruni Shikshan Natika was replete with threats of gender trouble. Kanitkar believed that the English education of native women would bring "immense harm to the males of his Community."[78] As he stated, the "teaching of the English language and English ways to young women ... [is] enervating, immasculating [sic]."[79] The English language and English cultural ways potentially blurred gender roles and could subsequently hurt Indian *men*. Furthermore, "if women ... imitate men ... they will desire the alien religion, they will mix the simple and pure Marathi language with English words to create a weak combination.... Obscene books will spoil their minds, they will drink alcohol with men, will want to dance in the English way, they will want to have love marriages, ask for divorces, prefer the path of elopement."[80] English would disrupt the fundamental markers of gender difference, encouraging women to appropriate westernized behavior and repudiate tradition. The blurring of gender roles and the outbreak of gender chaos was implied by bringing certain signifiers into alliance. The desires of English-educated women would drive them to prostitution and alcoholism. And then English-educated women would want to become men.

If English produced a corrupted femininity in women, it could also turn men into enfeebled, undesirably emasculated subjects. In 1891, one Martand Narayan Davne wrote a musical play, *Sangeet Aadhunik Shikshan Vipaak Natika*. The play alleged that native boys were increasingly draining their energy by learning English and other subjects in the Western educational curriculum. This compromised them physically, leaving the male protagonists consumed, diseased, and debilitated. Significantly, it was the body of the native subject that would suffer for imbibing English. English would blur the polarities of gender difference; it would produce emasculated men and hypersexual women. This was its lasting and prohibitive cultural power.

Anxiety over native masculinity was especially articulated through a growing obsession with cultural mimicry. A few weeks before the Poona Native Girls' High School had been inaugurated, the native-managed English paper, the *Native Opinion*, declared:

Reading as we do the same books and learning the same sciences as are taught in English Universities . . . all our anxieties are chiefly directed to acquire the outward surroundings of the Englishman. . . . We are securing the appearances only without the moral condition of English civilisation [which is] the Englishman's energy, determination and dogged perseverance, love of manly exercises and sports, of constitutional liberty and fair play. . . . Again, while we deplore the fact that the education of our boys is given in a foreign language, what can be said of an attempt to repeat the same evil in educating our girls?[81]

The writer demanded instead "an elementary education, that will not make fluent readers and writers of a foreign language, but which will make them good housewives."[82]

Indian men, however, would benefit from imitating the best aspects of English culture. But this would be accomplished by directing the education of women. The opinions resonated with views expressed by Vishnushastri Chiplunkar. He believed that the English language would fortify masculinity, although some aspects of English culture could initiate a feminized predilection toward shallow mimicry. Masculinity was produced through a selective appropriation of "feminine" qualities; the two were not binary opposites but rather locked in a selectively reinforcing relationship. Closely echoing the cultural agenda expressed by Chiplunkar and corroborated through Ranade's domestic experiments (discussed in chapter 6), the *Native Opinion* also expressed the conviction that the antidote to charges of cultural mimicry and native effeminacy lay in the supervision of women's education.

Bonds between colonial and native men were strengthened in the masculine signifying economy.[83] Picking up almost verbatim on the questions raised in the *Native Opinion*, the bilingual *Mumbai Indu Prakash* seemed to corroborate this opinion.[84] But it cautioned the Poona students:

Steer clear of the Scylla and Charybdis of superficial and showy education on the one hand and of masculine education on the other. . . . [We deny that] imitation is at all a bad trait in our character, or that we are not fit to imitate Englishmen. Well directed imitation is one of the best means of improvement. . . . We need not be ashamed to imitate them in their energy, determination and dogged perseverance, their love of manly exercises and sports, their love of constitutional liberty and fair play. . . . We must continually strive to improve ourselves, and as part of such improvement we must educate our women.[85]

As the paper reiterated the following week, "If we are to become like the Englishman, energetic, persevering, and manly . . . if the Englishman's virtues are to be reproduced in India, his education must begin at home."[86] Strengthening male authority in the home would fortify a native masculinity otherwise enfeebled by its mimicry of European ways. The acquisition of English culture had to be nurtured in the home and by appropriately educating Indian mothers and sisters. The writer of these lines thus argued that British colonial modernity was supported by a chain of cultural control; desirable masculine traits of British culture would be strengthened among native men if those very men could define and control the education of the home. Native masculinity must orient itself toward the supposedly masculine aspects of English schoolboys and political culture, but that acquisition could only be cemented if native women were taught their correct domestic roles. The feminine had to be harnessed to the masculine to bring the latter to fruition.

The conflict over mimicry in these debates partially evokes Homi Bhabha's work on the "ambivalence of colonial discourse." Reading Macaulay's "Minute on Education" alongside other colonial texts, Bhabha has famously argued that the desire of white supremacy was enacted "through the repetition of partial presence, which is the basis of mimicry . . . [the production of] authorised versions of otherness . . . the figures of a doubling, the part-objects of a metonymy of colonial desire which alienates the modality and normality of those dominant discourses in which they emerge as inappropriate colonial subjects."[87] But the native mimic man clearly did not mark the end point of colonial cultural engineering. Instead, English-educated subjects immediately sought to ventriloquize Macaulay's desire by reaching out to their *own women*. In the process, they augmented their caste and class power. The success of colonial mimicry, therefore, lay in the way that English-educated Indians deployed gender to contain English within their caste and class locations, turning colonial desire for the native mimic man into a revitalized Indian hetero-nationalism.

Conclusion

Departing from analyses of the English-studies project that foreground the overarching power of the colonial state or that interpret "English" as a fixed linguistic form, I have tracked how colonized subjects retained control over the production of meaning, directing the internal elements of language—even languages of power—to force changes in symbolic power and social organization. The conflict over sexual difference and power gave the English language a native potency. English came to be yoked to masculine authority, which harnessed feminine power to realize its own potential. The very recognition that English possessed the power to shape native gender difference was accompanied by the move to discipline its phallogocentric power.

Colonial discourses on masculinity and female sexuality, while irrefutably powerful, were never translated seamlessly.[88] As the debates I have discussed here establish, native masculinity's own history and self-representation did not entirely replicate colonial allegations on the lack of gender difference between men and women. While native anxiety over masculine authority certainly fixed feminine difference, it did so not simply in a reactive mode, or to establish clear polarities between the masculine and the feminine. Rather, the debates over native masculinity provide important clues on the universalizing of Hindu upper-caste heteronormativity. Control over femininity bolstered the resilience and agency of native-caste masculinity.[89] To realize its own distinct potential, native masculinity had looked to the cultural practices of the Englishman, but to actually maintain that potential it had to simultaneously regulate caste hierarchies. The symbolic value of "woman" was to perform upper-caste standards of conjugal, reproductive sexuality in order to render them hegemonic. Those caste parameters would—as the following chapters illustrate—undergo a (superficial) secularization, especially in the changing climate of twentieth-century nation building.

In a recent study on the Western education of India, Sanjay Seth argued that "as with other debates concerning the woman's question on colonial India, debates on female education were not about women, but rather about what they signified or could be made to signify. But also at issue was *who* was signifying; who could claim to be legitimately authorized to modernize Indian women."[90] While recognizing that the significatory power of woman indicates a wider contest over social power, Seth accepts the logic of ameliorative reform.[91] Woman and gender remain in tight embrace. New avenues for secularizing caste, the production of new monopolies over knowledge and labor, and new rituals of sexual difference must inform our understanding of the colonial period. After all, woman was under construction even as "she" was deployed to render social power as transparent and static. By reconstructing when and how essentialized tropes of "mother," "widow," "prostitute," and "wife" were brought into comparison and competition with one another, we can appreciate which caste-specific codes gained authority through the symbolism of woman.

I have, in this chapter, tried to look beyond the empirical "fact" of woman, to write about gender despite "the tremendous resistance within the discipline of History to thinking theoretically."[92] As we have seen so far, in the 1880s certain words were being brought into relationship and conflict with one another and, as signs, they were not restricted to a particular language.[93] The consensus over sexual difference redirected the internal, constituent elements of language, even languages of power. Motherhood, the mother tongue, reproductive sexuality, and domesticity were brought into alliance; nonconjugal sex and English were thrown into an oppositional relationship. Never was this merely a battle over signs or linguistic terms. This endlessly deferred contest over signification resulted in institution-building, new family structures, and novel expressions of desire. In the process, upper-caste strictures were rendered invisible and universal. The potent re-signification of the words that encircled women stymied the critique of the upper-caste monopoly over knowledge. The significatory power of woman, moreover, was heightened by caste-specific concerns: the alliances of motherhood, indigenous culture, respectability, "touchability," reproduction, and domesticity. Woman was re-signified to protect the interests of the very social class that had accessed English education under Elphinstone's earliest politics. This infinite deferral of meaning endowed English with a native phallogocentric power that manifested in the ability to order gender difference, to influence (and corrupt) sexual desire, and to stage hierarchies between castes.

The power of English in colonial India thus arose from the re-signification of gender under way. These gendered battles further augmented its ability to signify, or materialize, sexual difference. With that, it served to thwart critiques—such as those launched by the Phules or Pandita Ramabai—that exposed the alliances between knowledge and power. This significatory power was never fixed in perpetuity, although it hovered over several sexed and gendered associations. The internal elements of language can be (and are) continuously challenged, producing polysemic effects that were actively decoded by a range of actors for multiple forms of political and social power. Consequently, some colonized subjects retained control over the production of meaning, successfully directing the internal elements of language—even the language of power—to fix sexuality and police social change. "Our women" became the referent that signaled the endlessly deferred, even impossible, access to "English" for those who were *not* to access the Brahman woman, those who were not Brahmans. As the following chapter discusses, even anti-caste efforts were themselves subsumed to this sexualized logic.

4

"A NEW GENERATION OF HIPLESS AND BREASTLESS WOMEN . . . TO THE FOREFRONT IN EUROPE AND AMERICA"

Literature, Social Class, and the Wider World of Indian English

While appearing conflicted over the content and purpose of an English education, all participants in the debate conceded that the phallogocentric power of English hinged on its ability to guide the subject's entry into the realm of social conventions, to direct sexual desire, and to enforce new hierarchies between castes, genders, and languages. This chapter continues to trace these connections, focusing on the history of the Indian Women's University from 1890 to 1920. Following the writings of its founder, Dhondo Keshav Karve, and his associate, G. M. Chiplunkar, I foreground wider, transnational connections between Japan, India, and Britain on the matter of English. I track the systematic linking of language with literature in the case of female education, and the process by which expectations of female affect and domestic labor coalesced with upper-caste interests and the logic of nation building. By attending to the history of one institution, I can analyze a number of twists in the story of English and thus foreground how a new English became acceptable for all Indian women.

By virtue of his political participation over an extraordinarily long life, D. K. Karve (1858–1963) bridged nineteenth-century social-reform politics, discussed in previous chapters, and the early twentieth-century politics of nation building. He was a key player in the history of women's education, and he exemplifies the connections between two distinct stages in western Indian history. Karve's interest in education, language, and gender reform evidences interesting personal transformations, from widow remarriage to women's education to a gradual acceptance of English in the curricula of educational institutions. To appreciate his flexible self-positioning amid wider social currents, we must distinguish between his ideals and how his colleagues and associates later institutionalized his vision.[1] His role in shaping the history of gender and pedagogy exceeds institutional power and success and, moreover, spills beyond national frames as modes of analysis.

Karve's determination to foreground the "mother tongue" in the cultural mission of the Indian Women's University forged new connections between intellectual and cultural capital on the one hand and the positioning of female sexuality on the other. His discussions of language expose the otherwise embedded relation between biological essentialism, class, and caste. Karve explicitly argued that the vernacular-language policies of his university were designed with the social and cultural needs of non-elite women in mind. His writings illuminate how the discourse of class was deployed to universalize upper-caste strictures and, in the process, render a certain type of English knowledge as acceptable for what he considered Indian womanhood. In the institutionalization of the Indian Women's University, in other words, we can observe the final transformation whereby English became domesticated and democratized through the caste and gender regimes of modern India. The battle over women's access to English sanctioned Brahmanical power, even as it served to disassociate caste from religious ritual. This secularization of caste, which relied on the universalizing of normative sexual standards, perpetuated the discriminatory nature of the modern knowledge economy.

Continuing with the theme introduced in the previous chapter, here too I delve into the shifting relationship between sexuality and gender ideals. While nineteenth-century colonial arguments about literature highlighted its liberal humanist and civilizational promises, the native debate gave literature even more power to regulate not simply sexual difference, but the psychic aspects of sexuality in a range of locations. The belief that literature was an emotional force rendered new distinctions from language. Along with the expectation that translation could import knowledge without disturbing cultural hierarchies, these beliefs worked to secure social class, linguistic differences, and new forms of transnational power.

From Social Reform to Nation Building:
Dhondo Keshav Karve (1858–1963)

In 1916 Dhondo Keshav Karve founded the first university for women in India, the Indian Women's University (IWU), later renamed Shreemati Nathibai Damodar Thakersay Indian Women's University, or SNDT. Karve also inaugurated other facilities for the education of Indian women and girls. He provided the most concrete structure of opportunity for his sister-in-law's intellectual ambitions (discussed in chapter 8). Karve was most driven by the determination to address the issue of access, particularly that of non-elite Indian women and girls to educational facilities that had traditionally been created for elite men. He resolutely believed that language lay at the heart of this problem of unequal opportunity. But rather than train women to learn those languages and attain knowledge similar to those pursued by men, Karve was committed to a contrary agenda: the formulation of a specifically feminine educational curriculum that reduced the presence of subjects that he considered masculine, like the English language. He categorically believed that Indian women must learn Indian languages and womanly subjects. Such training would reinforce their femininity and increase their contribution to contemporary society. In other words, the purpose behind the vernacular education of his students was to make them better women and, therefore, better Indians. His schools and university institutionalized this conviction.

But first I give a brief sketch of Karve, reconstructed largely from his own memoirs (published in 1928) and other writings. As with many memoirs written by men from this period in colonial India, the first part of Karve's autobiography focuses almost entirely on his own education, which itself centered on his indefatigable zeal to learn English.[3] Born in a small town in western India in 1858, Karve had accessed only the most rudimentary facilities for an English education. Initially his desire for English was connected to his goal of securing a government job. Once, at the age of seventeen, he walked 110 miles over four monsoon-soaked days to appear for an examination for a government post. His tireless quest for an English education propelled him to leave his village for the big city, in this case Bombay. There he entered the Robert Money School, a missionary school for boys, to secure an English education. He was painfully conscious of the relative deficiency in his knowledge, but he repeatedly reminds his readers that through continuous struggle and hard work he triumphed over this inadequacy. In his autobiography Karve recalls that had it not been for his exposure to English, at best he would have been teaching Marathi in a small village school all his life. He never forgot the transformative effect of English. Karve supplemented his income in Bombay by tutoring other students and older people to read English. Some of his students were girls.

With time, he developed a facility for natural philosophy and mathematics, although he remembers having to always struggle over English and history. In 1887, at the age of twenty-nine, Karve started teaching mathematics and science to the matriculation class of the Cathedral Girls' High School in Bombay. This school was among the most prestigious in Bombay; it admitted the daughters of Europeans and a few prominent Indians. Dadabhai Naoroji and Dr. Atmaram Pandurang both had their daughters in this school.[4] Karve also taught female students in the "Maratha High School"[5] and the Alexandra Native Girls' English Institution. He reveals how profoundly influenced he was by intellectual currents that upheld the promise of social transformation through ideas of incremental progress. Drawn to the writings of Gopal Ganesh Agarkar, as well as texts by Herbert Spencer and Charles Darwin, Karve's wider interests were also influenced by the compositions of John Stuart Mill, Jeremy Bentham, and Immanuel Kant.[6]

While he initially enrolled in Bombay's Wilson College, he later transferred to Elphinstone College to benefit from the English-literature lessons provided by the latter's famous Professor Wordsworth.[7] He successfully secured his BA as well as MA degrees from Bombay University. His stay in Bombay brought him closer to the social reformers of western India, and through their influence he began teaching for the Deccan Education Society in Poona. He remained a teacher and educational administrator all his life. Conscious of the entirely fortuitous turn of events by which he had managed to learn English and the thoroughly life-altering effect that this had on him, he declared that without English the potential of other such promising boys would always "remain dormant and [not] be realized."[8] One of his first philanthropic acts was to start a fund to help boys in his village learn English.

Soon after the birth of his oldest son from his first marriage, Karve decided that he would not send the boy to school. Karve was himself a schoolteacher, yet he provides no explanation for this decision. Instead his new wife, Radhabai, whom he had taught both Marathi and a little English, educated the boy.⁹ But Radhabai died soon after they were married. Within a few years of his wife's death, and after considerable turmoil, Karve performed a uniquely transgressive act. In 1893 he married a Brahman widow. Despite the many stated intentions of prominent social reformers from the 1850s, Karve's second marriage to a virgin child widow, Godubai, marked the first widow remarriage in western India. Godubai was the sister of Karve's childhood friend Naharpant. She was also the first student to enroll in Pandita Ramabai's Sharada Sadan, a school for Brahman widows; she was likely literate in both Marathi and English. In keeping with Brahmanical custom, Karve renamed her Anandibai. Unlike other social reformers, Karve was unusual for acting on his beliefs, openly and in the face of crushing social ostracism.¹⁰ The couple was immediately expelled by the Brahman community, threatened with excommunication, and refused housing and food by their own families, as well as by social reformist friends.¹¹ Anandibai was considered ritually impure. As Kosambi notes, even the one sympathetic friend who took them in decreed that Anandibai "eat by herself and not [be] allowed to touch cooked food and drinking water."¹²

Karve's was not the only act to challenge the punitive Brahmanical injunctions on female sexuality. Pandita Ramabai had also exposed some of the contradictions embedded in the liberal male reformists' support for widow remarriage.¹³ Ramabai's agenda was specifically that of educating Hindu widows. She did not herself reject the option of remarriage for widows; in fact she supported Godubai's remarriage to Karve with great fanfare. But her agenda was wider than merely legislating in favor of remarriage. She worked extensively to ensure that remarriage was not the only route for widows. Through her school for widows, the Sharada Sadan (Home of Wisdom founded in Bombay in 1889), she instituted a socially and economically viable educational curriculum in which widows were taught carpentry and English, among other subjects.¹⁴ Ramabai strove to make the students self-sufficient beyond the institution of marriage. But the overarching consensus between male Brahmanical power and Victorian separate spheres eventually undermined Ramabai's plans for gender transformation. Rumors that Ramabai was forcing her students to convert to Christianity spurred a furor in the conservative town of Poona. By 1896 the controversy had caused terrible breaches: once-supportive liberal reformers, prominently M. G. Ranade and R. G. Bhandarkar, resigned from the board of the Sharada Sadan; scores of students were forcibly withdrawn; and the institution was faced with the possibility of closure.[15]

Following these events, Karve purposefully decided to start a similar venture to continue Pandita Ramabai's work. Karve named his school for widows the Mahilashram, located outside Poona.[16] Contemporary sources indicated that the widow's school was also referred to as the Hindu Women's Home.[17] It catered to widows, which would have largely entailed women of the upper Hindu castes. Karve records that it was his experiences with the Mahilashram that spurred his later conviction in the Indian Women's University. In his autobiography, he never reflects on the slippage between upper caste, Hindu, and Indian that seems to have guided his choice of names. The course of instruction at the Mahilashram was almost entirely in Marathi, although a few girls were taught Sanskrit via Marathi.[18] Despite his seeming critique of upper-caste sexual practices, he upheld Sanskrit as expressing "Hindu" culture. The most advanced students received an introduction to the English language and, over time, the Mahilashram expanded to include the English fourth standard.[19]

Building on Ramabai's curricular vision, Karve also prioritized the economic self-sufficiency of the widow students. In other words, extending Ramabai's pedagogic goals, rather than the model of Bhandarkar and Ranade, Karve did not, at least initially, foreground either marriage or domesticity.[20] But this soon changed. He records that public interest in his schools rose rapidly and to such an extent that he was soon faced with queries on also educating unmarried students. In response, he set up a separate facility for unmarried students, the Mahilya Vidyalaya (Women's School), specifically aimed to make the students "good wives, good mothers, good neighbors."[21] Geraldine Forbes has encapsulated the magnitude of this intentional bifurcation. As she notes, Karve believed that widows needed an education "that would make them economically independent and would enable them to think for themselves," but unmarried girls "needed an education that would reinforce their dependence."[22] Diverting thus from Pandita Ramabai's plans, Karve's critique of Brahmanical sexual strictures was quite rapidly overshadowed by a renewed conviction in the supposed inevitability and desirability of reproduction and marriage for women. Thus, by the turn of the century Karve demonstrated a selective fusion of anti-caste critique, social gender reform, the cultivation of domesticity, and faith in a Sanskritic-Marathi cultural core. Far from being banished, English was prominently displayed alongside these elements.

Karve now turned toward a more broad-based agenda on women's education, making decisions that would bring more students into his school, rather than empower some women to reject the Brahmanical sexual and knowledge economy. At least initially, he seemed unperturbed by wider allegations that teaching women English would annihilate Marathi, although he was increasingly motivated by the conviction that women must learn "their own" languages. But that did not render English impermissible; unlike some of the opinions discussed in the previous chapters, Karve did not immediately believe that English and non-English languages were necessarily involved in a zero-sum game. While at the turn of the century the schools taught the first grade of English education, they offered no further facilities for English-language schooling. In 1907, he realized that some of his students could pass the matriculation examination of Bombay University.[23] At this time, the Poona Native Girls' High School was the most viable option for native girls and women. Curiously, though, he enrolled his senior students in the New English School for Boys, where he himself had once taught English. As we saw in the previous chapter, this school was portrayed as driven by an anticolonial nationalism and guided by upper-caste interests. Even by 1907, the school remained entirely administered by Indians but did not admit girls. Special provisions were thus made for Karve's female students.

Why did the boys' school—and this particular one at that—appear to present a more attractive option? Karve offered several explanations. For one, the Poona Native Girls' High School had been closed sporadically due to the outbreak of plague in the city. Furthermore, he found that the methods used to teach the students in the PNHS were so extremely "severe" that the experience served to discourage the students altogether.[24] Finally, he maintained that "girls deserved much greater encouragement than boys," revealing a belief in the distinction between the emotional qualities and requirements of boys and girls.[25] The decision, as well as the explanations, seems counterintuitive. It is possible, however, that the cultural and class profile signified by the PNHS seemed impractical for the widows and non-elite women Karve wanted to educate. Alternatively, he might have found it easier to manage gender difference under the conditions of this particular nationalist and native-managed boys' school.

It was around this time that Karve became increasingly attracted to the agenda of what he considered a practical education for women. Despite his experiments with coeducation, he believed that women should have an alternative to the matriculation examination, one specifically attuned to their maternal and domestic futures. Instead of geography and history, for instance, he believed that women should be schooled in practical subjects like child rearing, home medicine, and cooking. But he did state repeatedly that those women who had the means to, or who were unconcerned about time and money, be encouraged to pursue an English education. Like many of his peers schooled under the aegis of Elphinstone's directives, Karve had already deemed the study of English a "reward for merit in other studies."[26] But now he further segregated English by considering the possibility of institutionalizing differences between an elite English education and a practical, non-elite, domestic, Marathi-language education. The needs of most women, he believed, corresponded to the latter.

The Strain of English on Motherhood: Class-Specific Gender Expectations

In 1915 Karve was invited to address the annual meeting of the National Social Conference. The conference, the social reform counterpart of the Indian National Congress, had its roots in M. G. Ranade's vision of liberal social reform.[27] By 1915 it had quite thoroughly broken from the INC.[28] Its leadership continued to be predominantly Hindu and Parsi males. In his autobiography, Karve explains that while preparing his speech to this forum, he happened to recall a pamphlet that had been sent to him anonymously, some years earlier, on the Japan Women's University in Tokyo.[29] It is only later in his autobiography that he revealed that the pamphlet was sent to him by Babu Shivprasad Gupta of Benaras and Professor Vinay Kumar Sarkar of Calcutta. For some reason they had not wanted their names disclosed. Through this pamphlet, Karve had learned about the Japan Women's University, which was started in Japan by one Mr. Naruse.[30] Karve crafted his speech, incorporating references to Naruse's school and, more broadly, expressing admiration for the cultural and political vision articulated by contemporary Japanese intellectuals, an admiration then widely shared by some sections of the emerging Indian national leadership. Only a few years before Karve's speech, the Nobel laureate Rabindranath Tagore had expanded his school to the level of a university in Shantiniketan, outside Calcutta. Tagore, too, was deeply influenced by Japanese culture and considered Japan an exemplar for cultural reasons, although not for political ones.[31] Karve does not mention Tagore at this stage in his memoirs, although it is intriguing to consider that both men were simultaneously looking to Japan to provide the blueprint for their national-cultural self-fashioning.

In his speech, Karve discussed the principles that had motivated Mr. Naruse and the possibility of their application in the Indian context. Drawing similarities between the two nations through their confrontation with "Western thinking," Karve informed his audience that "sixty five or seventy years ago Japan and India were roughly similar in their social and educational standards . . . influenced by European traders . . . attracted to western thinking, discoveries, knowledge, literature, and arts." Japanese men also initially went to Europe and trained in Western intellectual discoveries, all of which broadened the "huge gulf between male and female ways of thinking." But rather than attempt to shrink this difference, at least in the case of Japan, "it struck people that this difference could prove beneficial to the nation."[32]

Following Naruse, Karve believed that modernizing nations should harness sexual difference for their own benefit. Mr. Naruse had been aware of this potential, for in establishing the women's university in Japan he declared that it was neither his goal to emulate institutions for women's higher learning as existed in "America and Europe," nor to compete against other universities for men's education as they existed in Japan. Karve quoted Naruse as stating that this uniquely feminine and indigenous effort would benefit women and "call forth their consciousness as personalities with infinite aspirations and longings." Naruse argued, "We cannot support another movement which aims at the so-called emancipation of women. . . . Our aim is to educate women that they shall come to realize their own special mission in life as free personal agents and as members of the Empire of Japan and that, as such they shall be able to perform their services as wives and mothers in a larger sense and more efficient manner than hitherto."[33] Mr. Naruse believed that a course of study especially adapted to the traditional needs of Japanese women would ensure national progress toward modernity. Naruse's antipathy for a feminist agenda, or one that denied intellectual, emotional, and, hence, physical differences between men and women, struck a powerful chord with Karve and his colleagues. But Naruse never mentioned the subject of language or of the mother tongue. For Karve, however, an educational agenda that specifically emphasized the distinctions between masculine and feminine capacities and social roles primarily had to do with language. Karve was no anomaly from the perspective of Indian history. While appearing to contradict the agenda of someone like Manockjee Cursetjee Shroff, who in 1860 supported educating women in English, in actuality Karve also pegged language as the most volatile and malleable aspect of political and cultural transformation. Thus he entered the lineage of Indian activists and reformers who perceived language as crucially bridging knowledge, power, and sexuality.

Building on the conviction that female students be taught a specifically feminine curriculum, Karve now proposed a university that differentiated between the social function and purpose of men and women. It would do this by foregrounding the role of language, dramatically distinguishing between the applicability of English and the vernacular to the cultural definition of the Indian woman. And so he declared to the National Social Conference:

Perhaps the most disastrous in its effects [is] that of the medium of instruction. It is indeed a painful anomaly, it has been sapping the energies and undermining the intellectual caliber of our youths all these years. In the case of boys there are perhaps reasons, other than educational, which may reconcile us to the present state of things. . . . These reasons, however, do not exist in the case of girls, most of whom will be called upon to fill the humbler office of the upholder of homes and hearths. The strain involved in receiving instruction through a foreign tongue that tells so severely upon the boy is bound to do greater harm to the girls. *We cannot afford to have the future motherhood of the land thus enfeebled and enervated by this extra and uncalled for strain.*[34]

English was responsible for sapping the energy of the native male youth, an anxiety referenced in a wide array of sources through the mid-nineteenth century.[35] But the problem did not end there. As I discussed in chapter 3, the relationship between masculinity and indigenous womanhood was energetically explored in the nineteenth century. In contrast to those debates, Karve believed that, while English might be draining the physical strength of Indian boys, it could not be eradicated from their lives. But this was not the case for women. Even a mediated form of English would damage female health because women were entirely defined by their reproductive duties. The English education of Indian women would not necessarily render them either masculine or unfeminine, but it could potentially strain and weaken the potential of "future motherhood." In alluding to sexual difference in this way, Karve stressed the inevitability of reproduction. He merged an anti-caste agenda with a pro-marriage one, and, as I argue here, he invoked social class to reiterate the inevitability of reproduction.

Karve thus informed the National Social Conference in 1915 that English was inapplicable, not to mention harmful, to the needs of Indian women. He now added another set of terms to the distinction between "English" and the "vernacular": that of social class. Karve carefully distinguished between the practical needs of the majority of women from the elite and privileged ones pursued by the minority. At the conference he argued that "those women who have the time, money and inclination, and can afford to go high enough on this ladder, are welcome to follow [that] course of study" laid out without any sensitivity to gender difference.[36] Elite women could, if they so desired, opt for an education that diminished gender difference. But according to him, the majority of women were destined for a married and domestic future, and the course of study presently available through the Bombay University failed to address this inevitable necessity. While English had been defined along the lines of class for over a century, Karve put an interesting twist on it. He shifted the object of reform by distinguishing between the majority of women and those who had the privilege to pursue a more elite education. As I demonstrated in the previous chapters, it was by virtue of the very connotations of privilege and upper-class westernization that English had once signified equality with colonial culture and social progress for some natives. Social reform energy had been directed at managing the lives of upper-class women, in order to control caste power. But here Karve's work with English marks a significant shift to concern for the non-elite Indian woman.

Karve opened the Indian Women's University (IWU) with five students. The institution was based on the recognition of two essential principles: "The most natural and therefore efficient medium of instruction is the learner's mother tongue and secondly, women as a class have different functions to fulfill in the social economy from those of men."[37] Immediately, and not unexpectedly, a furor arose from some sections of Indian social-reform circles. In Karve's terms, the controversy raged between those of "Western" minds versus those of the "older" way of thinking.[38] The former believed there should be no distinction between women and men's education, and that all education should be in English. The latter said there should be no higher education whatsoever for women. Karve claimed that his plan to favor the vernacular mediated those two extreme positions. Indeed, his decision to maintain English in the curriculum as a compulsory second language did mollify some of those people who had initially criticized his plan. Karve believed that, realistically, "the male educational curriculum [could never] benefit [women] in Hindustan. It will prove detrimental to women to be revolving around the western university system, with its unnecessary emphasis on English."[39]

The male educational system, characterized by its dependence on English, was not for all women. The polarization of masculine and feminine, of English and the vernacular, of foreign and native debated in the previous chapters was naturalized in the agenda of Karve's university. While he conceded that "those women who have the time, money and inclination" be allowed to pursue "men's education,"[40] for most women, learning English as men do would not necessarily provide any benefit over a Marathi education. Instead, because Karve believed that non-elite women who learned their subjects in the mother tongue would see better results. He actually corroborated the correspondence between class mobility and sexuality that had directed the history of English education in preceding years. His arguments were based on a conviction in the separate destinies and functions of men and women, in the discrete and mutually oppositional status of indigenous and foreign cultures, the mother tongue, and English. He alluded entirely to the reproductive function of women as shaping female identity and gender difference. Hindustan and the West became essential tools by which to sculpt gender difference, and to curtail the reach of English.[41]

Through the university's curriculum, Karve could institutionalize his investment in the primary, reproductive role of non-elite women. Not only did the IWU do away with the matriculation examination as its standard for admission (crafting instead its own entrance examination), but it replaced the designations of bachelor and master of arts. The equivalent to the BA was the GA, the Graduate of Arts or Grihitagma. The MA was replaced by the PA, Proficient in Arts or Pradegragma.[42] In addition to these new degrees, English became a compulsory subject in the curriculum. Within a year of its inauguration, the IWU stated that the medium of instruction would be the student's mother tongue, but that English would be a compulsory second language.[43]

"A NEW GENERATION . . ."

Public Evaluations: Support and Dissension over the Sexual Power of English

Despite his rigorous emphasis on the vernacular as the medium of instruction and English as a compulsory language, Karve faced criticism from a range of twentieth-century nationalists. First demanding that Karve change the title of the university to the Hindu Women's University, Bal Gangadhar Tilak dismissed Karve's agenda as seeking to dissolve the Hindu nation and gender difference. Writing specifically about the IWU, *The Mahratta* declared:

> We must provide our girls with a fair knowledge of hygiene, domestic economy, child nursing, cooking, sewing, and so forth. Next to this intelligent and instructed love of the Home comes all else that may serve to make a woman socially useful. A Hindu woman's social usefulness will depend on her sympathy with and grasp of our traditional literature. Efforts must therefore be made to introduce into the New University's course of studies a progressive series of texts dealing with the instructive part of our Pauranic and other religious literature. The religious temperament of the Hindu woman is a great asset and we must take care not to destroy it in our endeavours to "enlighten" her mind.[44]

The tightening connections between domesticity, "woman," Hinduism, India, and Brahmanism are evident here. Tilak was crafting a prescriptive, normative Brahman power, and he was doing so by citing the sanctity of women's domestic and reproductive roles.[45] The sexual availability and domestic labor of some women bolstered Tilak's claim as speaking for the Indian nation. Further criticism, although in a different vein, came in 1916 from Mohandas Karamchand Gandhi, recently returned from South Africa. Karve had initiated a meeting to discuss his ideas for the Indian Women's University, and Gandhi approved of all aspects of the plan: that the medium of instruction be the mother tongue, that mathematics remain optional, and that arithmetic, life sciences, and health sciences remain compulsory. But Gandhi completely disapproved of the fact that English was to be a mandatory subject. He wanted it to be optional.[46] Gandhi believed that English and the regional language could not coexist as required subjects in the curriculum. Of course, Gandhi himself had launched a very successful political career by virtue of his use of English. Despite that, in later writings he brought together his beliefs about female social roles with the need for female vernacular education. Gandhi, too, seemed to recognize the phallogocentric powers of the language. But for his part, Karve stood his ground, saying that he would be forced to carry out his work without Gandhi's support and could not allow English to be anything but compulsory for his students. Gandhi finally agreed: "Mr. Karve, because it is you, I concede. But I will always maintain that even for a woman's higher education, English should be optional."[47]

Karve traveled extensively across India trying to popularize the idea of the university. But the responses he received were rarely positive. He recorded, for instance, that among the "cosmopolitan crowd of Bombay," the need for a university in the "vernaculars as the medium of instruction is not that acutely felt."[48] But if the people he met in Bombay seemed averse to his policies because the vernacular negated the "cosmopolitan," he remembers receiving quite the opposite reaction in Calcutta. Here a member of an audience that Karve had been addressing declared that the presence of English in the curriculum would mean that women would "start to wear high heeled shoes . . . they will be haughty . . . they will indulge in flirting."[49] Recalling this and other such incidents in his memoirs, Karve discussed his reasons for keeping English compulsory in the university's curriculum. He believed that no equitable pedagogic agenda could deny women the opportunity to learn English beyond the secondary stage of their education.[50] But, as he argued, the more powerful sections of society were entirely "smitten" by the English language and hence unable to appreciate the enormous burden placed on students by learning in a foreign language.[51] People increasingly thought that a curriculum that had no English component was entirely useless.[52] Karve opposed such views, but he was simultaneously troubled by the mysterious power of the language to command the single-minded devotion of upper-class Indians, a power that he believed oriented the desires of all Indians. But he took care to maintain that despite the structure of desire, the need for English prevailed: "Today it is the language of the entire world. In our country too it brings together people who speak other languages and this will continue for some time. Today if Hindustan is one nation it is because of English. Therefore there is no difference of opinion that women too should learn this language well. The difference arises when there is an unnecessary emphasis placed on the language, or when it is argued that this and only this should be the medium of instruction."[53] Stating that the overwhelming preeminence of the English language in the curriculum was a product and producer of the colonized Indians "slave mentality," he argued that the "enchantment" with the English language had meant that women, regardless of their economic needs, were also pursuing the language like other "madmen."[54]

Support for Karve's ideals remained patchy; his work was often dismissed as patriarchal and archaic by other educationists and intellectuals. Despite the later success of the university, contemporary intellectuals and reformers remained largely opposed to his ideals. Critics proffered a range of arguments, disputing the university's conviction that the education be imparted in the mother tongue, or that the course of study address women's domestic and maternal destiny. In other words, not all observers conceded that a woman was defined by cultural and biological reproduction. The clearest, most consistent argument was carried out in the pages of the Bombay-based weekly the *Indian Social Reformer* (ISR). A vocal, progressive mouthpiece for caste and gender reform, it was founded in Madras in 1890 by Kamakashi Natarajan, himself a close associate of the founder of the English-language, Madras-based daily *The Hindu*, G. Subramaniam Iyer. Natarajan moved the ISR to Bombay because he found the politics of Madras too provincial for his political opinions. He was not a Chitpavan Brahman, and he had not forged his political views in the Poona-Bombay milieu. The paper staked important positions over the Age of Consent Bill and, in later years, amplified wide support for the anti-caste politics of Bhimrao Ambedkar.[55] The ISR ended its run in 1953. On the matter of the curriculum at the IWU, it stated that "there is no sex in knowledge" and declared its complete resistance to a separate university for women. A separate curriculum, moreover, was "reminiscent of the medieval Hindu prohibition of sacred learning to women and Shudras."[56] There are glimpses here of Mahatma Jotiba Phule's conviction (discussed in chapter 1) that Brahmanical power was ensured through a double-headed move: the ritualization of sexual difference yoked to the denial of learning. The ISR recognized that the battle over women's access to English produced fresh, non-religious rituals that elevated Brahmanical power. The proliferation of gender debate served to secularize caste.

The ISR identified the vital power of English as a form of knowledge, one that was in turn shaped in the battle over caste. A few years later, the journal described the university's annual ceremony. Sir Hormusji Wadya had presided over the event. Wadya was the president of the Deccan Sabha, a Bombay-based liberal social-reform organization that claimed affinities with the gradualist and conciliatory politics of the Poona Sarvajanik Sabha and with G. K. Gokhale's Servants of India Society. Reporting on the event, the ISR noted that in presiding over the ceremony, Wadya had "laid his finger on the weak spot of the Institution," which was the absence of the "English language and literature which must . . . remain the lingua franca of the Indian nation for a long time to come." The ISR reported Wadya as conceding that at best, "Professor Karve's experiment was well worth making if only to show that, in modern India, the idea of having a separate system of education has no chance of acceptance."[57]

The ISR continued its relentless criticism of Karve's work over the years. Natarajan and his editorial staff thus spread word on the work of the university beyond the reaches of the Marathi-speaking Bombay Presidency. Consistently decrying any gender-based differentiation in the curriculum, they drew attention to the intersections of caste and gender. In 1925 the paper stated that the IWU "represented a retrograde step in the movement for the elevation of the status of women in this country. . . . It was planned to suit the prejudices of the average Indian . . . [but] English [is] the one language common to the whole Indian continent, a modern world language capable of expressing all the latest ideas in Pure and Applied Sciences."[58]

The ISR was aware of the class-based agenda at the IWU, that it was essentially aimed at educating women of the middle and lower middle classes. Writing on the occasion of another annual day function in 1926, it went on to reveal that many of the men in the university's administrative body, all of whom belonged to the most prestigious families in Poona, actually preferred to send their own daughters to the coeducational colleges of the Bombay University. For all its pretensions of democratizing education, the university actually *legitimized* the new caste- and class-based knowledge economy. Upper-class women could, and did, escape the kind of gender differentiation now being applied to the women of Karve's university. Most significantly, the ISR queried the collapse between woman, marriage, and reproduction that the university openly institutionalized. It argued that this collapse was engineered by denying women access to English. It called out the "ideal of the Indian Women's University in which the 'fictitious importance' attached to English in the other Universities has been transferred to wifehood and motherhood."[59]

The paper drew attention to the proliferation of discourses over sexuality. Cogently lambasting the nation-building project for naturalizing conjugality and reproduction for some, the ISR exposed the relationship between institutionalized heterosexuality and social mobility. The newspaper recognized that Karve's university had replaced the otherwise hegemonic power of English with similarly potent and irrefutable ideas on the necessity of the maternal and conjugal role of women. Unlike other critics of the IWU, the ISR was far from opposed to the English education of women. Rather, it criticized the university for deploying ideas of sexual difference to restrict access to the language of power.[60]

Despite, or perhaps because of, these criticisms, Karve increasingly sought corroboration for his work from wider, international quarters. Beyond his invocation of Mr. Naruse's Women's University, over time he legitimized his beliefs by citing influential European psychobiological, sociological, and psychological theories. Many years after Karve's speech at the National Social Conference in 1916, the noted British sexologist Dr. Meyrick Booth published his findings on the subject of the physical, inviolable distinctions in the character and activities of men and women. Booth was a psychologist writing at the height of the ideological upheaval of the interwar years and the Great Depression. The period saw the elevated role of psychobiological interpretations in prescribing national social behavior in Britain, interpretations that drew afresh on eugenics and debates over the "Freudian Revolution."[61] Feminists came under renewed attack from Booth, especially those who voiced an interest in cultivating school curricula that did not differentiate between the sexes.[62] In his autobiography, Karve cited Booth's views from *Nineteenth Century and After*, which had appeared in August 1927. It is fascinating to note how Karve drew upon British intellectuals to craft difference both from Europe and from certain constituencies of Indians. Karve cited Booth (who was himself citing his own lecture at the Ethnological Society):

Owing to greater relative importance of the sympathetic nervous system in women, and its greater fineness, women are more capable than men of experiencing and expressing feelings, such as joy, fear, grief, hope and are more instinctive and subjective in all their reactions. Men will never equal women in intuition, quick receptivity, adaptability and "emotionality." On the other hand, the greater stability of the male nervous system is the result of a different constitution. . . . The refusal of feminists to accept sex distinction as a basic social principle [and] . . . the progress of modern feminism has come to mean little more in practice than the penetration of women into a man-made social and industrial system. Today it is the woman with her inborn pliability of character, who is busy adapting herself to all sorts of masculine careers. The girl of today has been hypnotised by male influence.[63]

Booth was writing against the feminist curricula of higher education that had appeared during this period in Britain. This program aimed to move beyond the ideology of separate spheres and to make women professionally competitive in the interwar industrialized economy. He exemplified the conservative backlash against new configurations between class and gender in Britain. Here he located the so-called real and natural distinction between masculine and feminine behavior, opportunities, and professions on the axis of reproduction. This itself was not novel. But what was new was the heightened emphasis on affective and emotive differences, and hence on the aesthetic dispositions of men and women. Evoking the psychobiological reasoning popularized since Freud's theories, the scientific management of sentimentality provided a new means by which to fix differences between male and female behavior and social roles. Booth believed that educational curricula must institute the training and development of emotive, psychic, and hence sexual difference. Women must be schooled into femininity. A controlled, institutionalized setting might diminish the influence of what he saw to be the dangerous tendencies of feminism to repudiate sexual difference.

Booth was participating in a fairly well-integrated coalition of eugenicists and class conservatives; his aversion to those who sought to conceal biological and hence temperamental differences was compounded by his conviction that society was witnessing a growth in masculine women and effeminate men. This "penetration of women into a man-made social and industrial system" exacerbated the occlusion of "real" gender difference, which, he believed, could only lead to social degeneration. Booth, in turn, drew extensively on the opinions of the writer and physician Dr. Arabella Kenealy (1859–1938).[64] Kenealy had also published a number of novels dealing with vampires, lesbians, and menopausal women.[65] Vociferously antagonistic to the kind of feminism that she identified as denying "natural" differences between the sexes, Kenealy has herself been characterized as a leading "Eugenic Feminist."[66] Her concerns with the engineering of the national population were aired most energetically in her *Feminism and Sex Extinction* (London, 1920), in which she argued that social welfare at large was dangerously undermined with growing evidence of masculinity in girls or women and degeneration, even femininity, in men. Like Booth,

Kenealy was especially perturbed by school curricula that denied gender difference.[67] She declared that in the "normal girl the feminine characteristics are dominant and the masculine recessive. But should the opposite sex characteristics be over developed, we get degeneracy. The forcing of girls along masculine lines may result in serious and lasting injury to health."[68] Kenealy and Booth were voicing their anxieties in the context of class and urban upheaval in interwar Britain, and Karve readily translated those into the language of anticolonial nationalism.

Karve's memoirs exemplify the transnational movement of ideas, nimbly bridging the Hindu, the cultural-nationalist, and the eugenicist feminist. Kenealy and Booth's works appeared many years after Karve had first discussed his own beliefs on the propagation of a "feminine" curriculum for women.[69] Despite his strong admiration for these various scholars and activists, he does not so much as gesture to the fact that neither Naruse, Booth, nor Kenealy ever explored the issue of language.[70]

The immense care that Karve lavished on the question of the medium of instruction, the curiously organic metaphors that he deployed over the matter of language, and the strong biological associations he drew between mother tongue and reproduction all shifted over the years. While as early as 1896 (through the *Mahilashram*) he had begun to develop the idea of gender-specific educational curricula, by 1915 it was language that had become central to his beliefs on the education of gender difference. By 1928, when his autobiography was published, he had, by way of the "scientific" and psychobiological, moved away from theories of liberal egalitarianism to a more recognizable, patriarchal investment in the relationship between essential biological differences and national culture. Transnational connections bolstered Karve's ability to legislate on indigenous culture. In his *Atmavrit*, he argued that all universities in Japan, whether coeducational or only for women, conducted their studies in Japanese. Those universities had translated all aspects of the Western educational curriculum into Japanese. Karve was adamant that a similar transformation be introduced to India. It is curious that Karve exhibits no ambivalence on the matter of translation; in fact, he seems not to have held any opinion on the content or the politics of the colonial translation project itself.[71] Perhaps expecting that translations from English texts would seamlessly render the content of one language into another, he seemed unperturbed by the unequal power relations encoded in the long colonial history of the English language. Especially pertinent to my argument, his opinions signal the conviction that English had been successfully subsumed within indigenous power structures.

Karve sifted through elements of the colonial humanist project so as to frame a particular, "Indian" cultural identity. Staking difference from the West was not his only purpose. Naturalizing sexual difference by deploying the upper-caste vocabulary of touchability-untouchability, Karve argued that English exerted an immense, almost destructive power over the mother tongue. "Because of the policies of this importance to the English language implemented in Universities throughout the country, we find the continuing prohibition of the mother tongue, so much so that the mother tongue has been rendered untouchable.... While the mother tongue has recently been receiving some support, its struggle against English continues."[72] The Marathi word that Karve used for "untouchable" was *vital*. Indicating impurity and pollution, menstrual discharge, and the need to expel, marginalize, or dispense with, this was the same word evoked in the 1880s to propel the argument on the contaminating effect of the English language.[73] The use of the term reveals not only the consensus over conjoining caste strictures with female sexuality, but also the upper-caste investments of the intended audience. Continuing with the strategy of sexualizing languages—the process by which notions of sexual difference were deployed to fill the space between English and non-English languages—Karve echoed statements voiced in the late nineteenth century on the danger of the weaker, more pliant "mother tongue" falling under the encroaching power of English. This resonated with modes of argumentation from earlier decades, as caste and gender were invoked to quell the apparent rise of the English language. By claiming to protect indigenous culture from loose ideas of an encroaching, global culture, Karve and other intellectuals rendered transparent their own sociocultural positioning. In the process, they continued to ritualize the standards of female sexuality, to ensure the availability of domestic labor, and to determine access to and hierarchies of knowledge.

Despite his use of sexualized, caste strategies to "preserve" the parameters of indigenous language, Karve energetically supported the transfer from English into the vernacular. But he made no mention of a similar transaction from the vernacular into English, this despite the fact that he was writing in Marathi. Bemoaning the absence of a better policy for the development and training of "national genius," Karve criticized the fact that in India, modern thought and modern science—the basis for the material progress of any nation—remained "locked up in a foreign language."[74] Karve cited a work conducted by officials of Hyderabad's Osmania University, *Japan and Its Educational System*, quoting (and then translating into Marathi) long passages from that text. The restriction of knowledge to English was "unnatural," for it undermined the "position which nature means the mother tongue to have."[75] Karve repeated the words of the officials of the Osmania University, who also deployed the feminized vernacular to normalize standards of natural and unnatural, mobilizing sexual difference to mark distinctions between indigenous and foreign. For both Karve as well as the Osmania University, the most effective way to enable students to assimilate knowledge and think for themselves would be to make "the process of thought as well as its expression as natural as possible. This can only be done by making the Vernaculars of India the media of instruction."[76]

Comparing the students who graduated from the Indian Women's University to those who graduated from the government-supported Bombay University, he argued that, just as *swadeshi* goods received no tariff reduction or government support,[77] similarly there was no support for the curriculum of his indigenous university.[78] The natural, the mother tongue, and the anticolonial were clustered together, and their convergence produced meanings that directed who could access English and to what extent. Karve pointedly invoked the majority as the non-elite and as the real Indians, this even as his university ultimately maintained the hierarchies between an anglicized and a vernacular language curriculum. Karve concluded his illustration of the language policy of the university by asking which of the two possibilities were more "useful [and] will benefit family and society. . . . The education that women have had through English, but that has no connection to life, or subjects learnt in the mother tongue like psychology, child development, health sciences, a study of the nervous system . . . which would be more useful?"[79] The inevitability of reproduction for Indian women turned English into an artificial and foreign language.

Despite claiming to be invested in defining the parameters of the local and indigenous, Karve actively sought out transnational audiences and employed modes of argumentation that naturalized the power of global culture. He countered allegations that the university and its authorities were "vernacularists pure and simple shut off from any direct touch with western science and culture"[80] by pointing to the continuing place of the

English language as a compulsory second language. The university presented itself as remaining steadfast in its commitment to correct prevalent "misunderstandings that a graduate of this university is shut off from the vast treasures of English literature. The University does recognise English as a language of world-wide culture and special importance to India on political and national grounds."[81]

The low enrollment and lack of funds that had dogged the university in its early years changed dramatically within a few years after its inauguration. In 1919 the Gujarati industrialist Sir Vithaldas Thakersay, long a supporter of the IWU, happened to visit the very same Japan Women's University in Tokyo that had inspired Karve. Compared to Karve's IWU, however, he found the education imparted there to be "less bookish and more practical," for it placed a greater emphasis on subjects like gardening, laundry, cooking, and home decoration.[82] His interaction with the faculty and students at the Japan Women's University convinced him to further his support for Karve's venture. Thakersay returned to Bombay and immediately provided a large amount of money for the university, on the condition that the institution now bear the name of his mother, Shreemati Nathabai Damodar Thakersay. The increased funds allowed Karve to encourage other girls' schools in the Presidency to operate as feeders for the university.

But the city of Bombay continued to shun Karve's efforts. As a result, Karve and his associates turned to smaller provincial towns, working diligently to turn low-level girls' schools in places such as Satara, Belgaum, and Sangli into feeders for the university. That was how the university increased its enrollments. The ultimate aim was to have separate women's universities for each linguistic region. Until that point could be reached, the university appointed a Board of Studies to recommend books to be used by those students who might come from regions outside Maharashtra and Gujarat. Karve maintained that it was already possible to cover the syllabus of the university without attending classes in Poona, for some students had done this "from home," working in regions outside Marathi- and Gujarati-speaking ones, and also in other regional languages.

Support now increased, especially from provincial towns in Maharashtra, though the university did not gain statutory recognition from the government of India until almost two decades after independence. The first meeting of the All India Women's Council, held in Poona in 1927, recommended that the government issue recognition to the university.

Simultaneously the council expressed its tremendous support for those syllabi that privileged "the ideals of motherhood and making the home beautiful and attractive."[83] In 1927 the Senate of the Andhra University, in referring to the case of the SNDT University, recommended that it too "consider the desirability of having separate courses of study, for women and to formulate proposals for giving effect to this policy."[84]

Karve concluded his memoirs in 1928 and then undertook a voyage around the world in 1929.[85] He was especially impressed with the recent change in language policies in Ireland, where, despite British colonization, it was now recognized that every child must receive "the Irish [language] along with their mother's milk."[86] This prompted him to ruminate on the order of linguistic teaching in India, concluding that, in Marathi-speaking India, students should first learn the mother tongue (Marathi), the national language (Hindi), and the international language (English), in that order. Karve made no mention of Gujarati, nor of other important languages of western India, such as Kannada; he never questioned the growing hegemony of Hindi itself in defining Indian culture.[87] His visit to the United States made a favorable impression on him, especially because of his observation that many women's colleges that he visited were, according to him, specifically attuned to producing a scientific body of knowledge about domesticity.

The "Scientific Basis of Women's Education": Literature and Gender Difference

Karve rarely, if ever, sought recognition or support from the colonial state. Despite inheriting a project defined by colonial cultural power, his long life exemplifies the receding importance of the state in the battle over gender and culture. Women's education itself had largely remained in non-state (private) hands, even though most of the participants in its long history remained attuned to colonial patronage as they framed curricula, claimed new forms of power, and stymied access to others. As Karve's work and memoirs demonstrate, it was not just that colonial power remained marginal to the terms of sociopolitical competition. Rather, native elites competed over a range of wider transnational registers. A relatively small community of Brahman men had secured bicultural capital by defining, as mutually reinforcing, the contours of the local, feminine, and indigenous.[88] "Europe"—as audience and as disciplining agent—was often marginal to this contest, even as it was named as the "other" of indigenous culture and hence as the focus of cultural critique. Karve's own interest in maneuvering transnational audiences and forms of differentiation stretching from the United States to Japan very early on superseded support or criticism of colonialism. This is not an insignificant point. Partha Chatterjee, among others, has argued that by the turn of the century, Indian nationalists had resolved the "woman's question" through the projection of an essential, feminized culture, and thus turned away from negotiating over it with the colonial state. This might appear to be the case, when European culture and colonial power are amalgamated, assumed to be the central point of reference, or positioned as the primary motor of change. But in the case of the history of education, the colonial state was always an ally for the nationalists. Furthermore, from the perspective of comprehending the ongoing, tenacious reach of power and social hierarchies, it is crucial to note how upper-caste strictures were repackaged through forging alliances with new and emerging forms of imperial power. The seemingly secular turn toward women's education was definitely a matter of internal caste competition. And in addition, the attempt to control women's reform enabled, in fact accelerated, the participation of some Indian intellectuals on a transnational level.

Karve's vision found wider institutional applicability over the years, as it was consistently furthered by friends, associates, and reformist sympathizers. Literature, "scientific and technical knowledge," and gender coalesced over time. In the process, caste distinctions between the sexual and the cerebral, labor and intellect, defined new parameters of Indian culture. Among Karve's closest associates was G. M. Chiplunkar, a social activist and reformer who taught at the women's university and who assisted Parvatibai Athavale (discussed in chapter 8) with writing her memoirs. Chiplunkar went on to publish *The Scientific Basis of Women's Education* in 1930.[89] Citing a range of intellectual influences, the work hammered home the relationship between language, literature, and sexual difference. Second, by claiming the ability to legislate on distinctions between indigenous and Western culture through a specifically hetero-masculine logic, Chiplunkar demonstrated the rise of a new Hindu upper-caste, Indian transnational power. Accepting a greater participation of women in the workplace, Chiplunkar's work also envisaged a future quite different from that which Karve imagined. Rather than rejecting female domesticity, however, Chiplunkar adeptly brought conjugality, child rearing, and Hindu motherhood in line with the potential of women's employment.

Chiplunkar's text saw the return of the British sociologist and sexologist Dr. Meyrick Booth, not simply as a scholarly citation exuding veracity but now very much as an active participant. Booth, whom Karve had cited so heavily in his *Atmavrit*, now wrote the introduction to Chiplunkar's text. In this he declared that the "backwardness of the East" might actually release Easterners from replicating those mistakes made in the West on the subject of women's education. He argued that rendering women subject to the "dominion of masculine values," as was done in the West, divorced women from their inner natures and also encouraged an inadequate system of education.[90] Booth used contemporary biological and psychological arguments to buttress his conviction that there were insurmountable distinctions between masculine and feminine cultures, between "East" and "West." But he made no mention of either language or religion when discussing his opinions.

Building on the binaries deployed by Booth, Chiplunkar devoted *The Scientific Basis of Women's Education* to explaining how best to address the specific needs and circumstances of Indian women. For Chiplunkar, too, the differences between East and West, women and men, native and foreign, were immutable. Any attempt to soften the distinctions between the terms in these pairs was unnatural. Moreover, the absolute difference between them was based on an ancient cultural logic evidenced by the unique knowledge contained in "Hindu religion, Hindu Medical Science, and Hindu Traditions."[91] The correct curriculum for the education of all Indian women must, Chiplunkar decreed, address specifically Indian needs. In keeping with the theme of the comparative advantage of Eastern backwardness proposed by Booth, Chiplunkar cited evidence on the evils of the women's educational system in the West, claiming in no uncertain terms what the extension of the system of education to women would mean: "A new generation of hipless, breastless women is coming to the forefront in America and Europe. These women may serve the purpose of intellectual companionship in companionate marriages but as far as motherhood is concerned, [the] future race of children, if they are given the right of self-determination, will not prefer them as their prospective mothers."[92] Chiplunkar might have been making a reference here to flappers.[93] More directly, he was distinguishing between wifehood and motherhood. Karve, too, had centered reproduction as the most essential feature of sexual difference, but Chiplunkar's critique appears all the more pointed in the aftermath of American journalist Katherine Mayo's hostile assessment of Indian womanhood.[94] The purported primacy of reproduction assisted Chiplunkar in debunking the nineteenth-century argument made in favor of "equal" curricula. For its earlier class beneficiaries, English had signaled the support of colonial modernity, new forms of elite ascendancy, and the desire for marital companionship. Chiplunkar found most of those ambitions irrelevant. He was more concerned about the resulting inferiority of the children of those women who did work within the masculinized social system. Very urgently, the new Western education system was part of a larger cultural development whereby "women are getting themselves masculinised.... In the West, woman bears a close resemblance to man."[95]

The "West," which had once signified social progress for the agenda of women's education, was now regarded as the source of untenable policies on gender and culture. Chiplunkar now combined his arguments. He believed it was only "natural" that women receive an education separate from men, and he yoked this together with his conviction in the "foreign" nature of the English language. Brought together, he maintained this to be the reason why women's education must be conducted in the "mother tongue," "the only natural and effective medium of instruction."[96] He thereby revealed his own investment in the phallogocentric power of English. By selectively consolidating modern psychology, biology, and Brahmanical scriptures, Chiplunkar concluded that "the higher education in India being imparted through a foreign language is likely to cause a comparative greater stress and strain of Indian girls."[97] Indeed, "English as a national language for India involves an inherent contradiction. The only Language that can be made national in India is Hindi. *For women at least a vernacular University is badly needed.*"[98]

A critical development in the history of language and gender in western India was the often uncomplicated acceptance that Hindi should serve as the national language, and that all Indians should learn it. As I discussed in chapter 1, this belief has its history in the elevation of Sanskrit in the repertoire of the new colonial Brahmans, the multilingual history of the Bombay Presidency, and the competition with Persian. While Karve thought that, at least in Marathi-speaking areas, all people should learn Marathi, Hindi, and English, in that order, Chiplunkar seemed to suggest that non-

English languages were interchangeable, that Hindi could replace Marathi because any vernacular would counter the ascendancy of English.

Like Karve, Chiplunkar, too, believed in the practical necessity of the English language, but his ideas were informed by a curious notion of linguistic balance amid the multilingual realities of western India:

> The advantages, secured by making the mother tongue as the medium of instruction and examination, will surely counterbalance any loss, incurred by the decreased fluency in English or a superficial knowledge of Shakespeare and Milton. The importance of the study of English is unnecessarily exaggerated in India and the knowledge of English is developed at the cost of vernaculars. . . . Indians study English literature not with the idea of culture but with the idea of coming in touch with the scientific, industrial and political ideas expressed in that language and many more study this language simply for getting jobs. A working knowledge of English is quite sufficient for the clerical and other scientific purposes.[99]

This was the "scientific" basis for women's education. The passage introduces Chiplunkar's distinction between English literature and the knowledge contained in English-language works. Presenting a distinctive break with Macaulay, who had believed that literature secured knowledge and culture, Chiplunkar argued that the knowledge, literature, and language of English were distinct entities: each could be pursued independently of the other. The knowledge of "Shakespeare and Milton" was incompatible with the pursuit of a scientific, industrial, and political knowledge. But Chiplunkar did not believe that literature was irrelevant for Indian women. Rather, the identification of the discrete elements of English knowledge now elevated literature to a place of unquestionable authority in the education of middle-class women.

In "Present Day Education of Girls," Meyrick Booth had declared that while boys might "excel in Classics, History, Geography, Mathematics and Science," there was sufficient evidence to observe that girls surpassed their peers in "the study of modern language, Literature, Music, Drawing, Domestic Subjects, and Gardening."[100] The distinctions between scientific and literary-domestic knowledge, between language and literature, and between mental and emotive capacities were to add themselves to the stockpile of strategic polarities accruing around the definition of gender. The disaggregating of "English" into the components of literature, language, and emotion rode on the elevation of the emotive and sentimental virtues of women. Hence, Chiplunkar could argue that "women are more emotional than men. Artistic 'imagination' and 'vision' appears [sic] to be closely allied with their emotional nature and from this reason it is obviously of vital importance in their education."[101]

Chiplunkar and Booth were not the only ones to identify emotions as a distinct force that clinched the coalition between literature and femininity. A range of prominent educators voiced their conviction in the role of literature as the manager of gender difference.[102] The greatest authentication of the universal gendered power of literature had appeared in the British government's Consultative Committee on curricular reform; the report fueled Chiplunkar's theories on the "scientific basis of women's education."[103] The report had cited evidence on psychobiological differences between boys and girls to argue for a more sensitively differentiated curriculum. Reifying distinctions between physical and mental faculties, the report assuredly stated that "the aggressive instinct ... (pugnacity with its correlated emotion of anger) ... acquisitiveness ... self assertion and constructiveness, seemed stronger in males; while the milder instincts—secretiveness with its correlated emotion of tenderness, ... perhaps self-subjection and gregariousness—appeared to be more intensely developed in females."[104] This was why, according to the report, literature maintains and determines gender; this was why literature had to be at the very heart of the differentiated curriculum: "There was almost general agreement among witnesses that girls as a rule showed equal or superior originality and capacity in English literature, History, Modern Languages, and possibly the Biological Sciences, but were definitely inferior to boys in Ancient Languages, especially Latin, in Mathematics, and in those branches of Natural Science which specially require a knowledge of Mathematics. Girls showed, as a rule, a greater power of expression in the English language, but boys were more original."[105] The advisors to the Consultative Committee suggested instead a system that would "introduce a more explicit differentiation in actual methods of teaching."[106] Girls were recognized to be "better in English and boys in Mathematics."[107] While girls might be more expressive than boys, they failed in "logical arrangement and sequence of thought." Hence despite the central importance of literature and the "beauty of [the] literary form," there was a "certain danger that girls may direct their attention too exclusively to the emotional and aesthetic aspects of the subject." To counter the natural inclination of the female sex toward the emotional, the report called for close monitoring of study materials, to ensure that "girls should study pieces of Literature selected chiefly for their logical structure and the accurate use of language."[108]

The discussion over English took place on the terrain of sexuality. Macaulay had once stated his belief in the disciplinary effect of English language and literature for the colonies. Literary studies were now directing the production of correct femininity in Britain. Both Karve and Chiplunkar believed that English should be a compulsory second language in the education of Indian women. Chiplunkar argued that "the education of a future wife and mother is bound to be wider than the education of a boy. It will include all the important cultural subjects that a boy learns in the secondary and college stage; besides these the course will include 1. household arithmetic. 2. unlimited literature. 3. hygiene. 4. housekeeping in all its aspects."[109] Literature and language were discrete entities; they would ensure the parameters of gender. Other subjects that Chiplunkar advocated were fine arts, child psychology, sex hygiene, and moral training. Despite all his concern about unnecessarily exerting women through the educational system, Chiplunkar's ideal curriculum seemed even more taxing than the putatively gender-free one that was applicable to Indian boys.

The Bombay University had allowed girls to appear for its matriculation examination as early as 1883. Karve believed that the people of Bombay and Poona considered his "Karve metric" to be neither as prestigious nor as competitive as the matriculation examination for the Bombay University.[110] Despite that, the IWU remained committed to its mission, sending out its first graduate in 1919.[111] The other purpose of Karve's goal to bring secondary education within the reach of the majority of women was also gradually attained. The teaching of the vernacular was widely held up as the means of lessening class differences in the emerging nation. The university's authorities discussed the widening gulf in social class and emphasized again that "the natural method of imparting education through the mother tongue is one of the ways to bridge the chasm. Further, the roles played by men and women in the social life of the country are different and differentiation in curricula to suit these requirements is necessary."[112]

When Sir Thakersey promised financial support for the university in 1919, he demanded that the institution ultimately receive government recognition for his grant to continue. But this recognition was not forthcoming, despite intense lobbying on the part of university officials. Finally in 1949, the matter was taken up in the legislative assembly of the post-independent Bombay state.[113] Mr. B. G. Kher, the state's chief minister, remarked that it was the exaggerated importance habitually given to English in British India that had led to the unfortunate neglect of the university. It was now time for the postcolonial nation to reverse that trend. But this was not to be done by introducing English; rather, it was by recognizing the university for having fulfilled a momentous social mission in privileging the study of the vernacular. Kher connected the use of language to the development of students' behavior and conduct, arguing that for education to most effectively influence the "the personality . . . character and capacities of the pupils, it should be imparted undoubtedly during the earlier stages and preferably even at the later states through the mother tongue which is the music and magic of language."[114]

Overwhelmingly, the speakers at this debate favored government recognition for the SNDT University. The legislators believed that such a step would rectify the deliberate disregard of the institution during British times, a disregard aimed at annulling the vernacular language itself. It was incumbent on the independent nation to belatedly recognize the work of the university that had preserved the mother tongue in the face of British hegemony. There was barely any opposition to the university or to its policies of gender differentiation, except for the provocative complaint from Mr. Purshottam Trikamdas, who claimed that any support for an institution such as this that differentiated its curriculum was tantamount to sending "women back to the purdah."[115] Rosalind O'Hanlon's careful delineation of the relative newness of the discourse around purdah among middle castes from the Maharashtrian nineteenth century serves us well here. O'Hanlon demonstrates important contradictions in the practice: the widening use of purdah was attuned toward claiming a Hindu identity by middle castes; simultaneously, and for that reason, it invoked the scorn of Brahman castes who derided it for being a Muslim practice.[116]

Questions raised during the legislative assembly debates on the specific language to be used in the university were hastily brushed aside. It seems to have been decided that the university would attend to the mother tongue of all students, be those Marathi, Gujarati, or Kannada. The university received its required government recognition with an overwhelming majority of votes. It continued to claim the emotive and aesthetic sensibilities of women, a training that evidently strengthened the purpose of an otherwise fraught nation. Speaking at an annual convocation ceremony around 1960, Govind Ballabh Pant, the Union Minister of Home Affairs, declared:

"A NEW GENERATION . . ."

The specific aim of women's education is to relate their unique endowments and aptitudes to what the nation needs. The finest gifts of kindness, broad sympathies, dignity, poise, compassion . . . are indissolubly connected with the ideal of womanhood. . . . The Gods have endowed women with the gift of intensity of feeling and wider capacity for tolerance, compassion and kindness. . . . The power of these sentiments is a tremendous force for social cohesion. Fissiparous tendencies are asserting themselves over the national scene. Even language and regional and provincial affiliations are creating barriers. . . . Women have the added opportunity of furthering the supreme cause of national solidarity through education as well as through the home.[117]

The sexually normative woman, the Hindu nation, and Indian modernity coalesced, and English was subsumed to the logic of India's caste regimes. Language continued to be the litmus test for Indian womanhood, for the organization of permissible Indian sexuality. India itself transcended regional difference, honored female domesticity, resisted "fissiparous tendencies," and naturalized Sanskritic culture. The control over English spilled beyond the private-public partnerships of the early twentieth century; the upper-class male mediation over gender and language was now official state policy. This was how English came to be contained within the gender economy of India.

Once framing his agenda on gender in terms of disputing caste, Karve and his successors very quickly elevated heteronormative expectations, specifically marriage and reproduction, in arguing in favor of women's English education. In fact, the history of English determined that anticaste efforts galvanize marriage and reproduction. Having traced the institutional history by which English came to be domesticated by changing gender norms, we now turn in part II to book-length publications by individuals involved in this effort. My aim is to elicit how caste was secularized through the individual desires of English-educated subjects, and, more particularly, how sexual desire regulated, and was further directed, by the power of Indian English. Part II turns to a range of actors—men and women—from a number of religious backgrounds, all of whom portrayed their subjectification within English, and all of whom produced the normative woman as the way to indigenize the colonial language of power.

PART TWO

5

"I SHALL READ PRETTY ENGLISH STORIES TO MY MOTHER AND TRANSLATE THEM INTO MARATHI FOR HER"

Widowhood, Virtue, and the Secularization of Caste

Published in 1890, a Marathi-language biography of a young female student at the Poona Native High School (PNHS) illuminates each intricate step by which an idealized, normative womanhood successfully domesticated the English language. *Sadgun Manjari: Eka Hatbhagya Strichya Charitra*, by Ganesh Janard Agashe, tells the story of Avadi Bhide (1869–1888), the first student to enroll in PNHS.[1] Both Avadi and her sister entered the school when it was inaugurated in 1884; Avadi would also have been the school's first matriculate had she not died tragically before the examination.[2] A young Brahman widow, she was married at eleven, widowed at seventeen, and dead at nineteen.[3] Avadi left behind a number of English- and Marathi-language letters written to a circle of school friends, teachers, and relatives, as well as her diary, written in Marathi, and her school books, containing essays and examination answers. Upon her death, and at the request of Avadi's reform-minded father, Rao Moreswar Bhide, Agashe used those written sources to compose a biography. The resulting work, which is presented as a life story (*charitra*) of her virtuous but tragic life, paradoxically illuminates instead the male intellectual's desire to produce, edit, narrate, and individuate the Brahman female subject as the paradigmatic custodian of an intensifying and sexually conservative Indian modernity.

Agashe accessed the words and documents of Avadibai Bhide to construct her strictly moral, virtuous, flawless life.[4] His assessment reveals how English came to be embedded in a host of mutually reinforcing social relations: widowhood, caste, gender, marriage, Hinduism, Marathi. The biography illuminates the process by which English was disciplined by "indigenous" gender orders even as it claimed the symbolic power to guide gender. In the process, Agashe's work provides crucial information on the secularization or re-ritualizing of caste through the vehicle of English. His work thus demonstrates how idealized standards of womanhood established the ultimate power of native men to domesticate the English language.

Agashe was a teacher by profession, a self-published poet,[5] and a scholar of some repute.[6] The frontispiece to the biography describes him as the headmaster of Dhule High School. He had also held the office of the president of the Poona Marathi Literary Society.[7] A close friend of the Bhide household, he lived nearby, visited the family frequently, and knew Avadi personally over several years.[8] Paramila Rao has recorded that Vishnu Moreshwar Bhide was one of the group of native moderates who mobilized in 1895 to grant educated women the right to vote on Congress Resolutions. As detailed above, the student body of the PNHS consisted of the wives and daughters of upper-caste liberal reformers such as G. K. Gokhale, H. N. Apte, and V. M. Bhide. The urge to extend the vote to educated women was one way some men sought to double their power within the Congress.

The work's genre and the history of family studies in western India suggest that Agashe's complicated text straddles the desires of multiple audiences. As a biography it provokes comparisons with an established literary form for western India, but its circulation amid an imagined community of liberal native reformers and social conservatives implies a twist in the biographical mode. Biography has a long history in western India and in the wider subcontinent. In her important analysis of the conventions that govern the creation and telling of life histories in the early modern Indo-Islamic cultural encounter, Barbara Metcalf has stressed that biographical writings characteristically produced the "relational self," one that explicated the network of social and communal relations.[9] To that extent, the significance of the individual life was noteworthy for its similarity to, not its difference from, a wider social context. Building on Metcalf and analyzing the mode of "telling lives" over the Indo-British period, David Arnold and Stuart Blackburn trace the history of the biographical form from the early Pali Buddhist sources to the contemporary period, concluding that "modernity did not replace traditional life histories so much as recast them."[10] The relational self endured, even if it was recast through the rise of an individuated authorship, print circulation, and the act of reading. Agashe's Avadi, too, is depicted through her relation to others, in the process serving to normalize the intellectual and sexual violence that consolidated upper-caste power. Avadi appears as an exemplary conformist, one whose life drew its singular purpose from serving others and thus in maintaining social relations and naturalizing power differences.

If Agashe's account fits within the biographical form in some ways, especially in conveying the modern relational self, in other ways it does not. In a detailed study of Marathi-language materials, V. D. Divekar argued in 1978 that the "first published biography in Marathi" appeared in 1816 and that until 1900 the number of such works amounted to 100.[11] But Divekar does not analyze the temporal politics of Marathi as a literary form-in-the-making, nor does he signal its relatively recent materialization through the nationalist recasting of social relations over the nineteenth century. Marathi is an already emergent, trans-historical whole. And Divekar makes absolutely no mention of Agashe's work in his otherwise painstaking compilation of published Marathi-language biographies of the nineteenth century. On the other hand, Divekar's work turns to the genre of family histories and their mode of staking prescriptive caste norms. Upwardly mobile caste groups demonstrated their purity to the state by parading the chastity of their women, and family history served to record the cultural power of the socially mobile caste groups. Agashe's *Sadgun Manjari* is not a family history in and of itself, but it does seem to bridge family and caste history with hagiography. In other words, Divekar's research, though it does not specifically grapple with *Sadgun Manjari*, suggests the possibility that Agashe's biography of Avadibai Bhide functioned between genres and thus satisfied multiple social interests.

Who, then, was Agashe writing for? The literary-historical genres that he straddles indicate his multiple audiences and authorial strategies. Addressing the "true well wisher of Hindustan, the gracious Sir William Wedderburn" and the "prestigious James Fergusson," governor of the Bombay Presidency, in his opening pages,[12] Agashe then references the opponents of English education.[13] He was well aware of allegations leveled against English-educated women in the popular press, and he wrote pointedly that he was writing to counter their fears.[14] In addition, by stressing the pain and loneliness of the child widow, as well as her delight with learning and desire to use her education for philanthropic purposes, Agashe addressed the concerns of the reform-minded progressive and elite anglicized Indian community. And finally, the Marathi-language biography was dedicated to Miss Hurford, the superintendent of the school, perhaps indicating that Agashe expected that it would be read by some of its teachers and students. If Agashe's choice of literary form tells us about his audience, then some reflection on his intended audience helps us appreciate his authorial strategy. His focus on the life of the abject widow, I would argue, enabled Agashe to bridge the overlapping conventions of biography, Marathi linguistic nationalism, and family history; it also allowed him to bring liberal strategies of affect in line with upper-caste strictures.

In his preface to the text, Agashe discusses the uncommon nature of his endeavor: to write the biography of a lesser-known figure. He then cites Max Mueller,[15] who formulated the three insights that a biography provides: the public, the personal, and the "mystery aspect which can be seen by only one entity: god . . . the inner traits that dwell in one's mind."[16] But if the *sarvatma parmeshvar*, or the supreme, non-human soul force was the only one to view the mysterious traits of the inner self, Agashe believed that the biographer or the poet could flesh these out through analysis. Hinting thus at his unique power to reveal and reproduce Avadi's inner being through the biographical form, Agashe locates his privileged insights within the literary textual tradition of modern upper-caste Hinduism, citing not only Max Mueller, but also Shakuntala and Kalidas.[17]

Writers such as Vishnushastri Chiplunkar, discussed in chapter 3, had worked to craft Marathi as a modern language of literary prose. The turn toward a supposedly higher connection with English and Sanskrit straddled the aim of introducing the literary and historical works from Europe to a largely lower- and middle-class Marathi reading public. Chiplunkar's reliance on a transnational support structure for modern Marathi prose resonated in the works of contemporary authors such as Agashe. The latter's own prose was far more accessible, but he too favorably highlighted Avadi's references to British writers and Sanskrit poets. Mirroring Chiplunkar's work, Agashe deputed Avadi in the service of crafting the unbroken genealogy of Marathi literature, even as he used her writings to discuss moral standards sponsored by European writers.

Agashe was operating amid the new print culture of western India.

Rosalind O'Hanlon has discussed the rise of this textual form in western India over this exact period, noting the wide circulation of the themes of "drunkenness, prostitution and adultery" and the "most extreme combination of misogynism, voyeuristic detail and heavy handed moralizing."[18] She situates Tarabai Shinde's 1882 Marathi text, *Stri Purush Tulana*, in this literary context, pointing out that Shinde's outrage was aimed at the trope of the prostitute, one that marked the limits of conjugal modernity and reaffirmed the veracity of patriarchal power over the domestic realm. Shinde had astutely connected a voyeuristic sexualization of some women as prostitutes with a terse critique of the institution of widowhood. Fears of female sexuality not bound to the monogamous strictures of marriage were amplified through the figure of the prostitute, in order to naturalize the sexual and physical availability of the widow and secure her property within the deceased husband's family.[19]

Unlike Shinde, however, Agashe's work does not directly challenge the misogyny, the conservative outrage, the titillation, or the resurgence of violence against upper-caste widows. Rather, it seems aimed at reassuring those already somewhat sympathetic to women's education but who might have been surprised by a rhetoric that called for widow remarriage and women's education. Agashe presented himself as a progressive Brahman man energetically opposed to the misery of the widow. Like other reform-minded men of the period he never criticized the wider social logic, the strictures around female sexuality that served to naturalize the caste division of labor. Instead, his strategy was to build a sympathetic audience by dwelling in piercing detail on the suffering of the Brahman widow. Agashe's zeal to reconstruct the minute details of Avadi's life—by examining her sentiments, her interiority, her desolation, and her unassailable fortitude—served to individuate his subject and dampen any possible criticism of caste patriarchy. He insistently revealed the exemplary suffering of this particular, yet autonomous, Brahman widowed subject. Agashe's aim was thus to mobilize guilt or pity in response to what he saw as Avadi's virtuous and dedicated suffering. He muted the criticism embedded in her own words, effectively producing her individual suffering as distinct from her social position. He thus deliberately disengaged Avadi's individual plight from the radical social critique being voiced by widows and other women at that time.[20] The sexual normativities of Hindu upper-caste nationalism were not merely left unexamined, but they were reinscribed as secular and exceptional.

Sadgun Manjari, the Biography

Agashe embarks on his venture by acknowledging the "uncommon" nature of his quest. Rather than producing another account of world-renowned statesmen and soldiers, he notes that he is attempting a biographical account of an unknown woman.[21] He then holds forth in some detail on the nature of knowledge (*vidya*) and the rare accomplishments the young girl attained before her untimely death.[22] Agashe tells us that Avadi was born in Ratnagiri in 1869; her father, Rao Bahadur Vishnu Moreshwar Bhide, was the *zilla* (district) deputy collector. Like other male advocates of female English education, Bhide was an English-educated bureaucrat serving the colonial state and motivated by the desire to teach English to his daughter. Similar to Manockjee Cursetjee and M. G. Ranade, whose pedagogic work brought Western education to their wives and daughters, Bhide also launched his experiment at home. He educated Avadi in reading, writing, and conversation in both Marathi and English.

Despite his somewhat unconventional pedagogic ambitions, Avadi's father did not postpone her marriage. As was common at the time, she was married at age eleven. Unfortunately, both her in-laws died months after the marriage and her husband died six years later in 1886.[23] The general consensus was that educated women were so unlucky that they would cause the deaths of their husbands, and Avadi's case might have appeared to corroborate this belief.[24] Agashe never tells us whether Avadi had been living in her husband's home at the time of his death, nor does he proffer any information on whether the marriage had been consummated. Perhaps because of the death of her in-laws, Avadi returned to her natal home, although the more common outcome would have been for her to continue to reside with her in-laws and provide constant labor once she was widowed. Instead, her father unequivocally supported her and her education.

At the time of her admission to the school, Avadi was certified as having read to the Marathi Fourth Standard; she had also read the English First Book at home and was thus admitted to the Second English Grade in the new school. She was about seventeen years of age. Agashe takes great pains to impress his readers with her diligence, conscientiousness, integrity, pleasing mannerisms, and wide popularity among students and teachers alike.[25] She appears to have been completing more than one year's work each year that she was in the school, ranking first in all examinations. Her teachers encouraged her to read, providing her with English books such as Pandita Ramabai's *High Caste Hindu Woman*.[26] The women who taught her English included Miss Mary Sorabji,[27] as well as Miss Bhor and Miss Hurford. Contrary to the fears voiced in *Kesari*,[28] English was not being taught by men, though often the teachers were European women and women of other religious communities. In her free time, Avadi read English books, and among her favorite poets was the English poet William Cowper. There was, according to Agashe, no other English poet as devout, gentle, mild, and measured as Cowper. Agashe reports that Cowper was *shhradhalu* (full of faith and belief), and reading him brought Avadi closer to God. She was also very fond of drawing and rather skilled in free-hand and model drawing. Avadi's letters reveal that she was friends with Cornelia Sorabji (1866–1954).[29]

Avadi was a model student. Agashe reports on her performance in an English scholarship examination conducted in 1887, noting both the value and beauty of her sentence construction as well as the sentiments it conveyed. Asked in this examination how she would use her education in her domestic life, Avadi answered that it would be of great use to her in the afterlife:

Having been cut off from the worldly affairs by the will of God, I mean to pass my life in helping others. . . . I shall help my mother in keeping accounts, in needle work, and in many other things. I shall read pretty English stories to my mother and translate them into Marathi for her. I shall also read and explain the old Sanskrit books to her. . . . Though it is not the wish of God that I should have any children, I shall instruct those of my dear sisters and friends; and in this way be useful to them. When I am with my dear father and brother, I shall not have to sit still as many poor girls in my position have to do. Then science and the higher subjects that I learn and mean to learn, will help me in talking with my father and brother, and I shall have the dear pleasure of seeing them pleased with me.[30]

As a child widow, popular opinion would have held that Avadi was socially useless, a carrier of bad luck, and that her education was responsible for initiating this unfortunate turn of events. Here she presents her situation as willed by divine purpose and characterizes her interest in charitable pedagogic activities. Ellen McDonald has explored in detail the confluence between English education and the rise of a socially responsible philanthropic inclination, but the gendered aspects of this "transmission" have yet to be examined, especially at the site of an evidently Protestant notion of a calling or vocation in the service of society.[31] Avadi's self-presentation focused on her thwarted reproductive and conjugal desires. Her female subjectivity was shaped by lack and by a longing for reproduction and domesticity. Her knowledge of English structured existing biological, filial, and domestic—non-sexual—relationships. She planned to read English stories in translation to her mother but discuss science and the "higher subjects" with her father and brother. In the case of educating her unschooled mother, she would take on the task of the "surrogate Englishman."[32] But rather than simply extending the colonial project with her knowledge of English, she sought to use her knowledge to reverse the parent-child role, becoming the pedagogic power and infantilizing her mother. Here she echoes the idealized conversation between Saguna and her mother, Parvati, discussed in chapter 2. Her knowledge of the "higher subjects," evidently borne by English, would permit her a closer proximity, albeit subservient, to the male members of her family. Continuing her answer, Avadi stated, "By the education I receive here, I shall also be able to get money, out of which I shall spend some in helping the poor; and it will also make me independent." She thus exemplified the fears that English-educated women would earn money, enter the professions, and emasculate male power. But she instantly allayed those concerns, appealing instead to the philanthropic sensibility: "I shall teach my country women (and this is the principal aim of my life) the subjects that they want to learn."[33] Whether it was for the facility she demonstrated with the English language in these lines or for the self-consolidating sentiments she espoused therein, her answer satisfied her examiners.[34] She was awarded thirty-nine out of forty points for this answer.

Agashe glowingly underscores that the examination answer captured Avadi's "entire" inner self.[35] Another of his key sources for understanding Avadi's inner being was her Marathi-language diary, which she kept between January 1 and June 10, 1887, and which provided evidence of her steadfast commitment to tradition and domestic bliss.[36] Although Agashe reports that "it was Avadi's ardent desire that this diary not come before the eyes of anybody,"[37] revealing Avadi's fear that her privacy might be "exposed," Agashe proceeds to do exactly that.[38] Avadi herself did not share her diary with anyone; she related therein an incident in which a close friend chanced upon the book and Avadi tore it from her hands. Admitting that the diary was written neither for public recognition nor for publication, Agashe claims that the diary was a minor work, a mere "scribbling book" to which Avadi turned for relief and comfort in the midst of her alienation.[39] As he then emphasizes, all her female companions were happy in their homes and with their families. While her mother loved her dearly, how could Avadi be expected to pour out her "personal interests" to her mother?[40] He positions the diary as the widow's autonomous (and ultimately inconsequential) solution—the quiet, creative substitute for intimacy and social belonging. Explaining away the fact that any discussion of her diary would be "not desirable to her," he continues nevertheless to report from it. Agashe believes he did so "in Avadibai's service. . . . By presenting her hurdles, public ill-treatment; her courage and devotion to the world, I disclose her diary to show fair-minded people how she lived her short life and to young girls as an example to follow."[41]

In some distinction to Agashe's editorial statements are Avadi's own entries. On the anniversary of her husband's death and within the first month of keeping her diary, Avadi stridently complained about her unhappiness and turbulence. People remained unaware of her misery, she wrote, because she took pains to appear peaceful and content.[42] Privately, however, she wrote at length about the tragedy of the separation. She pleaded with God never to bring such a situation upon another person. All that day she relived her memory of her husband's passing, yet she remained determined not to let others know of her misery. She wrote that the divergent and negative thoughts that entered her mind were not to be written down, because it would give her mind no rest if the diary were to come within the reach of another.[43] On a daily basis she would evade self-pity by remembering that her situation was the will of God. But on this anniversary, with the memories of her husband's death washing over her, it was impossible to maintain her equilibrium: there was "no solution or medicine to my affliction in this world other than the prospect of death."[44]

Agashe interjects here that her words evidenced her lifelong devotion to her husband, how Avadibai saw his image day and night, and how his death dealt a strong blow to her delicate heart.[45] Again depicting her suffering through the upper-caste emphasis on virtue, Agashe resolutely avoids Avadi's own critique of the social and personal punishment of the Brahman widow. He also never addresses her reference to death. Instead, he inserts his belief in the continuing conjugal devotion of the long-suffering wife. Avadi's awareness that suicide provided the only route for a refusal of gender norms did not alter Agashe's sober assessment.

In her diary, Avadi recalled a conversation with a widowed friend who had also expressed the conviction that nothing other than death would release her from the encompassing misery of her condition. The friend mentioned that her brothers taunted her for her social uselessness. Avadi recorded, "She said, 'Avadi hearing these words it feels like it is better to die. How are my brothers like this! They are enemies of my life. I find it strange [they] want to kick someone who is already dead!'"[46] At this point, Agashe discusses the unfairness of the situation, wondering whether a woman who no longer held "worldly" relations (a term used as a synonym for reproduction within the married bond) must be forced to live an empty or useless life. Turning then to the progress narrative of liberal feminism, Agashe invokes the work performed by Mary Carpenter and Florence Nightingale, women who were allowed to be socially useful and became world famous despite having never married. But he does not acknowledge the conditions that held certain sexual standards in place, nor does he criticize those who supported these sexual-caste alliances. Rather, he shapes Avadi's words into support of his agenda. Resonating here with themes on masculinity that I discussed in chapter 3, Agashe's gender is reliant on his being able to demonstrate the power to contain femininity. He then turns to a wide discussion of the public and the domestic. Lamenting the huge rift between the male and female worlds, he declares that though the outside world was situated in the nineteenth century, the home remained in the fourteenth or fifteenth century. Women spoke of superficial things, or of their children, or of religious stories, and—unlike Avadi—could not converse on art, handicrafts, or poetry.[47]

The latter half of the biography veers directly toward discussions of English and gender. In addition to the diary, Agashe also mined letters that Avadi wrote to her female friends. In one English-language letter, Avadi describes in vivid detail a trip to Ahamadnagar: "A clear moonlit night and the scenery along the line, chiefly extensive fields and woodlands, was grand and picturesque. The sky residing on the earth like a vast vault studded all over with bright stars looked very beautiful."[48] Agashe suggests that; as one example in a rigorously mediated text, the letter highlighted Avadi's use of English and her enjoyment of rural scenery. Agashe approvingly notes Avadi's pleasure in the rustic and the natural. Writing to a friend on her recent trip to Mahabaleswar, Avadi had recalled the "chains of high mountains and deep valleys . . . the rivers Krishna and Venya look like fine silvery ribbon[s] running through the valleys, from these high peaks."[49] The romanticist mode, with its urge to describe the magnificence and tranquility of nature, would itself have been a product of the seemingly benign Western education that she was receiving in school. Travel through apparently empty lands was lauded as a means of self-discovery for Western subjects.[50] For his part, Agashe emphasizes Avadi as a passive spectator of scenery, rendering her a tourist in rural Maharashtra. Writing on December 16, 1886, to Miss Sorabji,[51] Avadi declared, "I would like to study all my life, if I could." Of all the subjects that she was learning in school, drawing was her very favorite. She wrote that she would like to be an artist who could draw the "beautiful trees, flowers, hills" and, later in the same letter, that it would be "delightful to go abroad into the world and see many different countries." But she was well aware that this desire would never materialize, "as at present I have no prospects of going. But if not to other countries, I should like to travel all over my own country at least. We learn so much by travelling."[52]

As she had assured her examiners in the English scholarship examination, Avadi did indeed write to her father and brothers in English. The letters detail household events, her schoolwork, and the health of her family, especially of her sister who was terminally ill by 1887. In a letter to her brother on April 7, 1887, she describes her sister's symptoms and also gives details about her schoolwork. Performing the very role desired by male social reformers who were in favor of women's education, Avadi demonstrated that her ability to read and write enabled her to shoulder the task of managing the everyday requirements of a modern household.

Repeatedly, Agashe brings English to the fore to signify chaste femininity. Recalling in another English-language letter the drawing examination that she had recently taken, Avadi illustrates her discomfort at being immersed in a room full of boys, despite the fact that her two teachers sat on either side of her the whole time. Still, she writes, "I was trembling . . . perhaps because I had never sat among such a number of boys before, and for this reason, I did not do my model as well as the others."[53] English could be yoked to a demure femininity, but it remained burdened by the lurking presence of sexual power.

Some women in Avadi's social circle deployed English to express their Christian beliefs. For instance, upon her sister's death, letters poured in from teachers and friends at school. Jane Sorabji, who appears to have been a teacher, wrote a lengthy poem called "The Gardener and the Maid," which ended with this verse:

> *Your Master* points the way, my child
> If you will only see him;
> Through deserts dark and forests wild
> Look for all guidance to him.
> You know him not, but seek him dear;
> Your tree is in his garden.⁵⁴

The sentiments of some of her teachers brought together Christianity, a transcendental male vision, and English. But for Agashe, their words provided the foil against which Avadi's steady commitment to Marathi literature and Brahmanical devotion could be developed. First taking care to remind his readers that Avadi, too, had the opportunity to develop an admiration for Western literature, he then dwells in some detail on Avadi's great admiration for the poet William Cowper. Cowper regularly mobilized Christian imagery, but Agashe does not mention this.⁵⁵

Agashe foregrounds Avadi's use of English when she expresses conservative convictions. Occasionally, for example, she amplifies the veracity of her opinions by adopting the perspective of an Indian woman. While she did not regularly enact such a slippage (between her caste location, her class interests, and her ability to speak in the name of Indian women) in her self-presentation, there are nonetheless notable instances when she cites the "nation" to authenticate her sentiments. In an English-language letter to Lady Wedderburn from July 1887, Avadi discusses the recent Rakhmabai case:

> The general opinion among our women is against her. Among us, the idea of a woman refusing to live with her husband goes sorely against the train [*sic*]. . . . My private opinion is certainly not in her favour. She says she will even go to prison for the good of the women of India. Examples of this kind will only serve to retard our progress. Besides, her husband . . . is not what she calls him. He is not a coolie, he gets 40 RS. a month; he is not consumptive; and he is quite as well educated as herself. . . . Rakhmabai who thinks herself so highly educated (though she publishes articles written by another in her own name) and who is the head of the Arya Mahila Samaj in Bombay will never have the honour of having set a good example to her fellow countrywomen.⁵⁶

Avadi—herself highly conversant in English—argues that Rakhmabai could not have penned the letters of protest in the newspapers, as it was impossible for a woman to attain such a high facility with the English language.

Her words suggest her acquiescence that the language had to be mediated in its transfer to Indian women so that its purported proselytizing and sexual power be subsumed under native gender regimes.

The domestication of English emerges again in Avadi's correspondence to Cornelia Sorabji. In one letter, she mentions a specific session of the ladies organization (attended by Sorabji's mother and sister) and the essays prepared and discussed by the women present.[57] In this letter, she recommends the *Veni Samhara* from the *Mahabharat* and then writes to Sorabji, "You must have read so many nice English books, but don't you think you ought to read some in your own language? Of course there are very few nice books in Marathi, but I think you ought to write some pretty books in Marathi and increase the number, as you are so learned." Agashe immediately interjects that the lines evidence the deep love that Avadi had for her "own, national language." The word that he uses is *svadeshbhasha*, literally, language of one's nation; interestingly, he does not use the term "mother tongue." He then underscores her desire for more books in her "own language," her *svabhasha*, a laudatory desire that he believed should be encouraged by one and all.[58] Agashe uses both *svabhasha* and *svadeshbhasha*, and the proximity of the words in his analysis suggests a tightening correspondence between self and nation, a desire to endow individuality by naturalizing the national. He reiterates that Avadi regretted that so many people had become learned through knowledge attained in the foreign language but did not seek to bolster the knowledge available in the language of Maharashtra.

Unlike such people, Avadi would never allow English to dictate her intellectual and cultural desires. Shifting somewhat from his earlier stated motive to memorialize Avadibai Bhide, Agashe reiterates in the last part of the text that his primary agenda has been to reach out to those opposed to women's education. He now claims that his purpose is to convince a wider audience that educated women would not be obstinate or intractable. The common attitude, according to Agashe, is that highly educated women would misuse their learning, be contemptuous of their husbands' authority, and thus despoil their deportment.[59] While there was a minority that conceded the need for a degree of female education, even those people had strong reservations about English education for women. Here he asks: if a learned man errs, how could one expect that it was the fault of his wisdom or learning?

To reiterate Avadi's pure and devout inclinations, Agashe cites an English-language letter that Avadi wrote to a friend about a Marathi book called *Venu*, which she describes as "such a pretty story." The book is about Venu, married at the age of nine to a boy "given up to vice." Venu's in-laws were cruel; they were "so unkind to her that they even used to beat her sometimes." Despite that, as Avadi underscores, Venu mentioned none of this to her parents as "she thought it would hurt her father and mother." Venu suffered and endured the humiliation when "her husband used to go out at night," yet she would simply "cry to God with all her heart." Female misery again fuses the narrative and reformist mode. Avadi noted there were times when Venu would come close to giving up hope even in the act of calling out to God, but "her heart" constantly prevailed over the rare fluctuations in her faith. And indeed, "after many days her husband saw how she suffered and he began to take pity upon her and became a good husband and our poor Venu was happy and thankful."[60] As is his custom, Agashe interjects immediately. He writes that the letter demonstrated that Avadi had a great desire and love (*haus*) for Marathi books. By reading these she gained the strength to distinguish between good and bad. Venu's hope and faith gave Avadi the strength she needed in her own life, he claims. Agashe sees the story (and Avadi's commentary) as evidence of her unassailable spiritual conviction. He never interprets it as evidence that women were deliberately trained to discard any prospect of contesting sexual power through lived praxis. Instead he believes that Venu's devotion reflected Avadi's faith and should be an example to all women. The letter carried no disdain or scorn for social rules or conventions: Avadi neither critiqued the in-laws' behavior, nor did she question Venu's seemingly voluntary embrace of an inequitable conflict over sexuality. Agashe boldly states that Avadi's intentions (which he materializes through the invocation of faith, long-suffering conjugal commitment, and psychic misery) worked as a corrective to the prevalent conception that women's English education would upset social arrangements.

Agashe continues to marshal evidence to establish that, far from tainting Avadi, the language subsisted harmoniously around her and suitably expressed her docile and respectful behavior. Citing an English-language school essay she had written, Agashe notes approvingly how this particular work demonstrates the effect that Western-style English education had had on her. Her essay is on her "favourite poem"—the *Savitri Akhyana* by Moropant. According to Avadi, the poem tells the story of the princess Savitri, who fell in love with Satyavant, whom she happened to chance upon while traveling. "She was so struck with the polite manners and the beauty of the young prince, that she fell in love with him and married him," related Avadi. She added that Savitri only knew him to be living in the forest with his blind parents, although in reality his father was a deposed king. Savitri's father grudgingly gave his consent to the marriage and Savitri went to live in the forest with the young man.

Avadi's account of the poem is difficult to relate, not only because her own description and commentary stretch unsteadily over a rather convoluted story, but more so because Agashe constantly and clumsily interjects his own commentary into her prose. For instance, in her description, Avadi mentions that at one point in the story Savitri and her husband were returning from worshipping the tree of Vata. At this point Agashe notes in parentheses that the Puranas state that worshipping at this tree makes one's husband enjoy *deerghayushya*, long life. Once again, Agashe naturalizes caste through sexuality, and once again he does so by citing those texts that themselves would only recently have been privileged by Orientalist scholarship and its obsession with the textual life of upper-caste Hinduism. He thus obscures the power dynamics of Hindu Brahmanical culture by referencing the supposed inevitability of sexual difference. We are then taken back to Avadi's description of how, upon their return from the ritual, Satyavant was suddenly bitten by a serpent, fainted, and died almost instantly. Savitri "lamented over him so bitterly and prayed to God so earnestly that He restored her husband to life again." At this point, Avadi appears to shift from a descriptive commentary to an autonomous analysis: "The description of the beauty and grandeur of nature in the solitudes of the dense forest, the plain living and the deep feeling and tenderness of the lovers is represented in such a charming manner; the passage in which Savitri's deep sorrow at her husband's death is described, is so extremely touching that one cannot help shedding tears. Her joy and gratitude when her husband rises to life again (as if he had been asleep) is depicted so naturally—and her prayers to Yama, begging him not to take away her husband are so full of pathos that I think the poem of [sic] the most beautiful I have ever read."[61] Immediately following these lines appears Agashe's complacent observation: the essay was required as part of the school's regular curriculum, and in that context Avadi might well have cited the prestigious poets Shakespeare or Milton. Had she done so, he argues, her teachers—especially Miss Hurford—would have been pleased. Alternatively, she might have chosen to cite a poem by Kalidas or any other

Sanskrit-language poets. Instead, she chose a Marathi-language poet. Most significant, Agashe continues, is that Avadi reached for this particular poem by Moropant, who had composed works on countless different themes. According to Agashe, there was only one way to understand Avadi's nuanced decision to write about the poem. She "had always been one full of contentment, she had deep faith in god and these were the qualities that the poem emphasized." Her "true" subjectivity was revealed in her literary taste; her poetic choice established her spirituality. With that, Agashe clinched his argument in support of women's English education. Avadi's decision revealed that the English-educated woman would never—as was otherwise believed—upset social conventions, become obstinate, or disdain her husband's authority. Avadi demonstrated instead that the one who procures real wisdom will transcend the narrow cultural identifications of language. Avadi's dedication to the sexual standards of her caste would overcome the power of English. By consenting to upper-caste sexual strictures, she would contain English.

Agashe concludes by citing a school essay that Avadi had written in English entitled "The Ideal Woman," in which she passionately argued:

A woman should be physically strong, tall, well formed and pretty. She should be active and cheerful. A woman ought to be very gentle and modest. She should never be lazy or obstinate. She should be true, loving and obedient to her husband. She should always help him in his work, cheer him in his troubles and share in his happiness as well as in his sorrow. She ought to take great care of her children and instruct them so as to make them good. In this way she should be a good wife and good mother. She ought to be very gentle, kind and thoughtful and she ought to love and fear God. Above all, she should be strictly religious for without religion no woman can fulfill all that is required of her as maiden, wife, or mother.[62]

Avadi's model woman was culled from religious and reproductive ideals that could harmoniously coexist with knowledge of English. In fact, as in Avadi's own case, the language would provide the ideal woman with the syntax in which to express well-disciplined gendered desires. The evidence Agashe collected on Avadi conclusively established that English would not encroach on Marathi. Despite its phallogocentric power, it could be disciplined by sexual difference and Brahmanical culture. Ultimately, the correctly schooled Brahman woman would perform her knowledge of English and render caste and sexual difference unassailable.

The Secularization of Caste

The upper-caste monopoly over knowledge had historically been sanctioned through performing restrictions over female sexuality. These restrictions served as the symbolic means by which to naturalize distinctions between intellectual power on the one hand and sexual, physical, and domestic labor on the other. The punitive treatment of the Brahman widow ritualized the restriction of knowledge to members from other castes. What, then, does Agashe's presentation of Avadi's English education mean?

Agashe showcases Avadi's compliance with the requirements of lifelong conjugality and her desire for reproductive sexuality. He reiterates the primacy of conjugal-reproductive standards in rendering her as lacking and inadequate.[63] At the same time, and through his constant mediation of her words, Agashe underscores his power to reveal Avadi's inner being.[64] He presented his privileged access to her journal as evidence of his ability to witness her self in its entirety. In the process, he manufactured the hermetically sealed, interior and private individual. But it was Avadi's widowed status that enabled Agashe to indulge a certain degree of secrecy and hence individuality in her. Of course, even that bond could, and was, easily exposed in the service of narrating the long life of upper-caste regulations and their successful resistance to caste critique. His ability to individuate Avadi and to explicate her through what he saw as expressions of interiority, secrecy, and female bonding demonstrates his transcendental vision. For all his editorial zeal, Agashe never intervened to point out that the wider ostracism of the Brahman widow was a caste-specific and socially sanctioned phenomenon. Perhaps expectedly, he feels no reason to address his role in reconstructing her, even as he selectively editorializes and exposes her journal.

At one level, it appears as though Agashe works to secure his readers' outrage against the terrible injustices that characterized Avadi's life. But the very focus on her suffering actually reduces the institution of widowhood, its privileges and exclusions, to a matter of her personal feeling. I am reminded here of Wendy Brown's terse critique of depoliticizing discourses that "substitute emotional and personal vocabularies for political ones in formulating solutions to political problems. . . . When suffering is reduced to a problem of personal feeling, then the field of political battle and political formulation is replaced with an agenda of behavioral, attitudinal, and emotional practices."[65] Of course, as we know from social histories of South Asia, anti-caste leaders successfully deployed the language of suffering for (limited) promises of liberation, though this was a broad-based group agenda that did not numb social critique through individual stories of misery.

Individuation is absolutely central to Agashe's strategy of depoliticization.[66] With it, he establishes that Avadi selects lifelong devotion to her husband, Marathi literature, filial respect, and friendship as her consolations. Her devotion to her dead husband is presented as a choice in favor of widowhood. Her virtue is her choice; it rises above a cluster of other possible decisions. The very trope of the virtuous woman was, as I pointed out in chapter 3, a means of consolidating upper-caste strictures, a means of naturalizing power and violence within and between caste groups. Avadi chooses to perform the misery of the Brahmanical injunction, just as she manages the power of English. Here Agashe's editorial power is to demonstrate that English would not corrupt Avadi or her commitment to Marathi Brahmanism. In fact, as the paradigmatic bilingual virtuous woman, Avadi could and would discipline English.

In her recent work on the "caste question" in western India, the historian Anupama Rao has demonstrated how "caste was secularized," a process that unfolds through the sustained troubling of divides between the religious and the political: "Caste did not become completely political, nor did models of equality for a bourgeois subject of freedom ever adequately encompass Dalit entitlement to political discourses. Ultimately, liberal forms such as constituency and minority became means through which Dalits imagined community and pursued equality."[67]

Rao tracks the politics of liberalism, equality, enfranchisement, and exceptionalism over 100 years, cogently illuminating the long, somewhat contradictory relationship of lower-caste, Dalit identity to Indian democracy. I, too, have been tracking the secularization of caste, although my interest lies with explaining the rituals of upper-caste power and how divides between knowledge and sexuality continued, even if they were reinscribed through English. "Secularization" for me is not merely the separation of the religious from the political; instead, it is the process by which new, seemingly non-religious rituals have rendered caste invisible and hence hegemonic; the union with liberal discourses of individuation and melioration are key to this process of secularization. In other words, caste-specific rituals that performed the monopoly over knowledge and the restriction of female sexuality were normalized by the seemingly secular, liberal promise of English.

In chapter 3 I demonstrated how English provided the conduit for deviant sexual desire, such as that discussed in the Marathi play *Taruni Shikshan Natika*. But here Agashe deploys Avadi's self-willed choice of a virtuous upper-caste femininity as the referent against which to discipline English. Consciously seeking to refute the representations that polarized English and normative womanhood, Agashe's work thus enumerates the many ways by which English and native women could coexist, even beneficially reinforce one another, through the liberal caste contract. No disciplining patriarch, Agashe presented himself as a sympathetic and reform-minded male, sensitive to the plight of widowhood. Yet in producing Avadi as the paradigmatic virtuous woman, he adroitly projected his masculinity as itself produced by the containment of the feminine even as he protected himself from having to critique caste patriarchies. Normative sexuality served the secularization of Brahmanical power.

Agashe's selective showcasing of certain documents and his constant interjections and commentary could not obscure the engineering of upper-caste power. And Avadi's words linger on in his text, permitting startling glimpses of the process by which English was carefully domesticated by the gender regimes of nineteenth-century India. *Sadgun Manjari* thus illustrates how women were taught to perform their discerning acquisition of English so as to maintain the chimera of "Indian" culture. The process was fraught with immense turbulence. The urge to render English acceptable was immediately ventriloquized through women, a process that demonstrated the necessarily contrapuntal relationship between women's possession of English, tradition, masculinity, and the embrace of new regimes of sexual difference. English was domesticated by staging the "fact" of sexual difference. Crafted as admissible to indigenous womanhood, English was simultaneously mouthed back in the voice of a docile, traditional, reformed, and individuated womanhood. In Agashe's work, Avadi's words are refracted through the prism of caste, nationalism, and patriarchy in order to demonstrate that correctly educated women could be active agents, embrace individual autonomy, fortify masculinity, and uphold upper-caste strictures. Virtuous women would render English an Indian language.

Agashe's ventriloquizing of the monogamous fantasies of bourgeois

Brahmanical nationalism is only one example in this complicated process of cultural refashioning. Avadi moved in a world where other women—students and teachers alike—simultaneously enacted their mastery of English and revealed their compliance with the heteronormative social contract. On her death, the English-language letters and poems that poured in from teachers and school friends (all female) recalled without exception her meek temperament, amiability, diligent zeal, sisterly love, obedience, gentleness, and modest humility. Far from crafting new gender identities by reaching beyond the institution of marriage, as was alleged in sources like *Taruni Shikshan Natika*, English-educated women like Avadibai consistently exemplified the highest standards of conduct for traditional and obedient native women.

It is, in short, the virtuous woman who domesticates English. And Avadi's virtue is absolutely essential to establishing the superiority, even exceptionalism, of the Brahman caste. Her possession of English is thus not about democratizing or widening the reach of English. She epitomizes the sexual rituals of caste through the voluntary demonstration of choice, intellect, hard work, and domestic love. English itself is presented as an individuated desire, a secular form. In other words, Agashe's Avadi demonstrates how English could be embedded in the caste logic of western India—how discourses of liberalism could ultimately reinforce caste power, and re-ritualize it toward secular pretensions. As we see in the following chapter, English would enable some women to displace upper-caste battles upon seemingly secular modes of desire. Delving into the micro-histories of affect, we now examine the engineering of sexual desire through English—the processes by which the promise of individual self-realization was placed in the service of class, caste, and nation.

6

"WHY HAD I EVER BEGUN TO LEARN ENGLISH?"
Desire, Labor, and the Transregional Orientation of Caste

At the age of eleven, Ramabai Ranade was married to a thirty-two-year-old Poona-based widower, the nationalist and social reformer Mahadev Gopal Ranade. It was December 1873. The ceremony was surprisingly austere and, other than her father, Ramabai's closest family was absent. In her memoirs, Ramabai recalls the first evening that M. G. Ranade summoned her privately.[1] First inquiring whether her father had left, Ranade reiterated that he was indeed married to Ramabai. He then asked, "Do you know who I am and what my name is?" She said she did, and Ranade asked her to say his name out loud.[2] Recollecting that she did not know enough to be "shy," Ramabai did as she was commanded. Her response satisfied Ranade, even seemed to put him at ease. Learning then that Ramabai could neither read nor write, he immediately provided her with a slate and pencil and acquainted her with the first seven syllables of the religious address, *Shriganeshayanamah*. It took the young girl almost two hours to become familiar with those letters. From that point on, Ranade spent two hours every night teaching her to read and write the Marathi alphabet.

Ramabai acknowledged she was unaware at the time that speaking her husband's name constituted a grave taboo in Hindu Brahmanical culture, for it suggested his accessibility, equality, and perhaps even mortality. She was, however, conscious of the other prohibition breached that night—the one against women reading or writing. Ramabai was all too cognizant of the widely circulating beliefs that an educated woman would cause the death of her husband.[3] Ranade went on to tutor his young wife in the English language, encouraging her to publicly perform her knowledge of English to native and colonial audiences. As her memoirs attest, Ramabai's knowledge of English estranged her from the women of her marital home, and the public performances engendered tremendous physical and mental turmoil. Despite that, she grew closer to her husband, learning to actively desire the tight exclusive bond that this pedagogic experience fostered between them.[4]

In this chapter, I discuss two sources: the Marathi-language autobiography penned by Ramabai Ranade and an English-language novel written by Shevantibai Nikambe, the founder of a girls' school in Bombay. Both works have been recently reprinted, and Ramabai's text has also circulated through a number of English translations. As in the previous chapters, I follow the developing connections between English as language and as cultural sign, the production of gendered subjectivities, and the incorporation of the sexual power of English by native caste regimes. But in this chapter I push further, exploring the registers of authorship and publishing, transnational reading audiences, and the transregional reach of caste rituals. At the core of my analysis is the exploration of desire: the process by which the desire for English was displaced upon the putatively secular conjugal dyad within the modern nuclear family, and thus the way that English served to obscure the working of caste.[5] By reading the autobiography and the novel through the politics of sexuality, I illustrate how the desires of a transnational reading public were brought in line with the ritualization of upper-caste heterosexuality.

Language, Prohibition, and Taboo

Ramabai's memories of disrupting conventions by speaking her husband's name and writing the alphabet seemed to displace, if not prevent, the mention of other acts. The education project, in other words, was transferred upon the sexual awareness. The compulsory forging of apparently companionate bonds between husband and wife, Ranade's desire to serve as Ramabai's pedagogic master, their retreat into the private and affective realm, and their subsequent emergence as desiring subjects all marked the cultural contours of the nineteenth-century history of the English language in British India.

There is, of course, no way to know whether the marriage was consummated that night. Sexual relations were usually deferred until both partners were past puberty. M. K. Gandhi's autobiography—perhaps the least inhibited account of sex within marriage in western India in the late nineteenth century—suggests that he and his wife (both married at thirteen) were sexually active from the start.⁶ In the case of the Ranades, Ramabai Ranade bore no children. When voicing his initial opposition to marrying Ramabai, M. G. Ranade referred to himself as too old to do anything other than live a life of reflection.⁷ But the symbolic connection between this first nocturnal encounter and the power of heterosexual entitlement has also been noted by Uma Chakravarti, who has trenchantly queried, "Short of brutally consummating the marriage what would one do in such a situation except to begin teaching the illiterate wife the alphabet?"⁸

Apparently committed to the agenda of widow remarriage, Ranade's decision to marry the virgin Ramabai, so as to mollify his father, has been documented widely by historians of western India. What is even more striking is that, as Ramabai reports in her memoirs, Ranade voiced his fleeting opposition to his own remarriage by invoking the example of his widowed sister, Durga, who lived in his household and performed all the household tasks.⁹ Durga had been denied the opportunity to pursue her education because she was married at a young age, although, as Chakravarti has recorded, after becoming a widow she was "made literate, along with her stepmother, by her father partly to maintain household accounts."¹⁰ Ranade's sensitivity to the plight of his sister and political commitment to widow remarriage continued, even though he shunned the one chance he might have had to direct any personal change.

By 1896 he played an absolutely central role in universalizing Brahmanical strictures on female sexual purity through his involvement in shaping the Hindu Widow's Remarriage Act. Lucy Carroll has illustrated how the Widow Remarriage Act of 1856 'administered by Brahman lawyers and Victorian judges, tended to promote Brahmanical values which held widow remarriage in disrepute by driving out customary law, under which most widowed women had rights of inheritance in their husband's estates in favour of the statutory and Brahmanical book law which disinherited them."¹¹ Over time, Ranade intervened to redirect the act toward even greater upper-caste conservatism. Chakravarti has traced how the 1856 Hindu Widows Remarriage Act had initially made it seem as though the remarried widow would give up her entitlement to inheriting the property of her deceased (first) husband. Subsequent cases had successfully overturned that assumption, ruling in 1886 that "where caste usage permitted the widow to retain property inherited from her deceased husband the forfeiture clause of the 1856 Act would not be applicable."¹² But in 1896, a full bench of the Bombay High Court, comprising Justices Farran, Parsons, and M. G. Ranade, held that the forfeiture claim must be applied to all Hindu widows. This elevated Brahmanical caste practice and deliberately negated practices existent among many non-Brahman castes, which might have supported widow remarriage and widow inheritance. The new law erased the remarried widow's own history, treating her "as if she had died" for property purposes.[13] Ranade was well aware that the ban on widow remarriage was "a 'privilege' held on to by the Brahmans and the highest castes against the attempts by upwardly mobile low castes seeking to . . . claim high status for themselves throughout the eighteenth and nineteenth centuries."[14] Hence, his commitment to universalizing Brahmanical strictures against the widow's right to inherit her first husband's property "amounted to the Shastric position that a man's property was to be enjoyed only by the 'chaste' widow who lived up to the sacramental notion of 'Hindu marriage.'"[15] Extending western Indian Brahmanical practice to all Hindu communities, Ranade's role was to systematically homogenize the vast differences in customary law and caste practice to a pan-India level.

Ramabai's memoirs span these very years. The work offers a complex first-person account both of the process of pedagogic transfer and of the desires engendered by an English-language education. Ranade chose to be her first teacher. Starting Ramabai off with seven Marathi letters, Ranade taught her for two hours every night: grammar, arithmetic, the Modi script, and Marathi reading and writing. In her memoirs, Ramabai presents herself as surmounting the hurdles of tradition within the household, intellectually progressing from complete illiteracy to becoming conversant in several languages, and even speaking English for public audiences. Despite this sense of advancing intellectual progress, her memoirs provide recurring glimpses of the tension and ambivalence at the heart of the English-education project, a tension that cemented male authority, the heterosexual contract, the containment of the "feminine" by the masculine, and Ramabai's own formation as a docile, educated, and desiring subject.

Ramabai's relationship with her husband, filtered through his desire to educate her, generated deep conflict at many levels: with existing female domestic authority, with the public world of institutionalized education, and with new figures of power in the colonial milieu of the late nineteenth century. One of the most stressful moments occurred while she was still learning Marathi. Ranade had employed a female teacher (from the Poona teacher training school) for Ramabai, but the young girl deliberately ignored her studies, as well as her female teacher's authority. Ranade's disappointment at her willful disregard was striking. He expressed himself silently, without physical or verbal threats, and yet his quiet displeasure affected her gravely. She instantly became aware that she had disappointed him; it produced a sense of shame that propelled a tremendous sense of dismay. As Ramabai recalled, "That was the first time that I really felt ashamed of myself, I didn't want anyone to see, I wiped my tears and went downstairs. After that my childish mischievousness ended."[16] It is intriguing that the female teacher Ranade employed was unable to discipline or teach the young girl. The experience generated deep regret in Ramabai. The sentiment of shame was multiply productive: it led her to mature self-awareness, a new sense of herself as dependent on her husband's approval (hence an introduction to gendered conventions), and, as I demonstrate below, her entry into the English language. Ramabai's learning evoked shame in the context of the larger family unit as well. From the very first days of her life in the marital home, Ranade had her recite her lessons to him at night. Despite trying to lower her voice or soften her performance (Ranade would often order Ramabai to recite poetry and hymns in rhythm), his female relatives overheard her each time. The next day they would ridicule and mimic her performance, "teasing me and shaming me before all the older women, and then they would laugh hilariously."[17] The young wife's emotional experience reflects an awareness of her fragility within the vast shift in configurations of caste and domestic patriarchy in the late nineteenth century, themselves expressed through bitter contests over domestic hierarchies and domestic space.

Eve Sedgwick has dwelt on the possibility that shame "is the place where the question of identity arises most originally and most relationally."[18] Sedgwick's work is helpful in understanding how the experience of shame frames gender identity and ushers the subject into the realm of the symbolic (of social conventions expressed through representations). Ranade's disappointment at Ramabai's academic disregard engendered a deep sense of shame in her. Her educational experience evoked sensibilities that shaped her relative subservience to Ranade and thus an awareness of gender difference. Education nurtured new domestic patriarchies, in the process stimulating affective routes to gender awareness. Ramabai's invocation of shame actually resonates upon wider political changes. Historically for western India, the term was repeatedly invoked to control female sexuality and was increasingly disseminated through the female education project. Rosalind O'Hanlon has discussed how liberal reformers held that women were morally weak, open to vice and the temptation to commit adultery; for this reason, they should be taught to be sensitive to their shameful predilections. According to O'Hanlon, in 1882 the "Prarthana Samaj newspaper Subodh Patrika pointed to the temptations to vice and crime that widows were subject to, and urged that they should be educated as the means of avoiding them."[19] The prominent social reformer and prime minister of Baroda, T. Madhava Rao, published in the *Times of India* that adulterous widows should be made to publicly bear their shame: "Let her suffer the pain of shame which she had dreaded so much [by choosing infanticide]. Would not that be a sufficiently deterring punishment?"[20] Shame was the antidote for the supposed inability of women to check their sexual and murderous instincts. Moreover, women could be educated to turn away from this innate disposition to crime, vice, and lust.

Broadening the study of affect to the production of emotion in general, Sara Ahmed has argued that "emotions are crucial to how subjects become invested in relations of power."[21] Ramabai's emotional ferment signaled her sensitivity to the injustices and silences over sexuality and labor that hovered over elite Brahman families. Women's education nurtured a number of new social and affective networks, hence new configurations of power. Centrally, as Chakravarti notes, the "careers of many professional young men, who came to constitute an important segment of the middle class, were built upon the labour of the widowed women of their families."[22] The social reformers' turn to female education entailed that the selective agenda of women's education was also sustained through the expectation of the free availability of widowed labor. Women's education was integrally constitutive of nineteenth-century reformulations in social-intimate-political power, and the control over domestic labor would have been one of the most contentious aspects in the new arrangement.[23] One of Ramabai's harshest disciplinarians was Ranade's sister, Durga. The siblings had grown up together and been close companions as children, although Durga's education was terminated when she married while Ranade continued to live in his natal home and to study. Although Durga was younger than Ranade, she was widowed by the time Ranade and Ramabai married. She lived in Ranade's home and (from Ramabai's perspective) controlled the young wife's time, power, and leisure. Chakravarti has written at length about the triangulated relationship that unfolded between Ranade, Ramabai, and Durga.[24] Durga's later widowhood upset Ranade grievously, yet his only solution was to provide her with a place to live and to put her to the inevitable task of providing domestic labor.[25] From Ramabai's point of view, however, Durga had tremendous power within the household and disdained the prospect of Ramabai's leisured education, which she saw as possible only because of her married status. Durga's labor, marginalization, enforcement within the inner, domestic realm, and sexual punishment contrasted dramatically with the world of the young girl, who was being lovingly schooled into new forms of public and domestic authority. As the young wife, Ramabai would have been subject to the demands of Ranade's older female in-laws, although, as the only one who could potentially bear children, she might have carved a certain degree of authority for herself within the household. But she never realized the socio-domestic power of motherhood. The sentiment of shame that Ramabai describes as arising specifically in the context of her education thus provides important clues to her awareness of her complicity in the inequities sanctioned by her husband's modernizing ambitions, and of her unsteady reorientation toward the native "housewife" status that parasitically depended on the labor and compulsory segregation of the Brahman widow. Ramabai's "shame"—and her in-law's ability to produce it—exposes the symbolic power at the heart of upper-caste, bourgeois nationalism.

The spatial location of Ramabai's education, which was physically mapped in proximity to her husband and at a distance from the world downstairs (constituted by her teasing female in-laws), further tightened the ties of companionship and privacy that bound her to the newly fashioned nuclear and heterosexual coupling. Ramabai recalls how, with time, she was able to bear the humiliation of their continuous taunts, knowing that at night, when she ascended the stairs to the room she shared with Ranade, all memories of the day would leave her.[26] Her home schooling, already inflected by the taboo against women's education, was multiply marked; it was spatially, emotionally, and physically distinct. In addition, it was a source of comfort in a woman-dominated household from which she was alienated. Her knowledge of the English language came to rest upon this private, nocturnal, and demarcated experience.

Soon after starting on her Marathi-language education, Ramabai became aware that two of Ranade's step-brothers, who were about her age, had begun learning English. At that time, she was at the Marathi fifth-grade level. The knowledge that the boys were learning English filled her with a *bhari haus*, a deep stirring of desire and ambition.[27] When she told Ranade "shyly" that she would also like to learn English, he was "surprised and pleased." Ramabai's account of her self-initiated turn toward English is reminiscent of Sigmund Freud's reading of (bourgeois) female desire and the staging of lack. Most controversially, Freud argued that when confronted with the sight of the phallus, the little girl "behaves differently. She makes her judgment and her decision in a flash. She has seen it and knows that she is without it and wants to have it."[28] Reading Freud less literally and more with regard to symbolic power, I argue that this vignette from Ramabai's memories sheds light on the interface between English and sexual identity, between individual desire and social power. Indeed, in her reinterpretation of Freud, Rosalind Coward pushes us to appreciate the process by which phallocentric power comes to be embedded (even obscured) amid a host of social relations. Coward further argues that gender subjectivity must be seen as a process, one that is "not given by an intrinsic sexual disposition, but constructed through our entry into a culture polarized around anatomical difference."[29] Coward's work, I suggest, opens possibilities for comprehending the moments of desire and lack evidenced by Ramabai. Her individuated desire to possess the cultural power of English was interwoven with her awareness that it was her male relatives who were learning the language. Immediately, she turned to her husband to mediate the gendered disparity in symbolic power, hence magnifying his ability to settle disputes between gender and power. Far from staging any resistance to the culture of Brahmanical male authority, Ramabai reveals instead her compliance with the phallogocentric power of English, especially its alliance with masculine power.

Ranade responded in the affirmative to his wife's request. He decreed, however, that she must first complete her Marathi learning. After a few months, he began to personally teach her English. Ranade was one of the first Indians trained and rewarded by the logic and hierarchies of colonial education. Echoing Mountstuart Elphinstone's policy that "English be made a reward for merit in other studies," Ranade both established the superior status of English in regard to the other subjects Ramabai was learning and, simultaneously, extended himself to complete the task.[30] Not surprisingly, English swiftly exacerbated the existing spatial, temporal, and psychic rift growing within the household. It was no longer possible for Ramabai to study in the late night and early morning, for she often had to work for an additional hour every day, memorizing the vocabulary.³¹ Realizing that she could not study during the day downstairs, Ramabai would retreat to their room to pursue her lessons. This angered the other women even more, for they imagined her "shirking household tasks and slighting their authority."³² Their concerns were similar to other English-education opponents we saw above who argued that English-educated women would disdain their domestic roles and thus cease to respect gender markers. Indeed, Ramabai's English education evoked nagging questions on domestic authority. The conflict was additionally sharpened by their apprehension that Ranade's ability to mediate Ramabai's education elevated his own power within the household. Ramabai relates a time when she was "caught" trying to read an English newspaper downstairs. Immediately, her sister-in-law fulminated, "Your office is upstairs! There you can dance or study as you like, but do not dare insult us! Our older brother tried to teach his first wife too, and she could read and write. She was our age and despite that she never dared to read or write a single alphabet in our presence. A war was waged continuously for her to learn English, but she paid no heed [to Ranade's wishes]. Yet she remained his loyal wife . . . and not frivolous like you!"³³ It is significant that Durga identified the difference between education and English, and that she did so by pointing to levels of domestic authority.³⁴ Ramabai's English was a greater threat to female authority than education in general and it bolstered Ranade's domestic dominance. Perceptively connecting Ramabai's possession of English with new aspirations for subjectivity, the sister-in-law recognized that Ramabai's knowledge of English built on Ranade's power to erode female authority. English, in other words, symbolized new binaries between male and female. Ramabai's aspiration to cultural power was a threat and it was insulting. Durga's complex reactions averred that "English" was a mobile, linguistic sign of vast material ramifications, indicating, expressing, and actively shaping a new hetero-conjugal contract.

For her part, Ramabai recalled that "abuse" such as this went on daily, so much so that she was often at the point of weeping aloud, continuously wondering why she had "ever begun to learn English."³⁵ The answer to that question lay in the fact that English afforded her greater proximity to her husband. At one stage, Ranade was offered the opportunity to leave Poona for Nasik, and he decided to take Ramabai with him. He also decided to leave their female relatives behind in Poona. The move filled Ramabai with great elation, and she spent weeks planning the new household where she would have (what she perceived as) complete autonomy. The ideal of the new conjugal contract was thus achieved for the first time in Nasik, and it is no coincidence that she records that it was there that her education continued with even greater gusto. Ranade, too, was seized by a greater enthusiasm in performing his pedagogic role.

Many years later, when Ranade was posted to Calcutta, Ramabai actively refused to be taught by any other teacher and demanded that he teach her himself. As a result, they learned Bengali together. As an individuated subject who now knew how to phrase her desire in the symbolic vocabulary of the caste-gender-knowledge economy, Ramabai increasingly inhabited the affective space of the conjugal relationship. And yet there was a difference between the languages; her desire for English was sharpened through social prohibition, the disdain voiced by other people, and her husband's ambitions. Even though Bengali represented her desire for hetero-conjugal companionship, it did not seem to traffic among all those complicated forces in her case. Taught to desire in and through "English," Ramabai's sense of self was substantiated through the joint family's prohibition against new forms of conjugal exclusivity.[36] She complied by realizing every one of her husband's wishes, but in doing so she repudiated the organization of labor in the joint family household.

The transfer to Nasik was only the first in a series of moves that Ranade was to make over the next decade. His high-level post in the colonial administration and his interest in contemporary social-reform issues required him to travel widely through Maharashtra as well as India. But Ramabai could not always accompany him; often he decided that the best option was to leave her behind. It is telling that these decisions instantly reverberated in her desire for learning, especially her desire for her English lessons. The first time that they were to be separated, Ramabai recalls the gush of thoughts that overwhelmed her. She cried bitterly at the news and remembers that "I did not like any aspect of this decision. It made me feel tremendously miserable. The joy I should have felt at the promotion disappeared. How would I spend my days all alone, my English lessons would cease, even the time that I spent on my lessons would not pass any more, and there would be no comfort to my days."[37] Ramabai exposes in these lines the "metaphysics of [her] presence."[38] The temporary sense of control or even sovereignty that the web of English and conjugality provided was completely shattered by Ranade's potential absence. The lines are striking, especially for Ramabai's repeated use of the individuated subject, "I"—a style of self-presentation that she did not resort to frequently.[39] In this instance, as the subject "I," Ramabai reveals that she is the unstable effect of two kinds of social norms: English and the hetero-social caste contract.[40]

Ramabai's ambivalent realization of self through Ranade's absence sheds light on the constitution of gendered desire in a phallogocentric cultural space.[41] Her ability to expose the fragility of her subjectivity, its dependence on English and conjugal exclusivity, defies any easy history of the "spread" of the linguistic form of English. Even in claiming individualism—the subject "I"—Ramabai exhibits a curious distancing from self, an ambivalence, and in the process she reveals the gendered edifice upon which Indian English took shape in the nineteenth century. English functioned as language and as symbol; together it mediated access to the "world." Neither a mere linguistic form nor discrete words or symbols cut loose from history, Ramabai reveals instead that English is an unstable sign producing physical, political, and psychic possibilities, mediated by the gendered subject's access to the realm of caste conventions. Her words resonate with the statement produced by the students of the Female Normal School discussed in chapter 2. Herein lay the answer to Ramabai's own query about why she had begun to learn English. Despite the manifest violence encoded in its acquisition and display, she studied English as diligently as she did because it pleased Ranade. Pleasing her husband cemented a certain inviolable bond, an iota of autonomy and self-actualization that appeared to counter the arbitrary violence emanating from an otherwise ritualized space.

And it was through English that Ranade was able to contain Ramabai within his new patriarchal authority. Ranade, for example, was affiliated with the managerial structure of the Poona Native High School for girls. While Ramabai did not herself study at the school, Ranade frequently involved her in its ceremonies. Like the other men who directed the education of their women, Ranade, too, encouraged his wife to perform her recently acquired knowledge, especially in front of strangers of the same or higher social classes. With that, he would repeatedly unleash the chain of cultural and linguistic ventriloquism advocated by proponents of women's English education. For instance, recalling the various meetings and gatherings in the wake of the inauguration of the Poona Native High

School, Ramabai remembers the occasion when Ranade asked her to present the petition for the school to the governor of the Bombay Presidency, Sir James Fergusson. It was her first effort at reading an English address in front of a large audience, and Ranade had prepared the entire speech for her. Despite that and his careful coaching, when the time came she had an unsettling, physical reaction: "As I stood up to read, my hands and legs trembled, I lost my breath and my head and body seemed on fire. It was as though a stream of hot blood was submerging me!"[42] The tension dissipated only gradually, and she remembers reading the address aloud despite a continuing sense of anxiety.

Ranade's urge to display Ramabai's anglicized acquisitions was to grow over the years. As with the schools' efforts discussed in part I, here, too, the "teachability" of a select few secured upper-caste entitlement to mediate the terms of colonial modernity for all.[43] As Ranade's wife, Ramabai had to perform her acquiescence to new gender norms, as well as to anglicization. The intended audience included not only European and Indian elites but, importantly and implicitly, the Brahman widow. Hence the difference in reception: comfort in the minds of the male audience and terror for Ramabai. When her female in-laws learned that she had read an English address to a group of strangers, they attacked her. The women berated her and Ranade for her performance of her knowledge of English and, what's more, for having done so in front of male strangers. The harangue then led to a short lecture on the shifting meanings of romantic love, with one of the women declaring to them both: "In the days past women dared not even lift their heads in front of strangers. Did they not know love, were they not their husbands' darlings? Nowadays, love means that a woman must sit close to her husband as if their clothes are knotted together, bring their chairs close to sit as if inseparable, for a woman to write and speak like a man.... Were you not ashamed to see your wife reading an address in English in front of two thousand people? If you must teach them ... why must it be English? Give up all this English at least for the present."[44] English education threatened to disrupt existing domestic hierarchies and, by way of the "new" companionate love, to diminish the authority of other women in a female-centered household. Women educated in the English way would mimic masculine ways, enable the rise of new forms of masculine power, and disrupt the existing sexual division of labor within the home. "English" would corrupt gender performance: women would now "lift their heads" and sit "close to [their] husbands." Ramabai remembers that Durga was so upset that she "convinced herself that in learning English I had defied 'him' and was beyond 'his' control."[45]

Far from being beyond his control, Ramabai was entirely devoted to Ranade. As her female relative had intuited, the real power of English was that it introduced new emotive experiences to the conjugal unit; they demonstrated the incorporation of the female into the new native masculinity. Indeed, sentiments such as those expressed by Ramabai were refracted through a devotional prism that further elevated masculine authority. Ramabai remembers when watching Ranade meditate: "In the peace of the morning's light, seeing [his] countenance fill with worship, my own heart overflowed with tenderness and my love [for him], and my worship [of him] increased involuntarily. . . . In those morning hours I was conscious . . . of a kind of spiritual power in him, and I saw him as almost divine."[46]

The reinforcing relationship between the sexual with the spiritual, which served to magnify Ranade's domestic and conjugal power, followed after the nightly English lessons. Sheltered from the relentless dissonance and emotional turbulence articulated by Ranade's female relatives and the world outside, Ramabai's memories of the "morning after" her English lessons were experienced as comforting to the point of surpassing verbal description. The quiet and silence that she so cherishes stand in clear opposition to the vociferous conflict over caste that otherwise determined her life. Tranquility, tenderness, and involuntary subservience guided her memories, and all were expressed as devotional. In the process Ranade emerged as transcendent; he contained the sexual and emanated spiritual authority. Desire and devotion dovetailed for the English-educated, upper-caste wife, constituting a space of comfort in otherwise turbulent times.

"Then Let Yours Be Out Too, and We Shall Make It Our Guide in Life"

Tenuously at first, and then accelerating under the weight of social sanction, a polysemiotic English accompanied the national-bourgeois subject into the domain of heterosexual affect and the reproduction of national culture.[47] Indeed, in the late nineteenth century we can find wider assessments of the way that the gender rituals of upper-caste power served to link English to the normative Indian woman. Here I approach the fictional, English-language account written by the Bombay-based Christian convert and school founder Shevantibai Nikambe in 1895. Entitled *Ratanbai: A Sketch of a Bombay High Caste Hindu Young Wife*, the short novel depicted Ratanbai—a young, married, but virginal Brahman girl—and her tireless quest for an English education.⁴⁸ The novel was published in London by Marshall Brothers, a publishing house known for bringing works on imperial, religious, and missionary themes from the empire to an English reading public in Britain. The short work was made available both in Britain and the United States.⁴⁹ That an English-educated Indian woman would reach to the novel to amplify her support of the English education of native women establishes my point on the chains of cultural ventriloquism initiated by the English-education project in nineteenth-century India. Similar to Ramabai Ranade and Pandita Ramabai, Shevantibai Nikambe also started and administered a school for girls. The short novel posed the familiar binaries of the nineteenth century, focusing especially on the conflicts between tradition and modernity, darkness and light, older female relatives and English education, and caste and love. In a hundred pages the author resolves these conflicts, activating the phallogocentric power of English to establish the ultimate triumph of liberal sentiment over caste-bound, older, female, and illiterate adversaries.

Dedicated to "Her Gracious Majesty the Queen, Empress of India," the author's preface additionally emphasizes India's indebtedness to the "happy rule . . . brightening and enlightening the lives and homes of many Hindu women." Familiar themes are materialized in Nikambe's depiction of the tradition-bound, older female relatives of the household: the caste-specific ceremonies of Ratanbai's Saraswat Brahman family, the disturbing presence of the child widow, Tara, alongside Ratanbai's craving for education, the desire of reform-minded men like her father, and the gradual self-realization of Tara's subjectivity. The novel opens to quickly place Ratanbai in the class, caste, and gender terrain of Bombay city: "Her father . . . is a successful lawyer of the High Court . . . [in his] office room which is comfortably furnished. A rich carpet . . . cushioned sofa . . . handsome cabinet containing a large collection of law books . . . portraits of great men, mostly literary."⁵⁰ Ratanbai, "a pet with her father . . . dressed as all Hindu girls are in a shirt of the *khan* material, and a short sleeved satin jacket. Her tiny fair wrists are covered with gold bracelets . . . [and] round her neck is a mangalsutra." The smooth invocation of the class-caste-skin color nexus is significant—"her fair complexion made her to be classed amongst the pretty girls of Bombay"—as is the information that she "had been married two years before into a wealthy but an uneducated family. The promise was made . . . when the girl was a baby, and the arrangement had to be fulfilled, though it had been against the real wish of the educated father."⁵¹ In other words, Ratanbai had been betrothed to one Pratap Rao Khote, but she was still a child and their marriage was yet to be consummated. In the meanwhile, she lived in her father's home.

Her desire to attend school, protected and encouraged by her father, is portrayed as being increasingly thwarted by the dictates of caste, especially the heteronormative caste rituals of the Saraswat Brahman community.⁵² The fracture between tradition and modernity, inside and outside, female and male, appears to propel the narrative, as it moves from Ratanbai's great longing for an English education to her realization of love, comfort, and English by the end of the story. Nikambe's fictional documentation of individuality and agency as culminating in the realization of romantic love—classic features of the nineteenth-century novel—are necessarily and continually adumbrated by tradition, gender, and the lack of privacy. The details endorse the individual liberal notions of progress and personal affect. In the process, however, the silent coalition between caste, patriarchy, an "Indian" identity, and English is exposed. Built upon a binary opposition between the desire for English and the conservative adherence to Hindu ritual, the text simultaneously unravels the logic that cohered nineteenth-century Brahmanical patriarchy.

The social life of the novel and the reactions it has produced since its first publication provide important clues to how Nikambe accessed the demands and desires of a multiply located nineteenth-century transnational reading public. In her introduction to the reprint edition of 2004, entitled *Ratanbai: A High-Caste Child-Wife*, Chandini Lokuge examines the long life of the short novel. She notes that the reactions spanned the gamut from condescending praise to pity, amusement to ethnographic interest. Christian missionary tracts applauded the work for "raising the deep longing" that accompanied the native's desire to embrace Christianity. Over a half-century later, the novel was recalled for the authoritative cultural details that it provided on the inner lives of the "Maratha Brahmans."⁵³ Lokuge herself acknowledges that Nikambe's "social novel" appears to bolster the reformist agenda, even as it exposes the double standards of the same progressive male elite. In her estimation, Nikambe's ability to convey controversial feminist critiques to a traditional audience places her "in a literary tradition to which some of her western contemporary sister writers

—confronting similar conditions—belonged."⁵⁴ For Lokuge, the author's proto-feminism is encoded in her critique of native patriarchy. In many ways, therefore, Lokuge returns the novel to a fairly conventional space: "Read more than a century later, [the work] can be interpreted as a subversively rebellious socio-psychological novel inspired by the nineteenth-century woman writer's main source of inspiration—the female consciousness alive to change, striving for liberation from the restriction and tyranny of entrenched convention reinforced by reactionary ideology."⁵⁵

Lokuge's aim is to place Nikambe in the tradition of female writers like Charlotte Brontë and Jane Austen, who were writing to and around the desires of local patriarchy. I do not disagree with this analysis, although I would resist the urge to celebrate Nikambe's fit with the progress narrative of liberal feminism. Most critically, Nikambe was not writing for a traditional domestic audience. Rather, her encapsulation of the rituals of native patriarchy and apparent desire to critique its inner workings indicate audiences and interests far wider than a local or native one. Indian writers in English were feeding the insatiable liberal appetite for non-Western alterity, custom, and female misery. Nikambe's novel is fully conversant with the mode of argumentation forged by this generation of bilingual Indians, from Manockjee Cursetjee and G. A. Agashe to Pandita Ramabai. Rather than focus on a somewhat limited notion of feminism-as-critique, I maintain that it is important to draw attention to Nikambe's ability to guide the desires of nineteenth-century metropolitan and liberal audiences with her apparently privileged perspective on native patriarchy.⁵⁶ For my purposes, Nikambe's text can be put to work to portray how English—as language and as sign—consolidated new alliances between the desires of a transnational reading public on the one hand and upper-caste heteronormativity on the other.

The story moves from Ratanbai's alienation and suppression by female-dominated tradition and the awareness of widowhood to her individuated realization of her desire for English and human connection. Ratanbai's desire for English is continually thwarted by the dictates of native tradition, represented (much as in Ramabai Ranade's memoirs) by the older illiterate female relatives of her household. Caste endures and forges transnational connections with audiences beyond India. Ratanbai's craving for English is depicted as seething, fervent, and potentially disruptive of the basic pleasures of home and family that bourgeois Indian women were being educated into desiring. Her schooling competed openly with the requirement of female ritual labor, in which her mother and mother-in-law immersed her. The novel always casts the contest as a zero-sum game: Ratanbai can do one only at the expense of the other. Invariably it is the familial requirement of reproducing "tradition" that prevents her from being at school; the conflict over cultural power is resolved in the endurance of caste rituals. As the novel progresses, Ratanbai's mother-in-law, who is so opposed to the young girl's education and the "new or reformed ideas," increasingly prevents her from attending school.[57] For her part, Ratanbai admits that her mother-in-law's "remarks . . . hurt her" and made her "miserable." The prohibition against her English education fuels the story and produces Ratanbai as a desiring subject. For instance, describing her reaction after she had been removed from school for the second time (again on her in-laws' behest), Nikambe informs the reader that Ratan was "most miserable. . . . How often, with an aching heart, she would sit dreaming about the school life! Her teacher, her companions, the English lesson, the translation class, came before her, and then the longing would come: 'Oh! could I but go to school once again!'"[58]

Having established the weight of social structures—the family, the purported clash between modernity and tradition, and the close scrutiny of female sexuality—Nikambe's careful ethnographic delineation turns to details of dress, festivity, and interpersonal relations. The details establish that the text is composed to provide succor to a reading public that is fascinated by, and yet completely ignorant of, the coded struggle over caste. The home is presented as darker, encumbered, and fraught by the apparently unpredictable outbursts of Ratanbai's female relatives. Ratanbai's school, however, is a space of energy, light, and contained discipline. Nikambe launches her critique of the hypocrisies of caste, dwelling in detail on the presence of the older widow, Kakubai, and her misogynist treatment of the more junior child widow, Tarabai. In her depictions of the many festivals and rituals that result in keeping Ratanbai away from the school, Nikambe returns repeatedly to the distinction between touchable and untouchable.[59] Whether it was mourning over the death of Ratanbai's uncle or the "celebration" of Shanvar Padha, Ratanbai's family is materialized through their investment, even sanctification, of untouchability.[60] But Nikambe's "feminism" betrays her interests: she blithely fixes Brahmanical practice as Indian culture.

As long as she yearns for English, Ratanbai embodies the disruption of tradition in the face of profound personal disappointment and colossal punishment meted by native women. Her longing for English, portrayed as sensual, secretive, and forbidden, is ultimately a precursor to a more mature desire. Much like the women in *Taruni Shikshan Natika*, for Ratanbai, too, English is the object of desire—one that threatened social and personal disruption. Nikambe demonstrates how gender was policed by the ritualistic requirements of Saraswat Brahman society so as to naturalize a heteronormative lifecycle. As the embodiment of prohibited desire, English conflicted with the presentation of gender in Ratanbai's immediate social world.

Ultimately, it would be Ratanbai's husband—himself educated to the highest standards at a British university—who intervened to redirect her fevered desire for English. Prataprao Khote enters the narrative rather suddenly, soothing Ratanbai's tumultuous longing for education, as well as guiding that very desire. His power to direct Ratanbai's desire, and thus free her from the dictates of caste and tradition, becomes evident in Nikambe's intriguing depiction of their wedding night. Their first moments spent in complete solitude, otherwise synonymous with heterosexual intercourse, are narrated through the power of the English book. The young couple retires to the "newly furnished room upstairs."[61] It is here that they almost immediately discover their mutual awareness of, and attraction for, a particular "beautifully bound gild edged Book." Prataprao "looked into his young partner's face" to declare, "Then let yours be out too, and we shall make it our guide in life."[62] The novel comes to an immediate end with the lines: "Thus Prataprao Khote claims young Ratanbai as his partner in life. They begin life together, recognising the responsibilities and duties which lie before them, and which concern not only themselves but their people and their country."[63] Clearly, Ratanbai's husband enters the narrative solely to divert her longing away from one form of phallogocentric authority—the English education project. With that, he leads her to another—heterosexual romance, reproduction, and a nationalist sensibility. The book thus maps the route toward the benign and entirely conservative benefits of an English education. As the novel so powerfully demonstrates, English thrives in the spaces of heterosexual affect: the privacy of the home, the wedding ceremony, and the nation. Although it suggests the potential of English to disrupt gender order, ultimately the novel demonstrates the ways in which, eventually, a "new" reformed patriarchy would tether the phallogocentric power of English to normative gender roles.

"WHY HAD I EVER BEGUN TO LEARN ENGLISH?"

Despite the reductive power of colonial representations, bilingual Indians played simultaneously to multiple, transnational audiences. This was evidenced in the strategies of a range of actors, from M. G Ranade's humanist faith in English as progress to Nikambe's authorial abilities. Their deliberate and openly enacted bicultural referentiality was shaped in and through transnational debates about the volatile nature of indigenous sexuality and served to distinguish English from metropolitan histories. Both Ranade and Nikambe recognized that Indian English harnessed the ideal woman to the project of caste power.

As the memoirs of Ramabai Ranade and Nikambe's novel reveal, the normative heterosexual unit was consummated through an English education. In the case of Ramabai, English further separated the English-speaking woman from a preexisting female-dominated space. Ironically, her performance of the language of power marked the public as a space of unease and discomfort. Yet it drew her closer to her husband in a novel, companionate, and exclusionary bond. It enabled Ranade's display of patriarchal control—the successful containment of the feminine within the masculine. And yet it generated sentiments of shame, rage, and gendered subservience in Ramabai.

The tension and ambivalence at the heart of this sexual-linguistic project demonstrate that English was a dense cultural sign, one that evoked fear, anger, and desire in the minds of nineteenth-century subjects. Nikambe's novel illustrates perfectly how the individuated subject, activated by English, was produced through networks of social prohibition and within the inequities of domestic, representational, and social labor. Indian English was thus bound by the nineteenth-century, educated, gendered subject to a new and self-consciously indigenous heteropatriarchy. As numerous memoirs and novels testified, battles over caste authority and new rules for gender difference produced the phallogocentric power of English—particularly its ability to initiate desire, submission, and difference. As it systematically incorporated normative womanhood—the location for stable gender difference—into its path, Indian English voiced the process by which nineteenth-century native subjects were taught to guide their desire toward an investment in sexual difference. And, indeed, it was once English became yoked to, even indistinguishable from, Indian womanhood that it could be disengaged from its point of origin as a colonial imposition and, finally, take its place as an Indian language.

"WHY HAD I EVER BEGUN TO LEARN ENGLISH?"

7

DOSEBAI JESSAWALLA AND THE "MARCH OF ADVANCEMENT IN THE FACE OF OBLOQUY"

Passionately intent on establishing that she was the first Indian woman to have tasted the "sweets of an English education," Mrs. Dosebai Cowasjee Jessawalla wrote her memoirs in a 499-page English-language book entitled *The Story of My Life*.[1] Published just after her death in 1911, the volume details her memories of the years between 1830 and 1870, which bracket her youth, education, marriage, and global travels. It provides only scant details of the last decade of her life. The text is a voluminous and idealized reflection on the nineteenth century and on the gendered presentation of the twentieth-century Indian woman. Dosebai brings to life an Indian cosmopolitanism that is integrally enmeshed in national sexual norms, illuminating the nexus between heteronormativity and the cosmopolitan dreams of a new, globally mobile Indian. A symptomatic reading of *The Story of My Life* thus reveals how Indian English emerged from the tightening relationship between sex, memory, and gender presentation and came to be embodied by the globally mobile Indian subject.[2]

A member of the upper class of the Bombay-based Parsis, Jessawalla lived and moved in a world marked by native power over the transnational economies of cotton and opium. English is central to the narrativization, realization, and expression of these new connections. Jessawalla's English education provides her with the syntax to lay claim to a unique gendered standpoint. In her own reckoning, a possession of the language established civilizational progress, the "march of advancement in the face of obloquy."[3] English enabled her smooth adoption, in fact indigenization, of the feminized and racialized binaries of European Orientalism. These were continually fortified by her determination to adhere to customs and practices she believed to be "Indian," while also demonstrating her acquisition of the companionate and romantic aspects of Victorian gender regimes. In this deceptively simple narrative of self-actualization, English is materialized through its direct and symbolic association with new historical formations, notably the desiring individual as the subject of history; transnational colonial-bourgeois social power; the institutionalization and naturalization of heterosexual desire; the interplay between the national and the cosmopolitan; and the emergence of the cultural critic as imperial mediator. The Indian, liberal, and gendered individuality that Dosebai crafted reveals how an Indian woman could claim to disavow caste so as to claim bicultural authority. In contrast to Ramabai Ranade's strategies of ambivalence and Shevantibai Nikambe's distancing from caste, Dosebai Jessawalla's belief in the liberal and heterosocial promise of English also marked the triumph of the pan-regional Indian over caste-based rituals and the realm of native culture.

The Parsi community of western India was firmly situated within the practices of caste. While customary law was not always written down for the community as a whole, Jesse Palsetia has written that by the nineteenth century, western Indian Parsis considered themselves to be a caste.[4] The relationship of prominent Parsis to upper-caste Hindus is itself fascinating; for instance, the Parsi reformer Behramji Malabari worked assiduously, as Antoinette Burton has recorded, to reorganize "Hindu" gender practice. Furthermore, Burton has remarked that Malabari "was instrumental not just in refining the gendered dimensions of contests for cultural legitimacy and power in the western presidency, but in refiguring such contests for consumption by the British reform public at home as well."[5] I situate Jessawalla firmly in this tradition. Her distancing from a native particularity was essential for her access to transnational registers of consumption, performance, and mobility. Relegating caste, regional, and religious difference to the realm of the traditional, Jessawalla simultaneously claimed her unassailable access to the modern and established her authoritative distance, for an avidly India-conscious, global public, from the very rituals of tradition. Native customs were all too often synonymous for her with Muslim and Hindu cultural practices. In this text, she thus triangulates the imperial relationship—polarities between West and East, colonial and indigenous—in order to foreground her transcendent individuality. In the final analysis, *The Story of My Life* powerfully illustrates how the phallogocentric power of English was finally and fully domesticated by the new, cosmopolitan Indian gender order, one that sought to negate regional, caste, and communal distinctions, as it claimed authority over national and global access.

Jessawalla presented her English education as her most striking feature, something she credited entirely to her mother, Meheribai. Dedicating her autobiography to Meheribai, Dosebai emphasized in the frontispiece that it was "by giving me the privilege of being the first Indian girl to receive the benefits of English education" that Meheribai had, by the middle of the nineteenth century, established "the dissemination of higher culture among the women of his Majesty's culture and inspired me with that public spirit and self-sacrificing zeal which led me to pioneer many social reforms amongst my Indian sisters." She saw herself as embodying the selective reform project discussed in part I, whereby Indian women were deliberately trained to acquire and perform their knowledge of English so as to buttress native male claims to humanist equivalence with the colonizer, and thus to political authority. She established her willing embrace of the ventriloquizing power of colonial education—the "chains of control" that produced hierarchies between English-educated subjects who were bound together through social and philanthropic sensibilities. But, unlike other women who were taught by the male members of their families to acquire and then perform their knowledge of English, Jessawalla's acquisition was fueled by her mother's political and cultural ambitions. It was Meheribai who "made me the instrument of pioneering the noble cause of higher education among millions and millions of the gentler sex in India."[6] Furthermore, in contrast to Manockjee Cursetjee Shroff, Ramabai Ranade, Shevantibai Nikambe, or D. K. Karve, Jessawalla never sought to further extend her cultural power through pedagogic routes. Determined to tell her "story of progress and reform, of the victory of self sacrificing courage over narrow minded opposition," Jessawalla set out (in the "evening" of her life)[7] to publicize how English cemented her individuality and unique distinction from other Parsi and non-Parsi women of her age.

Her English education began in 1842. Though Dosebai Jessawalla acknowledged how hard her uncle, Cursetjee Shroff, worked in the field of women's education, she very clearly established that, despite his efforts, in her case it was her mother—a woman—who brought the idea of women's English education to fruition. "A feminine, not as is generally supposed, a masculine mind conceived the idea and . . . gave the first impetus to so preeminent an undertaking."[8]

The story of Jessawalla's mother, Meheribai, is an astonishing one. Voluntarily separated from her husband over a property dispute, she took refuge in her maternal home, where she supported her children and complained about her marital family, especially her father-in-law. Meheribai's husband, who had made a series of unfortunate speculations on the opium trade and was deeply opposed to the marital separation, committed suicide, an act that drew the "unmerciful enmity of all" against Meheribai.[9] But Meheribai's "indomitable courage, her sound judgment, inborn spirit of progress, and her aspirations for the good of her country enabled her . . . to brave the torrent of bigoted resistance." Dosebai asserts that these qualities were the very ones that propelled Meheribai to seek an English education and thus to "sow the seeds of that culture of which we are all now thankfully reaping the fruits."[10]

It was by virtue of being separated from her husband, and thus being free of the familial duties that would have been imposed on her, that Meheribai could seek out rather unconventional social opportunities.[11] Meheribai had two close English friends, and it was through them, Mrs. Ward and Mrs. Mackenzie, that she "acquired a taste for European manners and customs."[12] Her ability to transcend the social racism of Anglo-Indian society might have resulted from her class, gender, and Parsi identity, but it was further actualized through Dosebai's own determination to remember the nineteenth century through the veneer of cosmopolitan possibilities, especially as secured through language. One of the habits Meheribai developed was that of "enjoying the evening breeze," a practice that led to "contempt and suspicion poured upon her by her own people but applause and encouragement by the whole English community." Dosebai Jessawalla trenchantly noted how even this "harmless freedom . . . was an offence to orthodox Parsees. They, like bullocks in the mill, were content to tread in the beaten track of their forefathers. 'Keep the females stationary' was their motto. They were culpably negligent of the wants, physical and moral, of their wives and children, thought themselves foremost in every luxury and pleasure. With their fingers in every dish, from a pie to a pudding, they yet denied to their wives and daughters the simple diversion of an evening ramble."[13] Jessawalla minced no words in decrying the obstinacy of her fellow Parsis, holding them responsible for the neglect of female needs and for replicating only those comforts that secured patriarchy.

Meheribai's determination to mingle with the European community, to constantly question the customs of fellow Parsis as early as the 1820s, and to live apart from her husband suggests a rare approach to the world around her. Certainly, in comparison to the case of Dr. Rakhmabai, whereby the press, the law, and influential natives corresponded to crush Rakhmabai's critique of marital entitlements, Meheribai's story appears radical. Somewhat paralleling Pandita Ramabai's conviction in the power of English, Meheribai's zeal to reevaluate cultural norms found its most lucid expression in her determination to have her daughter educated in English.

Sending Jessawalla to school could not pass unnoticed in native society; it "stirred up the wrath of the entire male portion of the whole native community . . . wag[ing] war upon the custom of centuries." To make matters worse, the school was located in the European neighborhood of Bombay, an area "scrupulously avoided by native ladies." The sight of Meheribai's young daughter entering that area each day elicited a vicious reaction. The mother had to fend off the displeasure voiced by her in-laws and threatening letters addressed to her family "declaiming against the vices which English education would assuredly bring with it."[14] Some prominent Parsis resolved to evict her from her house and even excommunicate her. Meheribai herself was unperturbed. She reprimanded her critics with humor and in the strongest language possible. Jessawalla recalls how, at the height of the controversy, Meheribai wrote to one such instigator who had threatened her with excommunication, "begging him to make his decision public, in order that she might claim her right to provide herself and her family with a separate Tower of Silence for the reception of their bodies after death."[15]

It was only after Meheribai had been sending her daughter to Mrs. Ward's seminary for a while that "people began gradually to open their eyes to the vital importance of women's education." Among those was Bai Meheribai's brother-in-law, Cursetjee Shroff. Manockjee would later go on to found the Alexandra Native Girls' English Institution (discussed in chapter 2). When she learned about Manockjee's attempts to educate his daughter, Meheribai instantly wrote to her father-in-law, demanding to know why he was so opposed to her attempts to educate her daughter in English, but he seemed unconcerned when his son followed her example.[16] She further argued that it was she who had initiated this development, trenchantly stating that "as you, my noble benefactor, have seen your son in this instance following my footsteps, so you will, God willing, see many other salutary reforms introduced among the Parsees through my instrumentality."[17]

Meheribai deployed her daughter's English education to critique multiple aspects of native patriarchy: the patriarchal bond of grandfather, son, and grandson; the double standards that credited male agency and ignored female initiative; and the sequestering of women for social capital. As the repository of her mother's ambitions, Dosebai smoothly ventriloquized the agenda, although she rebutted the dictates of indigenous patriarchy with even greater severity by decrying the "backward" and the "superstitious" aspects of native culture. For example, as Jessawalla reminds the reader, "Previous to 1840 what little nominal education our Indian girl could get was imparted in an antiquated and clumsy fashion. A ground floor verandah in some prominent locality . . . boys and girls squatting . . . the young were taught according to the whims and capabilities of their native teachers. . . . Too often the very appearance and habits of these male teachers,—or Mehetajees as they were called—were not such as to command respect. . . . Like the Moolla (Mahomedan priest) calling the faithful to prayer, these teachers were wont to recite, at a bawling pitch of voice and in a state of dreamy sluggishness, the multiplication table."[18] In one swift move, and with her signature self-assuredness, Jessawalla characterized non-English education as repetitive, chaotic, and antiquated—all through comparisons with the "Mehetajee" and the "Moolla." That the meaning of both terms had to be explained suggests that Jessawalla might have expected her reading audience to be ignorant of basic cultural knowledge from India, or of the 1840s. As important, the denigration of the male teacher was completed by invoking the comparison with the Islamic priest. Her aim was to establish that her own learning had moved—in fact, progressed—from the regressive and the indigenous to the English. Jessawalla's education enabled her to rise above Eastern traditions and stasis, no longer "content to run in the same channel from one generation to another," passing her time as other women did in household chores and "sluggish idleness or gossip."[19] Jessawalla derived tremendous satisfaction from noting how her governess had inculcated in her strong habits of "gentleness, respect, order, tidiness and politeness"—so much so that her manners even "appeared affected . . . [and were] considered pretended coyness." She was proud to be differentiated from those "Parsee lad[ies] [who] would squat on the floor in company, talk in a loud tone while gesticulating freely." The binaries of tradition / modernity, stasis / movement, nature / culture, Islamic / English structured the unique and progressive nature of her education. While Meheribai's motivation might have been to deploy English education to illuminate the blind spots of Parsi upper-caste patriarchy, Jessawalla, for her part, turned her education toward deepening gendered and Orientalist binaries.

Historians of western India have demonstrated how the English education project nurtured the rise of a social reformist spirit among the socially mobile "native" (male) elite, especially the wealthy members of the minority Parsi community.[20] Wealthy Parsis drew their income from a range of economic activities, and Jessawalla's own family connections hint strongly that they benefited from the opium trade with China.[21] The philanthropic sensibility came coupled with a conviction that the English-education project would liberate English speakers from the thrall of colonial racism and usher them to positions of power in indigenous society.[22] Jessawalla, too, noted that her education compelled her to act in a public, self-sacrificing, and reformist manner among Indian women. My argument in chapter 2 on the cosmopolitan urges nurtured through the Western education project certainly reemerges in Dosebai Jessawalla. In her case, the desire for cultural equivalence and the ambition to pose as the enlightened critic and reformer of native society is voiced through her need to establish her individualism—her unique and originary subjectivity. As in the case of the male and female actors discussed throughout this book, what bears close scrutiny is Dosebai's need to naturalize sexual difference so as to consolidate this individualism. Here I would reconfigure Gayatri Spivak's formulation on female individualism as expressing an "ideology of imperialist axiomatics."[23] Spivak unearths how the positing of the white, stable, and female subject in colonialism is predicated on the civilizing of the "native," so as to enshrine certain cultural laws as universal and ultimately to sanction the violence of colonialism and occlude its economic ravages. Dosebai's drive to constitute herself as an autonomous liberal subject was reliant on naturalizing the civilizing dichotomy of colonialism, interwoven with the logic of caste heteronormativity.

Writing about that other Indian community that embraced women's English education—the Jewish community—Jessawalla further noted that "Jewesses of this country enjoy the privileges of an enlightened education, to which is frequently added the culture of travel, many having visited England, the Continent of Europe and the New World, and now live much as English ladies of the period do."²⁴ English education ranked castes and communities on a scale of civilization so much so that "the Marathas seem to have adopted English education after the Parsees and Jews, and subsequently the Banias, and lastly the Mahomedans, who, however, do not appear to have made any appreciable progress."²⁵

In 1852, ten years after having embarked on her English education, Jessawalla was married. On the events leading to her marriage, she recounted, "By my association with English ladies, I had come to the conviction that I had a right to either assent to or decline any proposed union, that I too had something to say in a matter of such grave importance to myself."²⁶ Jessawalla was committed to the possibility of "choice" in her entry into hetero-conjugality. She appears to mirror the discourse on companionate marriage circulating among British feminists, demonstrating that she could access the liberal benefits of European civilization through celebrating the power of sexual difference.²⁷

Jessawalla's desire for matrimonial companionate understanding was yoked to a solidifying sense of individuation and self. Together these aligned with a discerning consumerism and an appreciation for the anglicized tastes of her husband. Recalling in detail the "stockings, kid gloves, pieces of lace and tulle" that her husband gifted her on the "first day of my new life," Jessawalla's memoirs establish the mutually reinforcing relation between individual subjectivity, consumerism, and the taste for British manufactured goods, all of which contributed to the pleasures of the modern conjugal dyad. As she recalls, on the marriage night, the couple immediately set out to discuss his needs and her abilities: his being the need to maintain traditional ties in a large joint family (over sixty relatives, as she recalls) and her abilities, which entailed her English education and simultaneous knowledge of custom. He informed her that despite his family being large and rather traditional, she, being *"blessed with an English education as well as trained up in Parsee usages,"* would discern the route to "family concord" without having to deprive herself of those pleasures or habits to which she might have "from infancy been accustomed."²⁸ As she records her grateful memory of the discussion: "These kind words of confidence in me soothed my anxieties, and I offered fervent praise and thanksgiving to Almighty God for the happy lot he had ordained me. It would be out of my power to describe the thrill of ecstasy which the love of my husband excited in my hitherto virgin breast—what could I do, but strive to live in harmony with all the members of his family and act a mother's part to my step-children?"²⁹ Jessawalla's performative strategies reveal the very "fiction of heterosexual coherence" as it entrenches and anchors the "ideology of individualism."³⁰ Dosebai's memories of this first encounter enhance her self-aware, autonomous subjectivity. She exposes structural alliances between English, desire, consumption, and an upwardly mobile liberal individuality. Ultimately, Jessawalla's memoirs render explicit the role of heterosexual desire in consolidating the emergence of English. Her discerning choice of a marriage partner established her individual needs and ambitions and simultaneously signaled a meaningful—although deliberately incomplete—break with tradition. The economy of consumption was fundamental to this discriminating choice, her husband's presents confirming that he appreciated her anglicized and material tastes. The emphasis on choice, pleasure, and taste conjoined. Together they formed the illusion of the discerning individual, who then freely entered into sexual relations with her husband. Jessawalla naturalizes her individuated claim to the cosmopolitan promise of the English-speaking ecumene. As Nikambe's fictional account also suggests, here, too, English is domesticated by bringing it into the bedroom, where it assists or even stands in for sexual consummation. Dosebai's desire expresses the affinity between language and bourgeois conjugality but even more strikingly, her memories materialize the phallogocentric power of English, bridging the sign with its form.

English bound the individuated gendered subject to the discourse of sexual desire. Jessawalla's virginal "thrill of ecstasy" rendered transparent the connection between English, a companionate understanding between herself and her husband, and the power of a "reformed" patriarchy. Voiced through the inevitability of sexual consummation, Jessawalla revealed that her desire was to universalize the power of bourgeois heterosexuality and uphold the dictates of indigenous custom. Her desire was to be hailed by phallogocentric power. And so it was that her feelings overtook her words; as she noted, "It would be out of my power to describe the thrill of ecstasy which the love of my husband excited in my hitherto virginal breast."³¹ Dosebai's momentary thrill of ecstasy is enhanced by her husband's recognition of her English acquisition. With that, she enacts an individuated turn toward her husband as sexual partner, the marital union, and the amalgamation of modernity and tradition.

Dosebai Jessawalla came into her own as the wife of the senior member of a prestigious Bombay Parsi family, effecting wide-ranging changes in her marital family's practices. While referencing her unique perspective (produced, as she took care to demonstrate, through her English education), she was also keen to remind her reader of her ultimate respect for tradition. Her self-presentation after marriage increasingly entailed the depiction of herself as traditional and modern, alternative yet conventional. Detailing, for instance, the rituals around mourning, childbirth, and marriage that she chose to uphold, she noted at one point that it was the very fact of her "liberal education [that] stood me in good stead, for with keen zest and enjoyment, I performed the household duties which others felt to be drudgery."[32] Some time later, she also declared that although "I liked to deck myself out in English array and though I advocated many salutary reforms, it by no means followed that I would deviate from any rule laid down by our religion."[33]

The ability to cast herself as the individuated, traditional-modern subject was instantly yoked to her determination to mark herself apart from "native females." Whether dwelling on the state of female education, the attention to ancient ritual, or the choice of fashions, Jessawalla argued constantly that she alone was distinct from, and more reflexive than, other women. For instance, on the subject of fashion, she noted that "unlike the Europeans, native females do not annually change the fashions of their dress; I, however, do so every three or four years, consulting nobody's taste but my own, both in my clothes and jewels."[34] Speaking about the social class of Parsis, who were keen to send their daughters to the newly inaugurated Alexandra Native Girls' English Institution, she claimed first that "they had looked at my position amongst the English, and they saw the advisability of sending their daughters to an English school."[35] But ultimately, this was a shallow ambition:

Now-a-days English schools are springing up in all directions and governesses are within easy reach of all, but the adage "All learning and no knowledge" illustrates the present state of things amongst our girls. They do not evince the least interest in domestic affairs.... Daughters learn English but ignore the necessity of helping their mothers at home.... They ape the extravagant dress of their rich companions.... The case is not improved when these senseless girls marry, and many a young man is driven to dishonesty by the extravagance of his wife.... The daughters... though they learn the language, do not, it seems to me, acquire the polite manners of the English.[36]

Jessawalla forged distinctions between her authentic subjectivity and the superficial mimicry, among others, of European culture. Continuing with her critique of other English-educated native women, she declared that "they think themselves reformed away in European ladies, but like the loud note of an empty vessel, their very appearance is enough to convince one of their limited knowledge. It is easy to dress like an Englishwoman, but to imitate her virtues should be the aim of my countrywomen."[37] Posing herself as the supreme, erudite cultural critic, Jessawalla claimed a more robust self-awareness because of her deeper appreciation of European cultural practices; this was buttressed by a conscious distancing from native women, and by her unique ability to bring her experiences of the nineteenth century to bear on her social critique. Increasingly, the insights her English knowledge gave her were voiced through the imperatives of a new Indian identity.

It might appear that Jessawalla identified with the colonizer, flawlessly adopting the modes of cultural critique developed by British colonialism, assessing the "genuine" ability of Indians to attain the complete attributes of English culture. Following Homi Bhabha's insight on the split subject of Indian nationalist history, it is possible that Jessawalla, in effect, demystified the power of colonial judgments on "native" society.[38] But Bhabha's formulation fails to account for the ways colonized subjects actively shaped their subjectivity by staging complex moves of cooptation and distance from other natives. Far more useful in this context is Antoinette Burton's perceptive reading of Cornelia Sorabji. Burton posits Sorabji as an "emergent figure" of Indian modernity: "In her determination to excavate what was pure and precious about 'traditional' femininities, [she] constantly revealed her deep investment in being seen as the discerning professional woman—an identity that was clearly aligned with the secular, the modern, and the masculine. She was what Williams would call an 'emergent' historical figure: fully involved in producing new meanings and values, new practices and social relations—those belonging to the 'modern woman' whom she alternatively feared and scorned."[39] Dosebai Jessawalla was some thirty years older than Cornelia Sorabji, but the similarities in their strategies of self-presentation provide crucial insights into the emerging phenomenon of the Indian border intellectual produced through the Indo-British cultural encounter.[40] Gayatri Spivak's work on the relation between the "native informant" and the upwardly mobile third-world intellectual who traffics in the urge to comprehend, unearth, and perform national-cultural identity is also very productive here.[41] Preceding the neocolonial third-world intellectual by 100 years, Jessawalla could confidently claim that her individuality was the product of her singular ability to amalgamate tradition and modernity. Her sense of entitlement to the otherwise restricted privileges of colonial modernity rested easily alongside a "critical" skill in transcending, yet respecting, the modern and the non-modern, the European and the native. Operating through an oblique dialogue with the colonial and native (male) urge to distinguish "Indian womanhood" as traditional and exceptional, Jessawalla's sovereign English-educated subjectivity was impossible without a studied critical opinion on native womanhood at large. The unschooled native woman was the minor, "self consolidating other" upon which Jessawalla could train her superior and educated opinions.[42]

In 1860, after the birth of her sixth child, Jessawalla embarked on what is portrayed as the next stage of her life (following education and then marriage and family): travel. In discussing nineteenth-century cultures of travel, Inderpal Grewal notes: "More than a trope, travel is a metaphor that became an ontological discourse central to the relations between Self and Other, between different forms of alterity, between nationalisms, women, races and classes. . . . Whether travel is a metaphor of exile, mobility, difference, modernity, or hybridity, it suggests the particular ways in which knowledge of a Self, society, and nation was, and is, within European and North American culture, to be understood and obtained."[43]

Grewal maintains that some Indian women can be folded into this critique, specifically "Toru Dutt as an upper class, English educated Bengali woman [who] frames her narrative of her visit to England within this Euro-imperial discourse, [while] Pandita Ramabai's and Parvati Athavale's cannot be so contained."[44] Grewal draws our attention to stark differences between Dutt, on the one hand, and Ramabai and Athavale, on the other, by emphasizing the disparities in their access to English.[45]

Grewal's formulation sensitizes us to the differential access of gendered subjects to the "English" ecumene. Dosebai's first visit was to Poona, a momentous journey for someone who "had never been further than a couple of hours drive from Bombay."[46] At this time of her life she was mired in several recurring property disputes, and one objective of her book might have been to set the record straight on the developments over those years. The second and far more pressing purpose was to provide minute details of her ever-expanding travels. From the first visit to Poona, she rapidly gained confidence and expertise. Mahabaleshwar was the next place she visited; she recalled the baskets of strawberries brought to her by "emigrant Chinese" farmers and noted that "the cold of Mahabaleshwar is like what we had heard people tell of the English spring or autumn."[47] The work now introduces a twist in genre, from autobiography to exhaustive travelogue. The switch draws attention to a shift toward an imperial cosmopolitanism, this through her adoption of the scientific-autobiographical-travelogue. Her enthusiastic deployment of modes of expression otherwise resembling colonial discourse leaves us with an uneasy appreciation of the portability and conceit of such discourse and for her talent in managing any reductive binary between colonizer and colonized.

The Prince of Wales's 1875 visit to India provided Jessawalla with the opportunity to dwell once more on her regard for British rule and the support she enjoyed from Europeans. In that spirit she traveled to Delhi in 1877 to participate in the Delhi durbar. Here her delight at being misrecognized speaks once again to her urge toward exceptionalism—her desire to separate herself from the majority of natives, and especially other Indian women—by virtue of her intellectual and transregional credentials. She recorded somewhat gleefully on overhearing "opinion[s] as to my identity; some said I was a European, some took me for a Chinese, some for an Egyptian, a Turkish lady . . . but very few knew me as a Parsee, as they did not believe a Parsee lady would venture through such populous thoroughfares in an open carriage."[48] From Delhi, Jessawalla went on to Agra (where she incorrectly noted that the Taj Mahal contained Noor Jehan's ashes) and Lucknow ("landmark of British heroism").[49] Her travelogues focus primarily on monuments and, to a more limited extent, on educational institutions. She spared no words in her criticism of the hallmarks of the indigenous: in Benaras, the fabled home of Sanskritic learning that was increasingly synonymous with the exploitive "homes" for Hindu widows, she decided the city's "most striking features are heaps of rubbish and pools of mud."[50] While in Calcutta, "the most interesting and magnificent metropolis of India," she was introduced to the viceroy's wife, Lady Lytton.[51]

On returning to Bombay from her travels in north India, she learned that the "Hindoo teacher" who taught her sons had culled the details of her travels, as well as aspects of her mother's life. This unnamed man then attempted to have the information published in the form of a pamphlet. She immediately resolved to "suppress its publication," for "its appearance marred the prospects of the autobiography which I already had in contemplation."[52] The man readily handed over to her all copies of the pamphlet that he had written and she reimbursed him for his monetary loss. Interestingly enough, he had not placed his name on the work, a fact that struck her as curious. When she asked him why, he replied that he "wrote on diverse subjects and published them, sometimes under his own name, sometimes that of his brother, and at other times, as in this case, published them anonymously."[53]

Jessawalla's sense of ownership over the telling of her "own" story establishes her ambitious pursuit of an autonomous individuality. Following Foucault's work on authorship and modernity,[54] I see this brief encounter as establishing the manner in which the "author function" was produced through a negotiation between the "Hindoo" reporter and the named autobiographer who sought to publicly situate herself as the "first" and most accomplished exponent of the multifarious aspects of an English education. The former was marked as indigenous; he reproduced his work while remaining unconcerned with establishing his identity through authorship. He could be compensated for the loss of his words and time, as well as subsumed by Jessawalla's more ambitious, wealthy, and individuated desires.

In 1878, Jessawalla traveled abroad and her narrative style shifted once more. Taking the ship to Britain, she was gratified to make the acquaintance of British officials and their families heading back to Europe. Reaching the Waterloo Bridge Station, she "set foot at last in London . . . [and thus] the great aim of [her] life was realised."[55] Once in England, she was especially pleased to identify herself as of the "same race as Sir Jamsetjee" —who was well known in certain social circles as a benevolent philanthropist.[56] More than her social or kin connections, it was her dress and appearance that immediately catapulted her to celebrity status. As she explained, while Indian and even Parsi women had visited or lived in Britain before her (including her daughter), they had readily adapted their clothes to the English styles. But Jessawalla maintained her "traditional" dress and found herself to be the center of attention, much to her own satisfaction. Here she performed the "traditional" to claim an individuated Indian subjectivity.

At this point, Jessawalla turns even more quickly from one narrative mode to another, especially after she begins to encounter what would (for most colonial subjects, even those of her social class) have been the hyperprivileged and elusive. Antoinette Burton's work on Indians "at the heart of empire" has called attention to "how elusive the goal of feeling comfortably 'at home' as a British colonial subject in domestic imperial culture could be."⁵⁷ Jessawalla records no such apprehension or anxiety. But the clues lie in her irregular grasp of a range of narrative strategies. Her mode of observation becomes intriguingly encyclopedic, distant, and impersonal, suggesting her uneasy fit within the expressive modes of English in the imperial capital.

Her tours in London included visits to the Crystal Palace and Madame Tussaud's. Outside the city, she immediately took recourse in the Romanticist mode, lavishly describing the "verdant land . . . the rich velvety grass spun by Nature's hand, the cooling green foliage."⁵⁸ Her observations contained images that were mirror opposites of those produced by British women who traveled to the "Orient," making evident that the "picturesque" for her was about claiming an English idiom and documenting her arrival upon the scene of metropolitan modernity. Jessawalla's desires echo (and do not repeat) the observations that manifested English female power in India.⁵⁹ She focused most on those markers—the great exhibitions, the monuments of steel and glass—that marked Europe at the pinnacle of material difference. But far from the accounts of the enervating, sequestering gender practices of the Orient were her observations on English women: "In the evening [we] went for a walk. On seeing a number of beautiful girls alight from every omnibus that I saw, I asked them if they all were coming from school, when they replied that they were shop girls. In the large shops hundreds of girls are employed as saleswomen and seamstresses. To see these girls was to love them, so beautifully fair and young were they. I was forcibly reminded of those tales in which even kings were willing enough to be led in silken chains by girls of plebeian birth, and what to me at one time seemed only fiction seemed now very likely to be the truth."⁶⁰ Differing markedly from Agashe's characterization of Avadi as the passive spectator of scenery and social customs, Jessawalla unabashedly appreciates women for their beauty and sensual power. Even more significantly, these are English, working-class women, configured by her as "girls."⁶¹ Maintaining her signature self-confidence, negating any sense of an inhibited colonized view or solidarity with the classed subjects of British power, Jessawalla succeeds in turning saleswomen and seamstresses into objects of delight. While recording few opinions on English men, she did note her pleasure on their admiration for the fact that she could converse with them in "their own tongue," suggesting in other words that her knowledge of English produced parity with Englishmen.[62] Jessawalla derived no end of pleasure from being the unique, traditional, and modern subject of the British Empire. Her writing on the imperial project was entirely laudatory; she approvingly noted the victorious reception of the dignitaries returning from the Berlin Congress, "having established peace in Europe without bloodshed."

In addition, and as important, she performed caste-specific actions in the heart of European and Christian civilization with ease and agility. For instance, when she visited Rome, she secured a private, hour-long meeting with Pope Leo XIII. The pope admired her clothes and ornaments, despite her stressing that she was not traveling with clothes as suitable as she would have liked to display when meeting so eminent a person. At this meeting, she rejected any requirements that would have clashed with her own faith: she refused to kiss the pope's toe, even though she was informed that this was required of all those who met him. She informed his secretary that according to Parsi doctrine this would be polluting, and the secretary excused her from this act.

After her travels in England, Jessawalla went on to Paris for the Great Exhibition of 1878. While there, she went up in a hot air balloon. The experience filled her with prophetic, inspired observations. As the "earth reced[ed] from beneath" her, she turned immediately to a reflection on education and progress, asking herself how long her "wealthy sisters shut themselves up in their old habits and prejudices, shunning the healthy and ennobling pleasures . . . alluringly at their very door!" Once again using "native womanhood" as the means by which to present her exceptionalism, she continued with her query: "Why do they cling so tenaciously to their idle crude custom, and know no higher ambition than to glide along in the same groove as their ancestors, instead of . . . basking in the free air of enlightenment!"[63] The experience of being suspended above the Great Exhibition, in other words, sparked her disclosure that her knowledge and power over English signified an intellectual, spiritual, as well as spatial progress over her "sisters" who were trapped by custom.

On returning to India, Jessawalla once more resumed her travels through the country. Her visit to Kashmir led her to note the exquisite beauty of Kashmiri women, a beauty that was "none the less noticeable than that of the women of an European nation. One can compare it with Circassian beauty."[64] In her eyes, India is open for description, for visual consumption. Most significant, in this portion of the text, Jessawalla, as the subject

"I," almost entirely disappears. Her description of the "mountainous regions surrounded by lofty hills and the wonderful riches of the gloriously coloured foliage and groves and avenues upon the banks of the vale of Cashmere" suggest the voice of a third person, one attuned to the significance of claiming nature to mark human subjectivity.[65] By this stage in her memoirs, her observations are far more attuned to an amalgamation of the Orientalist and the picturesque. She visited South India to record the "indolent" and polyandrous Todas, explicating details of their dress, appearance, and homes.[66] Descriptions of nature are immediately and regularly accompanied by observations on gender and sexual relations. Her appreciation of the feminine and the natural is then counterpoised with an insight on modern progress: in her travels through Kashmir she bemoaned that "almost all the high officials . . . downwards are men of great culture, yet it was disappointing to notice that education amongst the gentler sex had not made any advancement in such a well-refined State."[67]

In 1906, Dosebai Jessawalla made her second trip to England, this time via Ceylon and Hong Kong. Living in London (the "Home of the British Empire"), she attended a Parliament session and was standing so close to the royal entrance that "their Majesties" passed her and she was able to exchange greetings with them. It was during this trip that she learned to drive a car and finally, through her connection with Lord Lytton, was invited to meet the king and queen at a tea party at Windsor Castle. She recalls her excitement, for "to be presented to our Sovereign and Queen had been the most ardent wish of my life, and in the evening of my career it was about to be fulfilled."[68] At the party, she reminded the king that "we Parsees" were extremely satisfied with his "benign rule." She records that she was "charmed with his affability."[69]

By the end of her gigantic self-memorialization, Jessawalla comfortably cements the multiple connections between English, individual sovereign autonomy, and her mastery over the tradition-modernity binary. It should be of no surprise, then, that she chose to end her book with a newspaper article that initiated the quest for women's English education in 1842.[70] Criticizing the prominence given to a male figure in the article, Jessawalla nevertheless agreed with many of the other sentiments expressed in the piece, which contrasted English knowledge with ignorance, and the progress of the West with the weighty traditions of the East. The writer naturalized these connections by invoking conjugality and companionate love:

[A] woman's power of pleasing mainly depend[s] upon her capabilities to participate in feelings and in objects common to both her husband and herself—that man of education can have but little community of sentiment with women whose knowledge is confined to the acquirements filling them merely for the household drudgery of superior domestic selves. The experience of the wo[r]ld teaches us, that from such an ill-assorted association, nothing but disgust must eventually ensue and mutual estrangement is . . . commonly the result. This in Eastern nations evinces itself in a toleration of a plurality of wives, and concubinage. . . . From such a fate, from such a degradation, from such a prostitution of the ends and objects of marriage the liberal minded Parsee bids fair to rescue his child.[71]

But Jessawalla pointedly rejected any attempt to be cast as the passive receptacle for patriarchal or colonialist reform ideology.[72] Her sense of agency and self-actualization effectively illuminates the role of normative sexual difference in enabling the raced and gendered subjects' access to the secular, colonial-national public.

It is upon the willing bourgeois female subject that the axis of national, familial, and public-commercial relations turned. Dosebai ultimately (even if inadvertently) exposes in her memoirs the connection between English, sexual difference, heterosexual desire, bourgeois individuality, and the emergence of bicultural national authority in an imperial frame. Consistently, Jessawalla crafts cultural capital from her performance of upper-class cosmopolitan femininity. At the same time, she never ceases to remind us of the intellectual and sartorial work—including the deliberate strategies of distancing and disavowal—that goes into maintaining national-femininity.[73] Her unflagging desire to be remembered as the first Indian woman to have learned English immediately opens up our understanding of the close connections between bourgeois cosmopolitanism, normative and transnational sexualities, internal discomfort over proximity to other Indians, and the bridging of tradition with modernity in shaping global access. As the fulcrum between the memory of the native nineteenth century and the secularization of caste in the Indian twentieth, the text constitutes an act of translation, exposing the lives of those who domesticated English through new gender performativities so as to claim a transnational and cosmopolitan legibility.

8

EPILOGUE:

"I AM AN INDIAN. I HAVE NO LANGUAGE"

Parvatibai Athavale and the

Limits to English

The successful, even if ambivalent, attainment of English by a range of gendered subjects has shaped the focus of this book. But nowhere is the compact between gender, conjugality, and English more apparent than in the continuous failure of one woman—a Brahman widow—to learn English.[1] For these reasons, I conclude with the Marathi-language biography of Parvatibai Athavale (1870–1937). English continued to reinforce caste exclusivity and conjugal heteronormativity in tandem, and, as Athavale reveals, it did so even in transnational locations. Exposing the conflict between speaking, reading, and writing, she draws attention to the performativity of English in changing times. When she suggests her failure to learn the language, she sheds light on the fresh pressure of symbolic and social arrangements between normative gender and the twentieth-century Indian nation, and on the radical failure of language to transcend social context. Thus I do not conclude with a triumphalist narrative of the gendered subject's mastery over English. Rather, by probing the theme of failure suggested by Athavale, this chapter reveals how circuits of national and transnational gender served to limit English even from the upper-caste subject.

Repeatedly interpellated by the requirements of class, gender, nationalism, and religion, Parvati Athavale conveys how her desire to learn English took her from Poona to Bombay and then to the United States. And yet, she returned to India believing that she had failed to learn English and convinced more than ever that national identity and companionate conjugality reinforce each other. Parvati Athavale was Dhondo Keshav Karve's sister-in-law and, as mentioned in chapter 4, Karve had (in)famously married the widow Godubai, Parvati's sister. Athavale published *Mazi Kahani* (My story) in 1928 and made special note of the considerable assistance she received from G. M. Chiplunkar (discussed in chapter 4) in this endeavour.

Born one year after Avadi Bhide, in 1870, in a small village in the Ratnagiri District of western India, Athavale recalls that a girls' education in those days required that she know how to prepare for religious rituals, clean the rice and dirty plates, bathe younger children, and feed them; this knowledge comprised the equivalent of the matriculation examination for all girls in her village.[2] Athavale states that she had passed this standard at the age of eleven, humorously critiquing the conception that formal education was not gendered. One of her earliest memories was of her mother's constant labor in the fields and the kitchen. Athavale and her sisters would try to lighten their mother's burden, but they were keenly aware that the most effective way to actually do so would be to marry and leave the house.[3] Girls were usually committed to their future husbands by the age of five. Parvati was a teenager when her husband died, leaving her with a young son; in fact, all her sisters were soon widowed. Their brother, Naharpant, had been living and studying in Bombay and he had enrolled the oldest sister—Baya—in Pandita Ramabai's Sharada Sadan, a home for Hindu widows. Baya was Ramabai's first student. Naharpant was a close friend of Dhondo Keshav Karve's and the two men would often discuss matters related to social reform and education. Karve's first wife had died recently and he had stated he was so strongly committed to changing social customs that he would marry a *Brahman balvidhva*.[4] Naharpant successfully encouraged Karve to consider marrying Baya.

Parvatibai Athavale records that her sister's engagement provided the turning point in her own life. Instead of being forced to spend her life in Deorukh, bemoaning her fate and facing endless social reproach (which she says would have been the destiny of any Brahman widow), Athavale left with her sister for Poona. Here Karve tried to encourage her to begin to work for the widow's school—the Anathbalikashram—that he had started. Rather than have her help with the school's cooking and cleaning, Karve wanted Athavale to educate herself and then take on the role of teacher or administrator at the institute. And so, at twenty-six years of age, Parvatibai Athavale, an orthodox and shaven widow who had spent her entire life in a village, was enrolled in a school in Poona.[5] She never tells us the name of the school, although she does remember that the school made her very conscious of her difference from the other students, that she was a shaven widow, not well off, and much older than the others.

The teachers frequently ignored her, and Karve soon decided that Athavale might benefit more from private lessons at home. He sent her to learn with Gopal Agarkar's wife. As discussed in chapter 3, Gopal Agarkar was a highly respected upper-caste social reformer, an advocate of women's education, and, over time, a critic of Tilak's Hindu nationalist politics. Karve had always maintained a steady admiration for his ideals. Agarkar's wife was also considered too advanced in age to be sent to school and hence was being taught at home. Athavale recalls that she learned the "alphabet, 1st Marathi book, [and] multiplication to 14 and 100 numbers" in these home sessions.[6] The experience convinced her that she should study further, but the only school in the area that would provide a more advanced education was the Poona High School for Native Girls.[7] Athavale enrolled in the school's Marathi second grade. Once again she became deeply conscious that her shaven appearance, her relatively lower class, and her advanced age set her apart from the other students in her class—most of whom were from the more prestigious Poona families and were no more than ten years old. Despite all her fears and uncertainties, however, Athavale did very well in school and received a scholarship for further study, as well as a teacher-training certificate. But she makes no mention in her memoir of having learned any English in the school. By this time, Karve had eighteen students enrolled in his ashram and he asked Athavale to begin her work there.

Recalling the radical changes in her life since her sister's remarriage, Athavale states that earlier she "had no idea of what education was. So where would the question of national service arise?"[8] Parvati's connection between education and a national philanthropic social conscience speaks both to the liberal history of the colonial English-education curriculum, as well as to the obvious influence of G. M. Chiplunkar in shaping her memoirs.[9] Extending that to Sanjay Seth's argument on the essential pedagogic nature of Western education, it becomes evident that, at least by 1928, Athavale was sensitive to the belief that it was incumbent on an educated Indian to strengthen the links between teaching, reform, and the nation. But she indicates her discomfort at entering into wider battles over concepts such as "Hindustan," and national service. In her case, nationalist, reformist sensibilities were refracted through Karve's pedagogic mission, Chiplunkar's heteronormative Brahmanism, her sister's marriage, and her specific awareness of gender through the experience of widowhood.

Simultaneously, Athavale sheds light on the connection between education and the expectation of national service, raising intriguing questions about the power of caste in the face of liberal notions of individual autonomy. In December 1904, she was invited to address the annual meeting of the National Social Conference. This was twelve years before Karve was asked to do the same. Athavale spoke in Marathi and delivered a rousing speech in which she argued that women must certainly be "given" an education. Despite all the talk on women's social reform and education, the real and desired effects of education were not being felt by the women themselves, as they remained buried under mundane household tasks.[10] But most memorably, she condemned the westernized, socially reformed women and men of the large cities. She lashed out against the manners of the so-called emancipated women of Bombay and also against the way they dressed. Responding to this "bomb-shell" of a speech, *Kesari* applauded Athavale's deft exposure of the hypocrisy of westernized social reformers. Karve, on the other hand, was besieged with complaints on the sentiments expressed by Athavale, which forced him to worry that the cause of women's education and reform would now be thwarted.[11]

Soon after beginning work with Karve, Athavale tried to learn English. She bought herself an English primer the day she completed her studies at the teacher-training college. But she never got a chance to pursue her ambition because shortly after concluding her studies in 1904, she started traveling on behalf of the ashram. Although the demands of this work prevented her from learning English, she was aware that her efforts actually enabled "50 other widows to learn English."[12] Eventually, this very work convinced her once more of the need to learn the language. In 1906, shortly after Karve had an accident, Athavale realized that the responsibility of looking after the ashram should not fall solely on his shoulders. She took on the task of fund-raising—a duty that had kept Karve away from Hingne for weeks at a stretch, but that also required a certain confidence with public speaking and travel. Karve encouraged her decision. Parvatibai's account of traveling across the country in search of funds for the cause of Hindu women's education is a remarkable one. She had readily mastered her initial trepidation and was soon addressing large social gatherings and even going from door to door in unfamiliar cities to discuss her message with people and raise funds for the ashram. When her work took her beyond Marathi-speaking areas, as it often did, she would use a translator. But other aspects of language continued to challenge her work and travels. Once, not being able to read the names on the railway platforms, she disembarked at the wrong stop. She often had to visit the homes of the more prominent people in strange towns, but this was more difficult because she could not read their names, written in English, on the doors to their houses. She tells us that it was the nature of this work and her inability to communicate in languages other than Marathi that once again spurred her onto learning English.

Athavale's recognition of her need to learn English indicates the limits of operating within a particular regional language. She remembers each of those encounters as troubling because of her inability to read and communicate in languages other than Marathi, not because she was a female in unfamiliar surroundings. Her memory of those years foregrounds her discomfort with being linguistically unprepared. But she never recalls how she might have been received, dressed in a white sari, with her non-tonsured hair, traversing new neighborhoods, localities, and towns.

According to Athavale, thinking about pedagogy and national service led her to consider the plight of widows with a newfound critical awareness. And a few years after beginning to work with Karve, she began to grow out her own hair. A radical step by any standards, it is, however, crucial to note that she did not stop dressing in white. She rejected the Brahmanical injunction on widow tonsuring, but not on widow mourning. She was thirty-eight when she decided to do this, remarking that the most useful change initiated by the Sudharaks was the change effected in the lives of widows.[13] It was essential for her, however, to establish that she never lost her dedication to established social mores. She notes that she never considered herself a Sudharak and remained stridently opposed to notions of "individual freedom and equality."[14]

English hovers over this clash between caste and liberalism. In 1912, Athavale bought herself another English primer and again attempted to learn the language. Karve tried to help her, but his own work and commitments made this difficult. Then in 1914, one of Karve's associates wrote to them and mentioned the missionary-run Bandra Convent School in Bombay, suggesting that Parvatibai go there to complete her education. There were many other people working for the ashram by this point, and Athavale remembers that she did not feel much remorse about leaving Karve and his institute to go learn English in Bombay.

But once there, she soon discovered that her advanced age posed an insurmountable barrier. She was forty-two years old and felt isolated from the majority of students and thus from the activities in the school. Perhaps as a concession to her age, she was given her own room in the hostel, but this only heightened her general sense of alienation. The teachers would not admit her to the more elementary classes; rather, in the afternoons a "Hindu girl who had become a Christian" would teach her some English for about an hour.[15] Athavale found the entire experience useless and began to worry whether she would ever learn any English. It is curious that Karve never enrolled her in a Poona school, even the New English School for boys, as he had done with some of his other students. After all, it seems that Parvatibai (at least initially) had only wanted to read English. Even more curiously, he was teaching English to the girls in his own ashram by this point, but Parvatibai never mentioned the ashram as a possibility. The decision to pursue English in a missionary school was generally one made by the more upper-class Indian families, and it was synonymous with the acquisition of westernized social mores and manners. Athavale never tells us why Karve ignored the native-administered facilities available for women's English education in Poona and instead chose an option mediated by Europeans in a different town.

Parvatibai's reasons for learning English and her conception of the language as a means to travel, read, and speak change continuously over the years. The shift in her ambitions points to distinctions between reading and speaking. Moreover, they indicate the moving significance, the widening symbolic power of English, and its ability to transport her beyond a caste-specific regionalism and to reorient her memories of gender and nationalism. Athavale soon tired of her fruitless experiences at the Bandra Convent School and transferred to the Scot Mission School on Grant Road in South Bombay.[16] Once more, her advanced age prevented her from mixing freely with the students, and the teacher would not hold Athavale to the same standards as the other students. But here she could spend her free time collecting funds for the ashram. She remained at the school for three years, from 1915 to 1918, and passed the English second and third classes. Yet even this amount of English was not satisfactory for Athavale. She writes that while she had learned to read a little English, she made no progress in speaking the language; and so her expectation that the language would help her with her work remained unrealized. This presents an interesting contradiction, for her initial desire to learn English was motivated by her inability to read English names and places, not to converse in it.

One of Karve's sons advised her to live with a European family for a short while to learn English through the "direct method," but they were unable to find a host family. It was then that Karve and Athavale decided that she should travel abroad to learn English, hoping that she would be so entirely immersed in the culture that she would start speaking the language. It is striking that they believed she should be sent across the world to learn a language that would ultimately enable her to travel across India. An immediate storm of disapproval arose among Karve's associates; they thought he should send a younger woman, or at least a graduate for such "higher" studies, and not Athavale, who (by her own description) was "an old woman and close to death."[17] Parvatibai was forty-six years old at the time and her son had just completed his master's degree.

Parvati believed that Karve supported her because there was no other woman in the ashram who had shown such dedication to a course of study. In addition, he knew she would support herself and also collect funds for the ashram while abroad. Athavale emphasized the fact that far fewer Indian women than men went on this type of voyage to study abroad. On the other hand, she reasoned that the foreigner "has power because of a superior knowledge, social reform and social organization."[18] It was her duty, she says, to compare such social issues and to study the various institutions created abroad for women's education, while learning English. This, and her conviction that she could continue to collect funds for the institute, inspired her to carry out her plan. "But about this I told no one," she writes.[19] She revises her reasons for learning English, and these come intertwined with fresh incentives for going abroad. She recalls telling people that she was simply interested in learning English, although she informs her reader (over a decade later) that she secretly planned to collect funds for the institute. But later, when recalling her actual years in the United States, she would maintain that her overriding ambition was to learn about the family structure there.

A reference to Avadi Bhide is appropriate here. Bhide had declared that she would have liked to travel abroad, because that would have helped her learn and grow intellectually. What's more, Avadi was of the same age cohort as Athavale, and had she lived would have had similar opportunities. But in the 1880s, Avadi knew that she could not actually travel abroad; she knew herself to be caught in the shadow of widowhood, illness, and paternal support. Athavale's ability to travel independently further establishes Karve's unusual authority and her attainment of a professional role through the institute.

Karve decided that Athavale should arrive in the United States in the company of Professor Dharmanand Kosambi, who, along with his son and daughter, was leaving for Harvard University to teach Pali. Kosambi had lived in the United States, so he advised Parvatibai on the articles she would need during the voyage and through her stay abroad. She took with her "four Gujarati silk saris, seven sari blouses, one overcoat, a night gown, six cotton petticoats and two pairs of shoes." The voyage took them via Singapore and Tokyo, ending in San Francisco.[20] They made several stops along the way, and Athavale recalls the delight with which she viewed the Japan Women's University when they stopped in Tokyo. But otherwise, the trip proved to be excruciating. She was baffled by every detail: the bathing and sleeping arrangements, her first experience with wearing closed shoes, and the insurmountable problems eating. Athavale was a Konkanastha Brahman and thus a vegetarian. While some of the Indian families on board the ship shared their food with her, she was usually limited to bread, butter, and milk. She soon fell terribly ill and, in fact, by the time they reached San Francisco, she was unable to travel any further. According to the initial plan, Athavale was to accompany the Kosambi family to Boston, where she would earn her keep by cooking and cleaning for them while attending evening classes to learn English. But Kosambi had to leave immediately for the East Coast and could not wait for the infirm Athavale any longer. He entrusted her to the people at the local YWCA, requesting that they send Athavale back to India if her health did not improve, or send her to Boston once she recovered. And so, exhausted and invalid, Parvatibai Athavale was suddenly entirely alone in a foreign country, where she spoke but a few words of the language and ate very little of the food. Eventually, however, she conquered her sickness and the situation.

The majority of her experiences in the United States revolved around her constant struggle to learn the language she could not speak, and without which she was severely socially challenged. She moved from home to home, working as a domestic cleaner, trying to learn English and earn some money. Her English, she recalls, was very poor and, although she could understand a little, she could not speak any. Even the little she understood depended on how slowly people spoke to her, which was obviously out of her control. As a result, many interactions confused or alarmed her. One of the first places Athavale worked was the "Missionary Home of Peace" outside San Francisco. It turned out that the superintendent of the home had worked in India and so proceeded to question Athavale closely on the missionary activities in Ahmednagar, as well as on Pandita Ramabai's Sharada Sadan in Khedgaon. Stating that "earlier Jesus sent Ramabai here to study and so has sent you," this woman set Parvatibai to cleaning floors and carpets, washing plates, and cleaning windows. Here she was often approached by other missionaries, who would try to talk to her about Christianity, saying that "unless you accept Christianity neither you nor your country can be saved."[21] Athavale recalls very clearly being read as Indian, heathen, and in need of saving: constructed as text and emptied of volition. But she astutely turned the situation around to her advantage, replying that "if you teach me English then I can compare your religion to mine through study and [then] the religion I like, I shall accept."[22] This did, indeed, prove successful. One of the women in the home began teaching her to read the Bible.[23] Athavale remembers how rudimentary her English reading skills were at the time, and how pleased she was to finally be pursuing the goal she had in mind.

Soon, however, she began to worry about the future. The company of retired missionaries and their constant proselytizing gave her "no peace," and within ten days of being in the home, she began to worry that she would never be able to leave. She felt trapped in the Missionary Home of Peace and reiterates in her memoirs that no matter how desperate her situation, she would never consider changing her religion. Such a resolute reframing of caste-as-Hinduism-as-Indian culture was common among those who traveled abroad at the time: Anandibai Joshi, too, underwent a similar experience, as did Mohandas Gandhi. Athavale contacted the Young India Organisation and, through the assistance of three young Maharashtrian men at the University of California, Berkeley, was finally able to leave the missionary home. Her gratitude for these young students was unbounded; they had "saved her" from the missionaries. For that reason, to her they were the very "incarnations of Brahma, Vishnu and Shiva."[24]

Athavale moved in with these young men and fell into a markedly feminized and domesticated pattern, cooking and cleaning for them at home while they worked in their various offices and laboratories.²⁵ Sharply returned to gender, via her own assessment of their Hindu male power, she was again placed in the role of the Indian woman. And again, she grew restless. She soon decided to leave for the East Coast and, with the assistance of an unnamed Maharashtrian gentleman in New York State, she purchased a train ticket to Schenectady, New York. The journey took six days and she had to change trains twice. Athavale recalls her trepidation at the start and her continuing discomfort during the journey. Not only was she in a strange country with unfamiliar customs, but her problems were severely compounded by her ignorance of English. Furthermore, because of the prohibitive price of food and her vegetarian requirements, she was forced to subsist on a meager ration of bread and peanuts. And yet she was determined to complete her voyage. Chicago was the first stop. She got off the train, approached someone, and said, "I am Indian. I have no language. Will you help me to change the car?"²⁶ That is how Parvatibai Athavale managed to reach Schenectady.

There she worked in a series of homes as a live-in maid, stating that this secured one of her objectives, to become acquainted with "American families." But she changed jobs incessantly, moving from town to town in search of employment that would allow her to support herself and meet the goals that she had brought with her to the United States. Her difficulties were undoubtedly compounded by the arbitrary, unprotected, and illegal nature of her situation and the work she was performing. As she recalls, it was while working for a family in Schenectady that a young Bengali man discovered her "slavery." He learned that Athavale had been cleaning the houses of local families and confronted her rather brusquely about it. Curiously enough, Athavale does not mention the language they conversed in; it almost certainly could not have been Bengali or Marathi.²⁷ In her memory of that fraught interaction, the nation smoothly superseded the region for all concerned. The gentleman was horrified to hear that she—a "high caste Brahman"—had been working as a servant for "foreigners." Berating her for her actions, he exclaimed that Karve's "mistake" reflected badly on the national pride of all Indians and insisted that she leave the United States immediately and return to India. Toward this end, he brought her to New York. Just before she was to board the steamer for India, however, some other Indian men intervened and decided that there was no harm in her continuing with her work and efforts to learn English; her ticket was canceled and she stayed in the United States.

"I AM AN INDIAN. I HAVE NO LANGUAGE"

The incident is entirely perplexing. The first gentleman exhibited a paternalism even greater than that of the students in Berkeley. The others, though supportive of Athavale, also had greater power in defining her plans than she herself did. Although Athavale claims to have had her own opinions on the matter, she kept them to herself, appearing at the actual moment to have concurred with the actions of the men in all these situations. It is only in her memoirs that she voices her critique. The "patriotism" expressed by this Bengali man was "false," but she then explains that she did not want to argue with a fellow Indian in front of foreigners. So she agreed to his plans. Her ambition and independence seem to have instantly and inexplicably crumbled in the face of the power exerted by these various people and an imagined audience of invested "foreigners" (by which she means non-Indians). Here, one can no more lose sight of G. M. Chiplunkar's role in editing her memoirs—hence, in literally shaping her memories—than one can ignore the scripted ease with which her passivity, silence, and consent sealed her compliance with upper-caste male entitlement amplified as nationalism.

After reaching New York City, Athavale began to work in the home of Ms. O'Reilly, an Irish woman. O'Reilly was a committed nationalist whose support for Irish independence was so fierce that Athavale found herself galvanized into working for the cause of the ashram. Recalling this brave and courageous woman, Athavale stated that the cause of Irish nationalism was obviously blessed, for "people who had such women were bound to get independence."[28] Athavale started attending night classes to learn English. Her contacts in the city were proving useful: she was asked to speak at the International Workers' Conference of 1919 that was to be held in Washington, D.C. This was one of the more important postwar conferences, drawing representatives from several countries including India. Athavale was to represent women workers from India. The representatives were asked to write and then read their speeches in their native languages and then have an interpreter read out English translations.

Athavale's knowledge of English must have improved considerably by this point, for she recalls that she wrote her speech in both English and Marathi. But at the very last minute, the conference organizers canceled the presentations by the Irish and Indian delegations. She makes no mention of this being deliberately anti-Indian (or Irish). She seemed satisfied simply to have been listed as a delegate at the conference. Athavale returned to New York and began to live and work with Ms. O'Reilly, who bought her an English primer and had her mother teach English to Parvatibai. This is the last time that we hear anything about Athavale's desire to learn English. Parvatibai writes with great admiration for Ms. O'Reilly's political views, as well as her unbounded energy and determination. O'Reilly helped her address several influential gatherings, which allowed her to spread the word about Karve's ashram and to collect money for the cause.

Athavale finally left the United States for India on April 20, 1920. There is no reference at this point in her memoirs as to whether her desire to learn English, supposedly her primary reason for traveling around the world, had been realized. She stopped in London and Paris and continued to try to publicize the ashram. While in Paris, she attended a gathering addressed by Rabindranath Tagore. Here Tagore lashed out against the mounting urge among his countrymen to learn English and the concomitant neglect of Indian languages that resulted. Indian languages, said Tagore, were like sisters to one another. They were being devastated by the encroaching power of the English language.[29] Tagore's words reveal the upper-caste nationalist's conviction in the essential familial connection between otherwise disparate subcontinental regions. Her memory of Tagore's speech suggests the sedimentation of a wider, pan-Indian identity among the new bicultural and globally mobile nationalist elite. It was a transregional identity that relied on hetero-symbolic logic—an indigenous versus foreign binary articulated through the symbolism of the "vernaculars" as feminine and violated versus "English" as the aggressor. Tagore's nationalist perspective occluded the role of caste difference within the history of the vernacular and English, the power of caste in fueling Indian nationalism, and the social value accrued by English over two hundred years. At the same time, the reach of such opinions, which cast English as colonizing and foreign, and the vernacular as vulnerable and indigenous, help sensitize us to Athavale's predicament, her thwarted struggles to learn English, her turn from a once single-minded desire to master the language. How would she, who embodied the sartorial and sexual strictures of the Brahman caste, corroborate the Indian nationalist man's investment in rendering the heteronormative-caste contract as transparent?[30]

Athavale returned to Bombay on July 15, 1920, after which she relates very few incidents in her life. She does note, however, that her lengthy travels abroad and interaction with people of other cultures had equipped her to discuss issues related to marriage, family values, women's education, and the social mores of "Western" nations. Most crucially, both she and Karve seemed to believe that she knew no English, or, as Karve put it in his memoir, the little that she had learned was soon and rapidly forgotten for want of any practice.[31] Athavale's discourses on social issues coalesced immediately around the issues of marriage and desirable femininity. "Women are the future mothers of the nation," she stated emphatically, and hence the education they received must prepare them for this eventuality.[32]

The significant point here is the emergence of the tone of expertise. Connecting the non-differentiated curriculum in Western nations with what she perceived as constituting a decline in family values, Athavale declared that Indian educators and parents should be made aware of those mistakes and instead educate Indian women to strengthen their utility and authority within the household. Chiplunkar's beliefs possibly spur the change in her tone, no longer wavering or uncertain; here Athavale is authoritative and sure of herself. Her views on marriage were predictably shaped by similar beliefs in the different, but complementary, nature of masculine and feminine realms. Resonant with the beliefs of other nationalists, Athavale posed female sexuality as fixed, subservient to masculine power, and entirely subsumed to the family, the home, and thus to the nation. For this reason, educational institutions should educate girls to be "good natured, patriotic and cultured."[33] She had developed a deep regard for the socially and sexually companionate marriages she had observed while abroad, in which, she observed, the husband and wife consciously strove to maintain their partner's attraction and interest through the years of marriage. With that, Athavale transitions to a discussion of the dangers of female emancipation. Cautioning women that escaping servitude from men should not mean that they now accept the subjugation of jobs, Athavale stressed that "female emancipation" necessitated a clash with men and an unnatural adoption of masculine ways.

Her appreciation of companionate marriage remained locked within liberalism's own binaries of "India" and "the West." Athavale's discourse prominently evidences the successful amalgamation of liberal feminism with the upper-caste logic of the Hindu nation—by celebrating the conjugal bond. Significantly, her assessment of gender equality, companionate relations in the West, and the purpose of female education (the inculcation of modesty) spans a number of chapters at the end of her book. Her exposition on gender and conjugal matters stands in stark contrast to an earlier, hesitant style. Moreover, her observations contrast with another studied silence: she never again mentioned her earlier, once life-altering desire to learn English, other than to inform her reader that she had not been successful in her quest. It had once seemed entirely understandable to her that she would want to learn English so acutely that she would take up residence in Bombay on her own, study in schools with girls some twenty years younger than her, and then leave India for the United States in pursuit of this goal. Yet twenty years later, the very mention of English in her life seemed irrelevant or peculiar. Her desire to learn English unraveled in the face of her own textuality: her travels took her deeper into the confusing performativity of Indian womanhood and the Indian nation. Her voyages reinforced her experience of the power of gender, specifically of upper-caste widowhood in determining caste and nation. The only way to skirt the complex of meanings, heightened in transregional and transnational contexts, was to part ways with the symbolic power of English: Athavale reinterprets her knowledge of English. The self-assessment is intriguing, for she had clearly studied a good deal of English over her lifetime. Furthermore, she wrote her speech for the International Labor Conference in English and had traveled and lived in an English-speaking culture for two years, without the helpful insulation of a family or husband.

The pursuit of English took Athavale further away from a comfort zone of kin and a caste network. But in the process, it amplified her cultural meaning as an "Indian woman," even as it highlighted the specificity of her widowhood. The English language was no formal, linguistic convention. Athavale's "failure" to remember the English she had learned and Karve's concurrence with this assessment does not speak to anticolonial scripts or to the separation of English from the native, the material from the spiritual. English was integral to the hierarchies of sexuality and caste. The meaningful ballast provided by the Brahman widow for the wife/prostitute binary of national-caste reproduction required that she remain an outsider, but a respectful observer, of the hetero-conjugal contract. Neither the proper wife depicted by Ramabai Ranade nor the woman-turned-prostitute via English so feared in *Taruni Shikshan Natika*, Athavale and her intelligibility in the gender logic of the Indian nation required that she concede to and then perform her alienation from national-caste reproduction. She remains outside English: an Indian but with "no language."

Athavale's early desire for English animated her critical appraisal of caste, gender, and liberalism. But her pursuit of the language propelled her into an arbitrary and bewildering journey through the symbolic registers of widowhood, class, and diasporic patriarchal desire for the "Indian woman." While her initial pursuit of the language as an object of study permitted her to travel abroad and live a somewhat independent life, as it had for Pandita Ramabai some forty years earlier, the experiences constantly returned her to native patriarchy, specifically heightened as diasporic patriarchy. In the course of her many travels, whatever syntax, signs, or sentences she had acquired in her pursuit of English were rendered indistinguishable, untranslatable for her, as she was engulfed by the reductive logic of the Hindu caste nation.

The declaration on her inability to remember English poses the need to revisit the self-presentation of other subjects discussed in this book, and to probe the connection between English and the production of gender. Athavale's studied failure emerged within an entire complex of immediate and long-term developments: G. M. Chiplunkar's editorial eye, the heightened nationalism produced in the wake of Katherine Mayo's "exposé" on Indian gender relations, her sensitivity to her widowed and middle-age appearance, and her awareness of her Indian and female identity in the face of Western categories of identification and Hindu-diasporic heteropatriarchy. Destabilizing any easy "relationship between the normative and the psychic,"[34] Athavale simultaneously reveals the vast symbolic and epistemic edifice for English, as well as its performative and disciplinary nature—and she reveals this at the site where the fabrication of sexual difference becomes national culture. Unlike Ramabai Ranade, Nikambe's Ramabai, or Dosebai Jessawalla, Athavale as a widow was required to embody the logic of the lifelong conjugal contract while performing her ostracism from it. Her semblance to the child widow Avadi Bhide is also striking. Necessary supplements to the wife/prostitute binary, they were of the same age. While Avadi's "possession" of English was recorded through her performance of virtuous suffering and longing for conjugality and reproduction, ultimately, her acquisition of English was celebrated because of her death. In other words, both Brahman widows failed to master "English" in their lifetimes. Athavale's unease over performing her knowledge of English suggests her inability to reject upper-caste Maharashtrian injunctions on widowhood or to gain access to the conjugal bedroom—the heterosexual companionate world in which English had been domesticated. Her story, therefore, takes us to an appreciation of contingency, how the social life of English was forged by gender. English cannot transcend the sociocultural histories of India; languages do not travel as linguistic forms. For Athavale and for Avadi, English did not produce the bicultural authority so adroitly crafted by Dosebai Jessawalla, M. G. Ranade, and Shevantibai Nikambe. But all women determine that Indian English is a critical effect of native regimes of sexuality; in its convergence with history, it becomes indistinguishable from the normative woman.

The Brahman widow domesticates English. But she does so not by learning it, but by proving herself incapable of mastering it. The symbolic authority of "English" lay in its capacity to influence the chain of signifiers that shaped the relationship between the normative "woman" as the locus for gender difference and the upper-caste Hindu nation. "English" and "woman" were historically produced, unstable signs that had to be brought into tendentious conversation with one another, encoding new forms of cultural consensus on national identity, caste, and sexuality. Both English and sexual difference were meaningless out of context; the Brahman widow's pursuit of English had to end with a parting of ways. The diligent student's failure to imbibe English corroborates its tremendous, phallogocentric power. This book has tracked twists in the relationship between English and gender and demonstrated how English was domesticated by the caste and gender regimes of modern India. The power of English endured, although in a native guise, and it was successfully redeployed to naturalize the turn toward heterosexual contracts and to silence battles over caste. By attributing new, gendered meanings and forms of power to "English," a range of British Indian men and women shaped the reach and location of English in modern India, limiting the language through the caste-specific logic of Indian conjugal modernities. It was, in other words, by shaping English studies to the requirements of "Indian" womanhood that Indians domesticated English and rendered it an Indian language.

SALAAMS

Research for this project was funded through an International Dissertation Research Fellowship from the Social Science Research Council and a junior long-term fellowship from the American Institute of Indian Studies. Writing support was made possible by the Andrew Mellon Dissertation Award of the Department of History, the Women's Studies Dissertation Writing Fellowship, and a Chimicles fellowship for the teaching of writing, all at the University of Pennsylvania. The project itself was first conceived under the supervision of David Ludden and Sumathi Ramaswamy. Between David's talent for identifying the "big picture" and Sumathi's intricate renditions, I was indeed well schooled. Thanks too to Lynn Lees, and to Web Keane's mind-altering class on Language and Culture. A wide community of excellent people in Ithaca, Philly, and South Hadley provided great ideas and fabulous times: Luther Adams, Kathleen Brown, Maya Capur, Brian Caton, Sasha Constanza Chock, Aiden Downey, Mandakini Dubey, Jude Fernando, Shelley Feldman, Geraldine Forbes, Khalid Hadeed, Eugenia Herbert, Sukanya Kulkarni, Ahmet Kuyas, Morana Lasic, Ritty Lukose, Abigail McGowan, Kalyani Menon, Mindy Peden, Indira Peterson, Ian Petrie, Gabriela Ramos, Yanna Yannakakis.

In Bombay, where the project really began to take shape, I was especially fortunate to meet and work with Mridula Ramanna. I will always recall with pleasure my conversations with J. V. Naik, Aroon Tikekar, Prabha Ganorkar, and Vasant Dahake on all aspects of western Indian history and literature. The librarians and staff at the Mumbai Marathi Granthasangrahalaya, the Maharashtra State Archives, and the Bombay University Library were superbly knowledgeable: I especially thank Mrs. Athaleye and Mrs. Tilaka Joseph for their guidance. In Poona, Pushpa Wagle welcomed me into her home and sorted out my research problems; additionally, I benefited from spirited conversations with Ram Bapat, Mary E. John, Vinaya Kharpedkar, and Lata and Sudha Lad. My stay in

London was enriched by Catherine Hall, Peter Morey, Rosalind O'Hanlon, Avrill Powell, and Amina Yaqin,

My first job, at the University of Illinois, Urbana-Champaign, introduced me to a brilliant world of interdisciplinary argumentation and intellectual debate. Here I have accrued debts too numerous to list. Antoinette Burton modeled a passion for innovative historical writing that infused this work and the early years of my professional development. Every aspect of my work life was smoothed and every possible load lightened by Tom Bedwell's loving professionalism. The Humanities Research Board, the Gender and Women's Studies Program, the History Department, and the Illinois Program for Research in the Humanities provided course relief and research assistance. Terri Barnes, Marilyn Booth, Chris D'Arpa, Tulsi Dharmarajan, Mark Diaz, Indranil Dutta, Ezekiel Flannery, Darakhshan Khan, Jaya Kolisetty, Trisch Loughran, Deepti Misri, Lucy Moynihan, Dana Rabin, Junaid Rana, Ra Ravishankar, David Roediger, Siobhan Somerville, Shivali Tukdeo: thanks to one and all. Along the way I have had the friendship of some magnificent folk, Ayaz Ahmed, Shehla Arif, Nikhil Aziz, Urvashi Buttalia, Rahee Dahake, Sonali Gulati, Anne Hugon, Shakti Jaising, Roshni Jayakrishnan, Punit Kohli, Viswas Kulkarni, Judi McCray, Catherine Marro, Mohamed Mehdi, Sahar Shafqat, Fasih Uddin Toor. Deep gratitude to Uma Chakravarti, who welcomed me into her home over a decade ago and then went on to read every draft and energetically answer every query on caste, on gender, and, over the years, on life itself.

New colleagues and some superb students at Washington University in St. Louis have supported and encouraged the book as I finalized it for publication. Special thanks to the International and Area Studies Program, Tim Parsons and Priscilla Stone for crucial assistance at a late moment. In addition, thanks for guidance and friendship to Andrea Friedman, Hillel Kieval, Sowande' Mustakeem, Sheryl Peltz, and Margaret Williams. Small portions of chapters 2, 3, 4, and 5 appeared in "Gendering English: Gender, Sexuality and the Language of Desire in Modern India 1850–1940," *Gender and History* 19, no. 2 (August 2007), 284–304. Portions of chapters 3, 6, and 7 appeared in "Mimicry, Masculinity and the Mystique of Indian English: Western India 1870–1900," *Journal of Asian Studies* 68, no. 1 (February 2009), 199–225. My thanks to both journals and to numerous anonymous readers for shaping my ideas and arguments. Miriam Angress at Duke University Press stood by me as I struggled through the travails of dissertation-to-book, Anitra Grisales stepped in at a formative stage; hers is indeed the magic touch. Four anonymous readers grappled tirelessly with this book, providing me with a wealth of ideas from which to claim as my own; Eric Schramm and Fred Kameny worked out the final kinks.

Salaams, and all my love, to the unflinching constants who map and materialize the very contours of my life: Saadia Toor, Yasser Toor, my brothers Ambarish and Amitabh, and Jean Allman. From an early age, my parents Shailaja and Ramesh Chandra showed me why it matters to work from the heart and still do a really good job. With her inimitable sense of humor and contagious enthusiasm for life, my mother Shailaja is the friend and cheerleader who holds it all together. All that and more to my grandmother, Lilla Wagle Dhume. Ai helped me with translations, widened my knowledge of nineteenth-century western India with her stories, and kept me committed to completing the project. My first and most inspiring teacher, she made English and history come alive for me, as she must have done for hundreds of her students in Bombay and Delhi. Her influence on my life has been incomparable. It is immensely satisfying, though not remotely enough, to dedicate this work to her.

NOTES

CHAPTER 1: LEARNING GENDER, KNOWING ENGLISH

1. Nagarkar, *Ravan and Eddie*, 180. Nagarkar is known for his Marathi-language script and fiction writing, but his introduction indicates that he wrote this particular novel in English.
2. The term "native" was used by the British and Europeans in India to indicate all inhabitants of the subcontinent. It was drenched in disparaging overtones, but, as is evident from later chapters, educated Indians chose to use the term to designate themselves. For instance, the Alexandra Native Girls' English Institution, inaugurated in the nineteenth century by natives, only dropped the term from its name in the 1920s.
3. Butler, *Gender Trouble*, 173.
4. Such an assessment of the way that things accrue social and cultural meaning through historically shaped social relationships is laid out in the wonderful collection of essays edited by Appadurai, *The Social Life of Things*.
5. Volosinov's assertion that "language acquires life and historically evolves precisely in concrete verbal communication, and not in the abstract linguistic system of language forms, nor in the individual psyche of speakers" is entirely relevant here, although it is vital to recognize that he was separating spoken acts from literary and textual ones. The distinction between the spoken and the literary is not as evident in the sources I approach here, although his point remains relevant to my interest in culling the "social life" of English. Volosinov *Marxism and the Philosophy of Language*, 58.
6. Especially helpful in directing my study, Nikolas Rose asks us to "question the whole tyranny of 'language' or communication or meaning that has been invoked by the social knowledges for so long in the course of their claims to be distinguished from the natural sciences . . . [to] *focus not on what language means but on what it does.*" Rose, *Inventing Our Selves*, 178 (my emphasis).
7. Scholars historicizing a range of cultural products, from "science" to "happiness," have employed a similar methodology. In *Another Reason*, Gyan Prakash argues that "science means not only what scientists did but also what science

stood for, the dazzling range of meanings and functions it represented" (7). In her study of happiness and the manner by which feelings can be attributed to objects, Sara Ahmed tracks "the word, asking what histories are evoked by the mobility of this word. . . . If I am following the word happiness, then I go where it goes. I thus do not go where the word happiness does not go." Ahmed, *The Promise of Happiness*, 14.

8. Two excellent edited collections, Sunder Rajan's *The Lie of the Land*, and Svati Joshi's *Rethinking English*, study the shaping of English studies in India and place it in historical perspective. Their focus is primarily on literary and curricular changes at the level of university education from the colonial to the contemporary period.

9. My reading of English is deeply indebted to Lauren Berlant's call to approach the "object of desire" as a "cluster of promises we want someone or something to make possible for us. . . . [These could be] embedded in a person, a thing, an institution, a text. . . . [Such a study might enable us to appreciate] what's incoherent or enigmatic in our attachments, not as confirmation of our irrationality but as an explanation for our sense of our endurance in the object." Berlant, *Cruel Optimism*, 33.

10. My study of the way discourses of sexuality direct the power of language builds upon Sumathi Ramaswamy's excavation of the gendered symbolism at the heart of the Tamil language. She elegantly elucidates the "structures of sentiment" that transformed the modern Tamil language into a multivalent repository of spiritual, filial, and erotic desire. Ramaswamy, *Passions of Tongue*, 117. For the English eighteenth century, Laura Runge discusses the vastly productive, symbolic role of sexual difference. She demonstrates how "the language of gender enters the critical discussion of the Restoration and eighteenth century in numerous places, in metaphor or allegory, in models of hierarchy. . . . Gender provides an everyday vocabulary through which the critic constructs literary distinctions." Runge, *Gender and Language in British Literary Criticism, 1660–1790*, 3.

11. My use of the term phallogocentric recognizes post-Lacanian, feminist-deconstructivist assertions that the "phallus" indicates the symbolic power of patriarchy in orienting the subject's access to language, cultural knowledge, and power. The term suggests the power to control gender, to order the subject's relationship to the symbolic (the realm of social conventions expressed through representations), and to orient desire and affect. Not merely phallic or phallocentric, phallogocentric power thrives on binary distinctions.

12. David, "Beginnings of the Renaissance Movement in Maharashtra," 15–26; Ramanna, *English Education and Social Change in Bombay City*; Haynes, *Rhetoric and Ritual in Colonial India*.

13. Viswanathan, *Masks of Conquest*.

14. In very different ways, scholars such as Srinivas Aravamudan and Priya Joshi have illuminated the "native" history of English. Aravamudan explores the transnational uses of the language among "cosmopolitan" Indians. Joshi's interest is with reading practices in historical perspective; she accomplishes this through a study of the English novel in India. See, respectively, *Guru English* and *In Another Country*.
15. Judith Butler describes performativity as "that reiterative power of discourse to produce the phenomena that it regulates and constrains" *Bodies That Matter*, 2. The stylized repetition of acts creates the illusion of gender coherence; a study of performativity thus establishes that gender is always in the making and that there is no original sexual identity, only a constantly repeated imitation of the idea of the original.
16. As Sara Salih has explained, Derrida asserted that "signs can be transplanted into unforeseen contexts and cited in unexpected ways, an appropriation and relocation that he calls citational grafting." Salih, "On Judith Butler and Performativity," 91.
17. According to Spivak, the "subject effect . . . [elicits how] that which seems to operate as a subject may be part of an immense, discontinuous network . . . knottings and configurations . . . [that] produce the effect of an operating subject." Spivak, "Subaltern Studies: Deconstructing Historiography," 12–13.
18. Joan Scott's *Politics of the Veil* proposes a similar conception of the secular as the willed transparency of majority culture. Recent studies have corroborated that caste has staged alliances with secular discourses and repressed the visibility of religious rituals. For examples, see Lukose, *Liberalization's Children*; Slate, "Translating Race and Caste"; Gupta, *Interrogating Caste*. Most pertinent to my argument, Kamala Visweswaran has recently exposed the relationship between the putatively secular disciplines of anthropology and their reliance on a reductive notion of the "religious" in producing "caste." Visweswaran, *Un/Common Cultures*. While maintaining the definition of secular as nonreligious, Svati Joshi has suggested the role that English played in the secularization of caste, noting that the "colonial decision to introduce English literary studies derived partly from the policy of religious neutrality, or using English as a more secular substitute for religion." Joshi, *Rethinking English*, 13.
19. Macaulay served on the Supreme Council for the governor general and was specifically charged with legislative matters. Benson, "The British Debate over the Medium of Instruction in Indian Education," 1–12.
20. Sharp, *Selections from Educational Records, Part I (1781–1839)*, 107–17.
21. Ania Loomba points out that one of the most significant features of Macaulay's "Minute" was that he conflated Oriental scripture, literature, and language. Despite that, he was able-minded enough to distinguish between "the poetry of Milton, the metaphysics of Locke, and the physics of Newton." The

inability to explicate the constituent details of "Oriental" productions was itself essential to crafting the hierarchy between the "secular, refined, and identifiable works of Europe, versus the inexplicability of Eastern learning." This hierarchy goes to the heart of the history of "English education" in nineteenth-century British India. Loomba, *Colonialism/Postcolonialism*, 75.

22. Metcalf, *Ideologies of the Raj*.
23. Elphinstone, "Minute on Education"; Trevelyan, *On the Education of the People of India*; Mayhew, *Education of India*.
24. The prescription of the Parliamentary Act of 1813 was that a sum of one lakh of rupees be set apart "for the revival and promotion of literature and the encouragement of the learned natives of India, and for the introduction and promotion of a knowledge of sciences among the inhabitants of the British territories." This declaration was interpreted by colonial officials to mean that the East India Company would encourage the learning of native languages and knowledge. Macaulay was arguing against this Parliamentary Act of 1813 and, with that, giving voice to convictions shaped by preceding schooling experiments. As successive reports from the Director of Public Instruction attested, native languages themselves contained no literary content, and hence no ability to train the morality and integrity of these proposed intermediaries. For the primary debates see Director of Public Instruction, *Report of the Board of Education for the years 1847 and 1848*. For further reflection, see Chatterji, "Landmarks in Official Educational Policy"; Crook, ed., *The Transmission of Knowledge in South Asia*; Frykenburg, "Modern Education in South India, 1784–1854"; and S. G. Ghosh, "Bentinck, Macaulay and the Introduction of English Education in India."
25. Ganachari, "Imperialist Appropriation and Disciplining the Indian Mind."
26. Farooqui, *Opium City*.
27. Ramanna, "Indian Financial Support of Western Education," 105–22, offers a detailed account of the Anglo-vernacular controversy over Western education and language, specifically in Bombay. See also Fonseca, *An Analysis of the Relationship between the Political System and Education*.
28. David, "Beginnings of the Renaissance Movement in Maharashtra," 15–26; Hasan, *Knowledge, Power and Politics*.
29. Chakravarti, *Rewriting History*.
30. The four graduates were M. G. Ranade, Bal Mangesh Wagle, R. G. Bhandarkar, and V. A. Modak; as the following chapters elaborate, all were to play a vital role in determining the boundaries of English education. Tikekar, *The Cloister's Pale*.
31. Lal, *Domesticity and Power in the Early Mughal World*.
32. Kumar, *The History of Doing*; Sangari and Vaid, *Recasting Women*.

33. My use of gender as a generative force in history is indebted to Joan Scott's insistence that studies of gender elicit the symbolic and material organization of power in society. Gender for me is not an automatic reference to bodies or social roles. Rather, the study of gender must incorporate an appreciation for symbolic power and strive to reveal how the *knowledge* of sex and sexual difference is organized, in other words, to "historicize the ways that sex and sex difference have been conceived." Scott, AHR *Forum*, 1422–29. Put simply, my interest lies with tracking the generative power of gender.

34. Spodek, "Pluralist Politics in British India." Arguing that the colonies were ultimately secured through the collaboration of the many indigenous social classes that benefited most from the presence of the British Raj, these works approach the English language and its related structures of knowledge as shaping the political vocabulary for a rising intermediary class as it negotiated new, mutually beneficial relationships with the colonial government. Furthermore, the language is portrayed as cutting across ethnic and regional divides so as to permit greater collaboration between various sections of the male subcontinental elite. See McLane, *Indian Nationalism and the Early Congress*; Robinson, "Non-European Foundations of European Imperialism: Sketch for a Theory of Collaboration"; and Seal, *The Emergence of Indian Nationalism*. More recently, Douglas Haynes has explored the significatory role of English in his *Rhetoric and Ritual*.

35. Viswanathan, *Masks of Conquest*.

36. Although even in England, and well before colonial education policies had been institutionalized for cultivating the humanism of the other, English literature had been identified as a crucial tool for the training of the senses, emotions, and disposition of women. Rice, *A Lecture on the Importance and Necessity of Rendering the English Language a Peculiar Branch of Female Education*.

37. Viswanathan, *Masks of Conquest*, 2.

38. Ibid., 3.

39. In *Home and Harem*, Inderpal Grewal has established connections between English and transnational mobility over the colonial period, and Priya Joshi's *In Another Country* specifically studies reading practices in historical perspective.

40. Loomba argues that "one of the ideologies underpinning literary education was the assumption that there was an insurmountable cultural gap between those who had 'natural' access to literary culture, and those others who needed to be taught it." Loomba, *Colonialism/Postcolonialism*, 16.

41. Sangari, *Politics of the Possible*. See also her essay "Relating Histories: Definitions of Literacy, Literature, Gender in Nineteenth Century Calcutta and England," in Joshi, *Rethinking English*. Sangari's luminous study has been foundational to my investigation. It examines literary texts as they originated from

within, and then broke with, colonial power, how "literature was launched as a terrain of social history, law making et al., from within a conception of colonial utility." *Relating Histories*, 62. See also Trivedi, *Colonial Transactions*.

42. Gayatri Spivak has noted the alliance between postcolonial studies and literary studies: "One major difference between Subaltern Studies and Postcolonial Studies is that the disciplinary connection of postcolonial studies is to literary criticism rather than history and the social sciences." Spivak, "The New Subaltern: A Silent Interview," 31.

43. Sadana, "Two Tales of a City," 4. Pointing to the limits of the postcolonial understanding of English, Sadana argues instead for the "ability of English to mediate the sensibilities of other Indian languages" and explains how the "politics of language are intimate affairs in modern Indian life" (12). Sadana thus breaks away from the history of colonial texts and instead turns to the social context of modern India. Perhaps for exactly that reason, her work suggests tight affinities between the spoken and textual aspects of English, between its material and affective power in dense multilingual contexts.

44. Anderson, *Imagined Communities*, 90.

45. Viswanathan, "The Beginnings of English Literary Study in British India," 380 (my emphasis).

46. Bhabha, *The Location of Culture*, 87.

47. Seth, *Subject Lessons*, 195.

48. Veena Naregal, *Language Politics, Elites, and the Public Sphere*.

49. It was these very elite Marathi-speaking and writing classes of western India that were most invested in securing the new English education in order to "maintain by new methods the old aims of Brahmanical pre-eminence." Seal, "Imperialism and Nationalism in India."

50. Deshpande, *Creative Pasts*.

51. In reality, as Naregal has argued, those early Marathi works actively flourished in the "shadow of Sanskrit" and adopted a highly Sanskritized idiom. Medieval and early modern Marathi never existed in isolation or evidenced a popular folk tradition to the exclusion of Sanskrit. The transregional transition from Sanskrit to the vernacular attributed to the thirteenth century was not a subaltern process; it actually represented "attempts by local elites to re-articulate their authority in localised idioms." Naregal, *Language Politics, Elites, and the Public Sphere*, 15; see also Pollock, "India in the Vernacular Millennium." For a fascinating prehistory, and especially for his use of "domains of discourse" for language, see Pollock, "The Sanskrit Cosmopolis, 300–1300."

52. G. S. Sardesai, *A New History of the Marathas 1606–1707*. Sardesai further celebrated Shivaji's determined patronage of the Marathi language, although in actuality Marathi only rose to prominence in the last decades of the Peshwa (Brahman) court, in the second half of the eighteenth century.

53. Alam, "The Pursuit of Persian."
54. Gordon, *The Marathas 1600–1818*.
55. Even this Marathi was a "Persianised Brahman dialect . . . [with] a high level of Sanskritisation." Deshpande, *Sociolinguistic Attitudes in India*.
56. As Veena Naregal has argued, this ascendancy of Marathi formed a "pattern of vernacularisation" that was reiterated in the nineteenth century. At this later state, the emergence of a colonial-modern vernacular literate formation was impelled by the desire of ruling elites to re-create high discourses in local idioms, rather than the need of organic intellectuals to reach a popular audience. *Language Politics, Elites, and the Public Sphere*, 15 n. 21.
57. Tikekar, *The Cloister's Pale*.
58. See my discussion of the vernacular backlash against the English education of girls in the schools of the Students' Literary and Scientific Society (chapter 2), where Perry is caricatured as the officiating judge enjoying the sight of the "luckless husband" being castigated by his English-speaking "termagant" wife.
59. Perry, "On the Geographical Distribution of India, and the Feasibility of Introducing English as a Lingua Franca." Perry's linguistic policies are further discussed in Naregal, *Language Politics, Elites, and the Public Sphere*, 47.
60. Cashman, *Myth of the Lokmanya*, 37–38
61. Ibid., 40.
62. Bhatt, *Hindu Nationalism*, 33.
63. From the perspective of a narrow battle between westernization and indigeneity, the two would have disagreed over many subjects, and especially over English education See, for instance, Dobbin, *Urban Leadership in Western India*. But, as I discuss, the apparent divergence only papered over a deeper consensus. They were in complete agreement over the role of woman as primarily reproductive and over the centrality of Brahmanical culture to the definition of Indian culture, as well as in organizing the transfer of English.
64. "Report of School Final Examination," *Mahratta*, June 20, 1909.
65. All languages, including English, were referenced through the feminine pronoun in Marathi.
66. I am leaning on Pierre Bourdieu's notion of the "field," which he develops in *Distinction*. The field would be a relatively autonomous, structured social space where social actors were implicitly cognizant of and played by the rules, used social capital to evaluate their decisions, and communicated with one another on the basis of a shared conviction in inclusion and exclusion.
67. Sangari and Vaid, *Recasting Woman*.
68. Sarkar, *Hindu Wife, Hindu Nation*.
69. Fukazawa, *The Medieval Deccan*.
70. Bayly, *Caste, Society and Politics in India*, 55–56.

71. Chakravarti, *Rewriting History*.
72. Pratibha Ranade, *Stri Prashnanchi Charcha: Ekonisave Shatak* [The debate over the women's question: The nineteenth century].
73. O'Hanlon makes this assertion in her introduction to Shinde, *Stri Purush Tulana*, 13 n. 39. Specifically, she is citing Molesworth's *Dictionary*, 690.
74. O'Hanlon, "Introduction," 29.
75. The Derridean notion of the supplement is "that which conceptually undermines the binary of . . . inside / outside yet is crucial to the conceit of the integrity, autarky, self-sufficiency, and continuity of the dominant term." Quoted by Brown, *Regulating Aversion*, 27.
76. Anagol, *The Emergence of Feminism in India*.
77. Shinde, *Stri Purush Tulana*.
78. Saraswati, *The High Caste Hindu Woman*.
79. Chakravarti, *Rewriting History*. Neither Shinde nor Rakhmabai Sakharam were Brahmans. Pandita Ramabai disowned Brahmanism and converted to Christianity, a move that instantly alienated her from even the more moderate Brahmanical social reformers, such as M. G. Ranade.
80. Ramabai, *Stri Dharma Niti*. For a wider discussion of the content of the text, see Feldhaus, *Images of Women in Maharashtrian Society*, 199.
81. *Bombay Gazette*, September 12, 1882.
82. Kosambi, *Crossing Thresholds*.
83. Grewal, *Home and Harem*.
84. Ramabai did marry, but her husband was from a lower caste. Their marriage signaled a break from the endogamous requirements of caste.
85. Chakravarti, *Rewriting History*.
86. O'Hanlon, *Caste, Conflict and Ideology*.
87. Ibid.
88. Deshpande, *Selected Writings of Jotirao Phule*.
89. Keer, *Mahatma Jotirao Phooley: Father of the Indian Social Revolution*.
90. Naregal, *Language Politics, Elites, and the Public Sphere*, 90 n. 88.
91. O'Hanlon, "Introduction," relates that Tarabai Shinde was associated with Phule; she would have worked alongside him through the Satyashodhak Samaj (The Organisation for the Pursuit of Truth), the progressive, anti-caste organization that he directed and founded in 1873.
92. Omvedt, *Dalit Visions*, 21–23.
93. Keer, *Mahatma Jotirao Phooley*, 24.
94. Quoted in Gail Omvedt, "Why Dalits Want English," *Times of India*, November 9, 2006.
95. Phule, "Ingreji Mawli" [English is our mother, poem # 38], in Mali, *Savitribai Phule, Samagra Vanmaya* [Savitribai Phule, Collected Works].
96. My reading of transgression and positionality is indebted to Peter Stallybrass

and A. White, *The Politics and Poetics of Transgression*. As they argue (201), "Only a challenge to the hierarchy of sites of discourse, which usually comes from groups and classes 'situated' by the dominant in low or marginal positions, carries the promise of politically transformative power."

97. I am relying on Stuart Hall's early work on encoding messages and decoding for the politics of competing social groups here. Hall, "Encoding/Decoding," 128–38.

98. I have benefited from José Muñoz's theory of disidentification, which is "about recycling and rethinking encoded meaning. The process of disidentification scrambles and reconstructs the encoded message of a cultural text in a fashion that both exposes the encoded message's universalizing and exclusionary mechanisms and re-circuits its workings to account for, include, and empower minority identities and identifications." Muñoz, *Disidentifications: Queers of Color and the Performance of Politics*, 31.

99. Ambedkar was a Dalit (the term "Dalit" indicates the position of those considered "untouchable" by the caste system) and a trained legal scholar who went on to chair the committee that drafted independent India's Constitution. According to Anupama Rao, Ambedkar "first used the term [Dalit] in his journal, *Bahishkrit Bharat* (Outcaste India) in 1928, where he characterized being Dalit as the experience of deprivation, marginalization and stigmatization." Rao, *The Caste Question*, 15. The term further swept into wider currency during the 1970s and through the work of the Dalit Panthers. For a wider etymology of the term, see Zelliot, "Introduction" to Moon, *Growing Up Untouchable in India*.

100. Ambedkar, "Caste Class, and Democracy," in *Essential Writings of B. R. Ambedkar*, 146.

101. Ibid., 326.

102. Ambedkar, "Castes in India," in *Essential Writings of B. R. Ambedkar*, 260.

103. Ambedkar's awareness of the restriction over knowledge was forged alongside his keen awareness of the sexual division of labor: "Brahmanism did succeed in making the shudras and the women the servile classes. Shudras the serfs to the three higher classes and the women the serfs to their husbands." Ambedkar, "Revolution and Counter Revolution," cited in Ambedkar, *Essential Writings of B. R. Ambedkar*, 50.

104. Ibid., 260. And further, as he recognized in his *Annihilation of Caste*, caste worked not as "a division of labour; [rather as] a division of labourers." See Omvedt, *Dalit Visions*, 49.

105. It might be evident that I divert from those studies of caste that have focused singularly on public practice and ritual or that have reinscribed "lower"-caste suffering and abjection. Building instead on Uma Chakravarti's trenchant assessment of the intimate histories of western India from a materialist and

anti-caste perspective, my interest lies in the consolidation of majoritarian power. My focus on Brahmanical and Parsi control over the knowledge economy of urban western India thus relies on the feminist documentation of the regionally specific route by which upper-caste patriarchy came to stand in for Indian culture itself. Chakravarti, *Rewriting History*; for Bengal, see Sarkar, *Hindu Wife, Hindu Nation*.

106. Sedgwick, *Between Men*, 86.
107. Najmabadi, "Gender and Secularism of Modernity," 246. In this particular article, Najmabadi tracks the history of the bread and the veil. Significantly for my methodology, she treats the veil as a sign that served as a repository for divergent sexual anxieties.
108. My reference to "queer theory" is shorthand for scholarship that excavates discourses of sexuality so as to destabilize the essentialism of some women studies. My investment lies in troubling the purported distinction between sex and gender, in maintaining that discourses over sex and sexual practices are always contingent and deeply vulnerable to historical pressures.
109. Cathy Cohen defines heteronormativity as the institutions and the assumptions that assume heterosexuality as fixed and inevitable, as "both those localized practices and those centralized institutions that legitimize and privilege heterosexuality and heterosexual relationships as fundamental and 'natural' within society." Cohen, "Punks, Bulldaggers and Welfare Queens," 39. Cohen's focus on institutions of power provides a more concrete direction to what Judith Butler had once argued for as an appreciation of "the regulatory fiction of heterosexual coherence." Butler, *Gender Trouble*, 173.
110. Hennessey, "Queer Theory, Left Politics," 101.
111. Building on Deleuze and Guattari's work on regimes of signs or "assemblages" as they shape subjectification, Rose inverts the focus and asks instead that we treat "language as assemblage [and study] the techniques, authorities, apparatuses" that produce the notion of the self. Rose, *Inventing Ourselves*, 178.
112. Barlow, *The Question of Woman in Chinese Modernity*, 10. As Barlow has argued, the study of gender in colonial modernity provides an important "speculative frame" by which to subvert simplistic distinctions, such as colonial versus anticolonial, modernity and tradition, global and local. Barlow, *Formations of Colonial Modernity in East Asia*, 6. See also Burton, "Introduction" to *Gender, Sexuality and Colonial Modernities*, and Sinha, *Spectres of Mother India*.
113. John and Nair, "Introduction" to *A Question of Silence?*, 1–50, 12.
114. Chatterjee, "The Nationalist Resolution of the Women's Question," 249.
115. The critiques posed by Bengali women from the nineteenth and twentieth centuries to the male fantasies resurrected by Chatterjee have been thoroughly documented by feminist scholars. The examples I discuss through the course of this book are not the only ones that fly in the face of Chatter-

jee's analyses. Contemporaneously—and in Bengal—women adroitly manipulated the categories of social organization to expose collusions between state and native male power. The most obvious work is Rokeya Sakhawat Hussain's satirical "Sultana's Dream," first published in 1905. Extensive research by Mahua Sarkar, *Visible Histories, Disappearing Women*, and by the historian Tanika Sarkar provide important counterevidence to Chatterjee's deterministic analyses.

116. Partha Chatterjee, "The Nation and Its Women," in *The Nation and Its Fragments*, 128.
117. Respectively: Chakravarti, *Rewriting History*; Anagol, *The Emergence of Feminism in India*; Banerji, "Pygmalion Nation," 34–34; and Sinha, *Spectres of Mother India*.
118. Duara, *Sovereignty and Authenticity*.
119. Prakash, *Another Reason*; Seth, *Subject Lessons*; and Chakrabarty, *Provincializing Europe*.
120. For instance, recentering Hindu upper-caste desires in valorizing what he sees as the native critique of liberalism, Dipesh Chakrabarty has argued that "the highest form of personhood [for women] was one constituted by the idea of self-sacrifice, the idea of living for others, not in the spirit of civic virtue that Rousseau would have applauded, but in a spirit of subordination to nonsecular and parochial principle of dharma. The idea . . . was not at all innocent of power, domination and even cruelty but, whatever else it may have been, it was never merely a ruse for staging the secular-historicist project of the citizen subject." Chakrabarty, "The Difference-Deferral of (a) Colonial Modernity," 50–89. It is no coincidence then that the native critique of European universalism so celebrated by these historians revolves around the outpourings of a predictable cast of upper-caste nationalist male characters: Rabindranath Tagore, Nirad C. Choudhury, and Swami Vivekananda and their conjugal companions.
121. *The Nation and Its Fragments*, 131–32.
122. In a trenchant exposé of the theoretical maneuvers of the Subalternist School's assessment of the "woman's question," Himani Bannerjee notes that "these historians cannot disentangle their own thesis of successful decolonisation from that of Hindu revivalist nationalism, and are thus forced to '(counter) narrate' their own position on the nation through a patriarchal imaginary." Banerji, *Pygmalion Nation*, 64. See also Visweswaran, *Fiction of Feminist Ethnography*.
123. Gupta, *Sexuality, Obscenity, Community*, 29.
124. Ratna Kapur, *Erotic Justice*, 31. Kapur also concurs that "neither postcolonial theory nor subaltern scholarship has brought an adequate account of gender or sexuality to its position" (23).

125. Ibid., 35.
126. I would reiterate Julian Carter's insight on the "theory wars" of the 1990s. Carter states that the most unfortunate fallout of the so-called linguistic turn has been a consistent, deepening divide between the discipline of history and studies of sexuality, so much so that today "few Ph.D. candidates in history are being trained to use the kind of theoretical and interpretative tools that scholars in interdisciplinary sexuality studies find most useful." See Carter, *The Heart of Whiteness*, 170 n. 62. This is particularly so in the case of South Asian history wherein sexuality is often described through the socio-historicist mode, covering the long history of "same-sex" desire, without attention to power, the manufacture of desire, or the contestation over social categories. Far too often is the "homosexual" celebrated and then fixed within already familiar historical narratives and within the very same sex / gender binary that scholars of sexuality have long discounted. For a longer elaboration of this critique, see Toor, "The Erotics and Politics of Sexuality," 12.

CHAPTER 2: "THE PRUDENT AND CAUTIOUS ENGRAFTING OF ENGLISH"

1. Elphinstone, "Minute on Education," 2.
2. Sahitya Academy, *The Encyclopedia of Indian Literature*, Vol. 1. According to the entry on awards for Marathi literature (303–5), the Dakshina Prize was controlled by Peshwa families and specifically awarded to Brahmans.
3. Naregal, *Language Politics, Elites, and the Public Sphere*.
4. Records of the American Missionary Society and the Church Missionary Society, as well as texts such as *Kutumbacha Mitra* [Children's friend] and the newspaper *Dnyanodaya*, all record the role of simple, moralizing Christian messages translated into native languages for the use of female students.
5. Reflecting the tightening interconnections between colony and metropole, the term only gained popular usage in Britain after 1818. Mehta, *Liberalism and Empire*, 11.
6. Prachi Deshpande has noted that Elphinstone was educated at the University of Edinburgh in the late eighteenth century and he drew his ideas on human progress through history from the teachings of the Scottish Enlightenment. Human actions were marked on a gradual, evolutionary scale from barbaric to civilized, but ultimately were marked by their "natural" and environmental locations. Elphinstone was a proponent of the Orientalist research into the texts of Hindu antiquity, and very critical of the Utilitarianism—and notion of instrumentalist reform—propagated by James Mill in his *History of India* (1818). However, with Mill he believed in the virtues of "philosophical history," the "urge to provide a narrative of India from ancient to present . . . a comprehensive understanding of its people, their predilections, and their achieve-

ments in the context of the progress of human civilization." Deshpande, *Creative Pasts*, 73–74.
7. Naregal, *Language Politics, Elites, and the Public Sphere*, 89–94.
8. N. Krishnaswamy and Lalitha Krishnaswamy, *The Story of English in India*, 47–51.
9. Ajgaonkar, *The Problem of the Higher Education of Girls in the Bombay Presidency*. J. M. Masselos describes Cursetjee's father as a member of the "quasi aristocracy" of the Parsi commercial class, tracing his efforts within the Parsi Panchayat in the 1820s. The Parsi Panchayat legislated on gender, prohibiting women from participating in Hindu and Muslim festivals; it was both "puritanical as well as revivalist." Masselos, *Towards Nationalism*, 19.
10. *Report of the Alexandra Native Girls' English Institution from the Year 1886 to 1887*.
11. Social histories focusing specifically on the Parsi community are relatively scarce, although any major work on urban social change is by necessity replete with details of Parsi entrepreneurship and enterprise. For example, see Dobbin, *Urban Leadership in Western India*, and Farooqui, *Opium City*. A recent work focusing primarily on the Parsi community of western India is Luhrmann, *The Good Parsi*. Luhrmann argues that the Parsi leadership in the nineteenth century saw itself as the privileged node between the colonial state and native society, hence readily adopting and ritualizing selective aspects of British culture. Especially pertinent to my work is Luhrmann's observation that the later marginalizing of the community as a whole in the politics of modern India led to a marked cultural disillusionment that was reworked as an internal critique of failed masculinity.
12. Jeejeebhoy was the first Indian to be knighted by the British Crown in 1842 and to receive a baronetcy in 1857. Jeejeebhoy was related to Dosebai Jessawalla (discussed in chapter 8). Amar Farooqui has discussed Jeejeebhoy's role in the consolidation of Indian transnational capital. He dominated the opium trade in Bombay city and by 1820 emerged as the leading supplier of opium to the largest opium trading network in China. Farooqui, *Opium City*, 26–28.
13. Ajgaonkar, *The Problem of the Higher Education of Girls*, 44.
14. J. E. D. Bethune (sometimes credited as the progenitor of nonreligious education for Indian women) arrived in India in April 1848 as a legal member of the Governor General's Council. He was appointed as president of the Council of Education in Calcutta (the capital of British India) and was supported by a section of the upper-class Hindu Brahmans in his idea for a girls' school. The Calcutta Female School (unofficially known as "Bethune's School") was inaugurated in May 1849. Cursetjee was specifically inquiring about Bethune's school. For more details on that pedagogic venture, see Bagal, *Women's Education in Eastern India, the First Phase*. According to the records, Bethune re-

sponded to allegations on the possibility of religious conversation by emphasizing that the language of instruction would be the students' own language; in other words, Bethune was aware of the analogy between English and Christianity that some natives were making at the time. Bagal, *Women's Education in Eastern India*.

15. Cursetjee, *A Few Passing Ideas for the Benefit of India and Indians*, 26.
16. In Cursetjee's use, the term "vernacular" denoted the non-English languages of India. Obviously referencing the distinction between Latin and other European languages, the very use of this word implicitly elevated English to the authoritative position of a classical language. Ramaswamy discusses how Tamil devotees rejected the term "vernacular" because it denoted the language of the slaves. Ramaswamy, *Passions of the Tongue*, 57. Cursetjee's project was to elevate English and not Marathi or Gujarati. Cursetjee, *A Few Passing Ideas for the Benefit of India and Indians*, 26.
17. Cursetjee, *A Few Passing Ideas for the Benefit of India and Indians*, 25.
18. Sumit Sarkar and Tanika Sarkar, *Women and Social Reform in Modern India: A Reader*.
19. Pollock, "The Cosmopolitan Vernacular," 6–37.
20. Naregal, *Language Politics, Elites, and the Public Sphere*.
21. I base this on Derrida's notion of citational grafting. Derrida argued that signs can be transplanted into unforeseen contexts and cited in unexpected ways, both through appropriation as well as through relocation. For this reason, signs need not conform to their speaker's or writer's original intentions. Rather than dismiss the grafting for being inaccurate, Derrida encourages the cultural analyst to recognize the instability, even failure, that is inherent in the making of the sign. Derrida, "Signature, Event, Context," 80–111.
22. Sumathi Ramaswamy, *Passions of the Tongue*, 17.
23. In her work on Tamil, Ramaswamy traces the "ideological devices and strategies of persuasion . . . deployed by Tamil's devotees to convince their fellow speakers of the natural and unshakeable bonds between themselves and their language." Ramaswamy, *Passions of the Tongue*, 7.
24. *Oriental Christian Spectator*, 1854, cited in Ramanna, "English Education and Social Change in Bombay City, 1815–1858," 392.
25. Cursetjee Shroff, *A Few Passing Ideas for the Benefit of India and Indians*, 80.
26. Alexandra Native Girls' English Institution (ANGEI), *Alexandra Native Girls' English Institution, Its Origin, Progress, and First Report 1863–64*.
27. Ibid.
28. *Times of India*, April 10, 1863.
29. ANGEI, *Report of the Alexandra Native Girls' English Institution, Read at a Meeting Held on the 10th of March 1865* (1865; my emphasis).
30. Missionary schools and boys' schools had been receiving this form of support

from the government ever since the recommendations of the 1854 Wood's Despatch, which had expressly stated that women's education required greater financial assistance from the government. The system of grants-in-aid was the way that the state could support education without having to be directly involved. Krishnaswamy, *The Story of English in India*, 47–51.

31. Letter from M. Cursetjee, Alexandra Native Girls' English Institution, "Application for a Grants-in-aid in amount of Rs. 40,000 or Rs. 50,000," November 11, 1867, *Education Department File (EDF)* 5 of 1868.
32. Ibid.
33. There were several such community-level boards for the Parsi community that legislated on caste, gender, and social practice. See Dobbin, "The Parsi Panchayat in Bombay City in the Nineteenth Century." Hindu castes also had Panchayats, which competed with one another to legislate on appropriate caste-specific behavior.
34. ANGEI (1876), 1878.
35. Ibid.
36. The reports mention that native men were accompanied by their wives. Bal Mangesh Wagle of the SLSS is recorded as being present with his wife.
37. Here Judith Butler's call to decode the process of being "hailed into gender" guides my attention toward the performative potential of the descriptive statements themselves. Butler has argued that the naming of the infant by sex ("It's a girl!") starts the process by which it is "systematically 'girled' [or] brought into the domain of language and kinship through the interpellation of gender." As they are reiterated through time, the statements serve to fix distinction, emphasize norms, and thus naturalize the "fact" of gender. Repeated, constative statements obscure the cultural codes that define gender and make it appear as though it is always and already fixed. Butler, *Bodies That Matter*, 7.
38. ANGEI, 1876.
39. Ibid.
40. Ibid.
41. ANGEI, 1876, 1877, and 1878.
42. Elphinstone, "Minute on Education," 3.
43. Naregal provides a close history of the Bombay Education Society. See *Language Politics, Elites, and the Public Sphere*, 66–67 nn. 23–24. Comprising in equal numbers European and native officials, the Education Society morphed into the Board of Education, specifically aimed to "diffuse the benefits of national education . . . to endeavour to obtain the co-operation of *influential Natives* in the efforts made by Government to improve the moral condition of the people" (my emphasis). Naregal relates that the native section of the Bombay Committee had an "equal" community-wise representation of Parsees, Hindus, and Muslims. Education Societies such as this were the first of their kind

to be set up in the colonial world and played a crucial role in establishing structures of ideological mediation. Most crucially, "the composition of the Education Society reflected the colonial view of the South Asian social structure . . . and were powerfully reproduced . . . especially in the field of education." *Language Politics, Elites, and the Public Sphere*, 67 n. 25.
44. Elphinstone, "Minute on Education," 20.
45. Naregal, *Language Politics, Elites, and the Public Sphere*, 69.
46. McDonald, "English Education and Social Reform in Late Nineteenth Century Bombay," 453–70.
47. Along with Bhandarkar and Ranade, Bal Mangesh Wagle was one of four students who graduated from Bombay University in its first degree-granting year. Chandavarkar would later be knighted as Sir Chandavarkar and Telang would rise to prominence as Justice Telang, renowned for his reinterpretation of scripture as the basis of Hindu law.
48. Conventionally dated to the territories acquired by the British after the loss of the North American colonies. See, for instance, Strobel, *European Women and the Second British Empire*.
49. For more information on Naoroji's moderate (pro-British, non-violent) brand of Anglicized nationalism, see Goswami, *Producing India*.
50. Students' Literary and Scientific Society (SLSS), *Students Literary and Scientific Society (1848–49 to 1947–48)*, 1950, 5.
51. SLSS Rules and Regulations (Bombay, 1872), 1, 4; SLSS, "Report for 1852" in Proceedings, 1853, 5–6, 24.
52. The report for the society's first meeting tells of the progress made in the Marathi Hindu girls' schools. The girls were taught reading, writing, arithmetic, singing, geography, history, popular science, domestic industry, and morality. In the second class, girls were reading Marathi translations of *Aesop's Fables*, while in the first class they were reading the text *Balamitra* [Children's friend]. In geography, these students had acquired a "general knowledge of the different quarters of the earth, [and could] point out and trace boundaries. They can point out the different countries in Asia, their capital towns, and the principal rivers and mountains; and evince a still more intimate knowledge of the geography of Hindustan." SLSS, *Report of the Students Literary and Scientific Society* (first report, published with the fourth report).
53. Perry, "On the Geographical Distribution of India, and the Feasibility of Introducing English as a Lingua Franca," 289–317.
54. Board of Education, Bombay 1850–51, 5.
55. SLSS, 1950, 10.
56. Ibid.
57. Quoted in the *Proceedings of the Students' Literary and Scientific Society, Bombay. For the Years 1854–55 and 1855–56*.

58. Arguing that she had been married to her husband as a child, and drawing attention to intellectual, moral, and physical incompatibilities, Rakhmabai (1862–1953) fought a four-year legal case in 1884 of regional, national, and international ramifications in which she actively resisted living with her husband. Rakhmabai's English education was repeatedly cited (especially in the press) as the reason for the "incompatibility." If we are to take the critique in the *Chabuk* as providing vital clues on the structural alliance between caste, knowledge, and sexuality, then all parameters of Rakhmabai's case appear entirely overdetermined. For more details on the years around the actual case, see chapter 3 and also, Anagol, *The Emergence of Feminism in India*, 184–91. For an assessment of the case from the perspective of Britain, see Burton, "From Child Bride to Hindu Widow," 1119–46.

59. Quoted in the *Proceedings of the Students' Literary and Scientific Society, Bombay. For the Years 1854–55 and 1855–56*. Emphases in proceedings report.

60. Quoted from Monthly Miscellany I, 6 (1850), 329, in Masselos, *Towards Nationalism*, 32.

61. In addition, the SLSS made no provisions to educate girls over the age of twelve; thus girls could not receive any instruction through the Society's schools beyond the Vernacular IV standard. Bombay Education Department rules had already legislated that all Indian students be trained in the vernacular until at least Standard IV. The fact that the Society would not impart any education to girls beyond the age of twelve (or the fourth grade) carried the implicit assurance that an English-language education would not be imparted at any level in its girls' schools. These policies would not be reversed for another thirty-five years.

62. Sumitra can be translated literally to mean "The Good Friend," a title that resembles many missionary tracts for early learners. However, in the *Ramayan*, Sumitra was the third wife of the king Dasharath; she was considered his wisest wife and the one who bore him the most sons.

63. At the Bombay University Library, I found Volume 1, issue 1, to Volume 2, issue 12 (July 1857), with several issues missing in between.

64. Although writing about eighteenth- and nineteenth-century England, Nancy Armstrong's demonstration of the increasing power of the domestic woman buttressed by the emerging print culture speaks to important similarities in a transnational Victorian gender order between upper-class India and England. Armstrong, *Desire and Domestic Fiction*. See also Mukherjee, *Realism and Reality*.

65. *Sumitra* 1:3 (1855), 57–60.

66. Articles such as this one, illustrating conversations between an educated and uneducated woman, were a common feature in many of the women's magazines of the late nineteenth century. See, for instance, other Marathi maga-

zines for women such as the *Arya Bhagini* [Arya sisters]. Examples abound from various parts of British India. From the Madras Presidency, see "A.L.O.E. 1880 The Planets," in the *Zenana Reader, Madras: The Christian Vernacular Education Society*, 1880. This is discussed in greater detail in Kent, *Converting Women*, Bagal, *Women's Education in Eastern India*, and Young, *Resistant Hinduism*.

67. *Sumitra* 1:3 (1855), 44.
68. Ibid., 24.
69. Frere was a multitalented meddler. See Davis's blistering account of Frere's deliberate racism in fanning the crushing famine of 1873 in the Bombay Presidency. Davis, *Late Victorian Holocausts*.
70. Thus, further pushing Seth's assertion that "the British claim that colonial rule was a pedagogic enterprise for the improvement of India, and that western education was one of the means toward this end, was largely accepted by the new elites emerging under British rule." Seth, *Subject Lessons*, 159.
71. *Report of the Students' Literary and Scientific Society and of the Vernacular Branch Societies, Together with the Reports of the Girls' Schools for the Session of 1862–63*.
72. Ibid.
73. Naregal points out that even the *Bombay Durpan*, the first Marathi-language newspaper, was possibly funded by Parsi seths. Naregal, *Language Politics, Elites, and the Public Sphere*, 175–78. The dominance of Parsi commercial interests in the Marathi print world would change with the inauguration of Arya Bhushan Press (a publishing house) in the late 1870s and the writings of Vishnushashtri Chiplunkar. Both are traced in the next chapter.
74. V. S. Mandlik was an "outstandingly successful" pleader in the Bombay courts and, according to Masselos, characterized the professional independence of the Young Bombay group of male intellectuals (Masselos, *Towards Nationalism*, 55). Mandlik founded the conservative Anglo-Marathi *Native Opinion* (discussed later in this chapter), which he edited until 1871. *Native Opinion* argued in 1870 that reformers cultivate an enlightened conservatism. See Dobbin, *Urban Leadership in Western India*, 76.
75. SLSS, *Report of the Students' Literary and Scientific Society and of the Vernacular Branch Societies, Together with the Reports of the Girls" Schools for the Session of 1863–64*, 1864.
76. Ibid.
77. Ibid.
78. English was never referred to as the mother tongue, except when it was yoked to parodies of masculinized women or sickened, debilitated men. When Savitribai Phule (chapter 1) referenced English as mother, she indicated that it was a time in history, a form of knowledge, and not the mother tongue.
79. According to the *Report of the Students' Literary and Scientific Society for the*

Session of 1873–74 (1875), "The girls in our schools are now taught Arithmetic up to the Rule of Three, the Geography of the World, but especially of our own country, and an elementary sketch of the history of the Mahrattas. They read the Marathi Books used in the Government Boys' Schools, and many of them are able to understand and fully explain easy passages in Marathi poetry. Sewing and Wool work is also taught regularly, and the performances of the girls have been pronounced very creditable by the examiners of the schools."

80. SLSS, 1950, 8.
81. Correspondence of November 5, 1867. EDF 4 of 1868, compilation number 14.
82. "Female Education in India," EDF 15 of 1877, compilation number 176.
83. Ibid.
84. Ibid.
85. An Anglo-vernacular standard entailed a mix of two or more languages. Generally, the curriculum was conducted in Marathi and Gujarati, while English existed as one subject in the curriculum.
86. *Report of the Director of Public Instruction in the Bombay Presidency for the Year 1870–71.*
87. The RNN was itself interestingly situated amid the class and caste politics of the time. In the case of the Bombay Presidency, the RNN began annual publication in 1868, and it was supervised by the Department of Translation. The reports carried English-language translations and synopses of prominent newspapers articles in the native press. RNNs were directed by the Reporter on the Vernacular Press, a post held successively by the bilingual Brahman beneficiaries of colonial English education, significantly Krishnashstri Chiplunkar (1824–76) and M. G. Ranade. For the year of 1868, the RNN recorded a range of critiques of the Normal Schools in several newspapers.
88. Director of Public Instruction for the Bombay Presidency, *Report of Native Newspapers*, 1868.
89. *Bombay Samachar*, September 9, 1869. The paper was the first vernacular newspaper from western India, dating back to 1822. Again, it was funded by Gujarati trading interests. Masselos, *Towards Nationalism*, 32.
90. This reflects the charges levied by the *Chabuk* over the Ladies Committee of the SLSS. This also anticipates my discussion of the Poona Native Girls' High School in chapter 3. In that case, the school's official biographer and former student had reacted to an allegation of the immorality of the school's students (expressed in *Kesari*), asking whether it had been possible for *Kesari* to make the allegation because the students had been taught by European women.
91. Chandrodaya, September 13, 1869. From Report on Native Newspapers, 1869.
92. "Female Training School in the Bombay Presidency," letter no. 234 of 1867 / 68. EDF 4 of 1869.

93. Ibid.
94. Ibid.
95. Ibid.
96. Ibid.
97. *EDF* 21 of 1875, compilation number 66.
98. "Female Normal School," *EDF* 3 of 1870, compilation number 5.
99. Ibid.
100. Elizabeth Povinelli's recent work on the world historical emergence of the liberal subject stresses the necessary relationship between individuation and constraint in the "Empire of Love." She draws attention to the reinforcing relationship between discourses, practices, and fantasies about "self-making, self-sovereignty, and the value of individual freedom associated with the Enlightenment project of contractual constitutional democracy and capitalism" on the one hand and "social constraints placed on the autological subject by various kinds of inheritances" on the other. Povinelli, *The Empire of Love*, 4–5.
101. "Female Normal School," *EDF* 3 of 1870, compilation number 5.
102. According to Masselos, the *Rast Goftar* was founded in Bombay in 1851 with the specific intention of addressing the failure of the Gujarati *shetia* classes during the Parsi-Muslim riots. Its first editor was Dadabhai Naoroji and it was financed by a syndicate of Parsi businessmen from the Cama, Bengallee, and Furdoonjee families. Entirely reformist, its subscription grew to twelve hundred by 1869, which is when it was considered the largest "native" newspaper in India. Masselos, *Towards Nationalism*, 32.
103. *Rast Goftar*, July 23, 1871. *Report of Native Newspapers for the Bombay Presidency for 1871*.
104. *EDF* 22 of 1873, compilation number 54.
105. See response from the *Parsi Chabuk* of 1851 on the English class of the Students' Literary and Scientific Society Schools, discussed earlier in this chapter.
106. For instance, the *Report of Native Newspapers for the Bombay Presidency* had printed a letter in 1872 from the *Belgaum Samachar*, signed by a "Public Woman," in which the writer had complained that it was a "great injustice that the girls and women of her class should be refused admission into the Government girls' schools. She says that they pay all State taxes as well as other people [do], and therefore are as much entitled as other people to get their children educated in government schools. . . . Knowledge and education are universally believed to be the most potent means of reclaiming people from ignorance and vice, and their children perhaps need more than others the benefit of the reclaiming agency of the schools." It is possible that the letter was written not by a "public woman," but by one who posed as such so as to oppose widening the class and caste base for female education.

107. *Report of the Director of Public Instruction for the Bombay Presidency* (1878–79), 71.
108. *Bombay Gazette*, September 5, 1882.
109. Elphinstone, "Minute on Education," 20.

CHAPTER 3: "THE LANGUAGE OF THE BEDROOM"

1. The matriculation examination secured entrance to undergraduate programs in the three colonial-administered Presidency universities. These universities were inaugurated in 1858 in Bombay, Calcutta, and Madras. Modeled on the curriculum of the University of London, the degrees offered at these institutions indicated the suitability of native men to undertake employment in the vast administrative apparatus that arose to support colonial rule.
2. "Higher education for women. Important government concessions, Poona." *Bombay Gazette*, August 12, 1884. Herself a Chitpavan Brahman, Pandita Ramabai was initially extolled by the new colonial Brahmans of western India for her exemplary learning; it was they who recognized her as the "Pandita" or highly learned woman. She was just as resolutely rejected when her conversion to Christianity and her rising critique of Brahmanical orthodoxy began to reach a Western audience. For more details, see Anagol, *The Emergence of Feminism in India*, 235.
3. Mote, *Vishrabdh Sharada*, 271. The justice M. G. Ranade (1842–1901) was among the first graduates of the Bombay University. Serving as a judge of the Bombay High Court, he worked with many regional caste leaders to found a number of liberal organizations such as the Indian National Congress, the National Social Reform Conference, Prarthana Samaj, and the Poona Sarvajanik Sabha. See chapter 6 for a longer discussion of his role in the Widow Remarriage Act of 1856.
4. "The higher education of native women," *Bombay Gazette*, July 26, 1884.
5. In her memoirs (which I discuss in detail in chapter 6), Ramabai Ranade wrote of how the AMS's sessions were regularly supervised by gentlemen from the community who would present lectures and then encourage the women to write and communicate their thoughts on a variety of issues. Ranade, *Aamchya Aayushyatil Kahee Aathavani*.
6. Johnson, "Chitpavan Brahmans and Politics in Western India in the Late Nineteenth and Early Twentieth Centuries," 95–118. Johnson (107) records that by the turn of the century more than 80 percent of the Marathi newspaper editors were Brahmans.
7. Recognizing that words are never transparent in their effect, Stuart Hall asked in 1982, "If the world has to be made to mean then how do certain meanings get privileged over others?" Hall, "The Rediscovery of 'Ideology,'" 67. Later, Hall discusses how, in the negotiation between "high" and "popular" cul-

ture, signs are being constantly provided with meaning depending on the group speaking. Intended audiences decode these differently. Hall, "For Allen White," 287–305.
8. Naregal, *Language Politics, Elites, and the Public Sphere*, 121.
9. Ibid., 256–57.
10. Tucker, *Ranade and the Roots of Indian Nationalism*, 182.
11. Naregal, *Language Politics, Elites, and the Public Sphere*, 253.
12. Deshpande, *Creative Pasts*, 101.
13. Ibid., 102. She is referencing his writings in *Nibandhamala* 1:1–7.
14. Ibid.
15. *Kesari*, edited by Agarkar for its first six years, was a Marathi-language paper, which posed itself as a bridge between new political debates and the Marathi-speaking population. The circulation figure given in the *Report for Native Newspapers* was two hundred (RNN 1881 [vol. 100 of Judicial Department 1881]). The English-language *Mahratta*, edited by Tilak until 1891, was similarly conservative in propagating an ideal Marathi-language literary political agenda. Circulation figures for the paper jumped considerably over the years; a more detailed account of the numbers is available in Reiner and Goldberg, *Tilak and the Struggle for Indian Freedom*, 435.
16. New English School, *The Annual Report of the New English School Poona for 1883*, Poona.
17. Naregal, *Language Politics, Elites, and the Public Sphere*, 69.
18. Phadke, *V. K. Chiploonkar*, 56.
19. Deeply appreciative of the tradition of English literature, Chiplunkar also dismissed the imperfect knowledge which British historians held on Asia, boldly writing against canonical literary figures and describing the political impact of the knowledge that European scholars constructed about the "East." "Itihaas," reprinted in Phadkule, *Nibandhmaleteel, Teen Nibandh*, 28–78.
20. *Nibandhamala*, 1882, 107. In the Marathi language all languages (Hindi, English, and Marathi itself) take the feminine gender; I have translated Chiplunkar's *nipajne* as "to turn out," although it can also mean "to be produced as" or "to be born as." I have translated *lenchapecha* as "irresolute" although it can also be translated as "weak" or "silly." I have translated the sentence maintaining the implicit masculine gender, which raises the question of whether Chiplunkar envisaged women to be in his reading audience.
21. Chiplunkar, *Nibandhamala*, 133.
22. In the *Myth of the Lokmanya*, Cashman discusses the history of the Bombay Gorakshak Mandali (Society for the Protection of Cows), founded in Bombay in 1887.
23. At the heart of colonial allegations on native effeminacy had been the assertion that Brahmans were like women in their demeanor, physique, and man-

nerisms. Perceptions of the lack of gender difference buttressed the British colonial discourse on "native masculinity." Drawing from the case of Bengal, Mrinalini Sinha made this important argument in 1995 in *Colonial Masculinity*.

24. Tilak resurrected the Ganpati and Shivaji festivals and, in *Kesari*, noted that the festivals were a means of "maintaining national vigor.... Celebrations like the one under consideration are intended rather as a tonic for the advancement of the general health and strength of the body politic than as medicine for any specific disease." *Kesari*, April 9, 1901, quoted by Deshpande, *Creative Pasts*, 189. As Deshpande notes, colonial celebration of the martial Marathas as a caste deliberately excluded Brahmans. If Tilak was reacting against that, so too perhaps Chiplunkar.

25. A recent study on nationalist Egypt has tracked similar associations in far greater depth. See Jacob, *Working Out Egypt*.

26. Analyses of present-day Indian masculinity have suggested that the demonstration of the female or the feminine within masculinity is an integral aspect of contemporary masculine performance. See Chopra, Osella, and Osella, *South Asian Masculinities*, and Nandy, *The Intimate Enemy*.

27. In the case of western India, and in the post-1857 climate, the Brahman caste was read against the more virile "Mahratta" peasant and warrior groups identified by colonial sociology.

28. "The Higher Education of Native Women," *Bombay Gazette*, July 26, 1884.

29. *Proceedings of a Deputation from the People of Poona Waited by Appointment upon His Excellency the Governor in the Council Hall, Poona, on Saturday the 9th of August, Re a High School for Native Girls*, 1884. As the deliberations over the Female Normal School (discussed in chapter 2) determined, the caste-based relationship between Ahmedabad, Bombay, and Poona was being played out over the issue of female education. All three cities were part of the Bombay Presidency.

30. According to the official history of the school, Miss Hurford of the Zenana Mission was its first lady superintendent. She had worked with the Bethune School in Calcutta and in Poona she worked through the Zenana Mission with the ladies of the Arya Mahila Samaj. She often went to these women's houses to teach them English and counted Ramabai Ranade, Pandita Ramabai, and Mrs. Bhandarkar (wife of the Orientalist and Sanskrit scholar R. G. Bhandarkar) among her students. The school had eighteen students on its rolls the first day, with Avadibai Bhide recorded as the first student enrolled (I discuss her biography in detail in chapter 5). A few years later the teacher-training school was amalgamated with this school. Of the seventy-four girls on the rolls at the end of the first year, twenty-four were married, six were widows, and sixteen were from outside Poona; the students ranged in age from seven to twenty-nine years old. The prize distribution held at the end of the first

year mentioned that Avadibai Bhide had secured the highest rank in her class, with her sister Ramabai Bhide second. Panse, *Pragati Pathavar: Svarn Mahotsav Smarak Granth* [On the road to progress: Golden jubilee commemorative volume].

31. *Report of the Proceedings Held on the 29th September 1884 in the Town Hall, Hirabaug.*

32. "Poona Native Girls High School: Provision of Funds in connection with the Poona Native Girls High School," EDF 47 of 1885. Other standards taught at this school can only be gleaned by reading the Indian Education Commission's report (also known as the Hunter Commission). Conducted in 1882, the study mentioned only the curriculum of boys' English schools in the Presidency. Given that the PNHS was expressly geared toward the state matriculation examination, its standards would have been on par with those at boys' schools. Students were required to learn one other language, and the other subjects included "Arithmetic, Algebra, Euclid, General Knowledge, History of England and India, Geography." Indian Education Commission, *Report of the Indian Education Commission, Appointed by the Resolution of the Government of India dated 3rd February 1882*. The PNHS had Sanskrit as an optional language, and the majority of students studied Marathi. Miss Hurford taught English songs. Although not included in the syllabus for the matriculation examination, the girls were also taught sewing, singing, and drawing. Panse, *Pragati Pathavar*.

33. The question of equivalence with Western culture informed much of Bhandarkar's work. Bhandarkar was one among four students to graduate from the Bombay University in its inaugural degree-granting year. A colleague and fellow ideologue of M. G. Ranade (who was also of this graduating class), Bhandarkar was educated entirely in colonial educational institutions. Rapidly espousing the tenets of liberalism, he was, as Deshpande has noted, an especially dedicated espouser of "objectivity and the search of truth . . . the conceptualization of history as an unbiased, chronological narrative of facts." Bhandarkar "resorted to an empiricist method and objectivity to contest the frequently sweeping, derogatory remarks make by European Indologists about Indian civilization . . . instead highlight[ing] the linguistic connections between classical languages like Greek and Sanskrit [to] claim parity with western civilization." Deshpande, *Creative Pasts*, 99–100.

34. Maharashtra Female Educational Society: Ceremony of October 9, 1891. EDF 60 of 1891, compilation number 87.

35. See Masselos, *Towards Nationalism*, 233, for a discussion of the growing rift between Tilak and Agarkar in the context of the Deccan Education Society (which they were credited as having founded along with V. S. Chiplunkar)

and the manner in which M. G. Ranade emerged as the bridge between the two factions.

36. "Stripurushanan Ekach Shikshan Ghyave, va Tehi Ekatra Ghyave!' [Men and women must get the same education, and together!], *Sudharak*, October 31, 1892.
37. In *Ranade and the Roots of Indian Nationalism*, Tucker discusses their disagreement in terms of the clash between extremist and moderate political positions.
38. "A High School for Native Girls," *Mahratta*, August 17, 1884.
39. "Strishikshanavar shevatche don shabd" [A few words on the subject of women's education], *Kesari*, September 16, 1884.
40. Vaze, *The AryaBhushan School Dictionary*, 501.
41. *Kunbi*: Marathi for peasant. "A High School for Native Girls," *Mahratta*, August 17, 1884.
42. Ibid.
43. It is significant that the debates over language in the girls' school never referred to the far more prevalent government-sponsored activity of rendering Marathi works into English. Orientalist translations from Indian languages had of course been far more invested in the classical languages and had only fleetingly taken account of the vernacular languages. The activity had peaked some sixty years earlier in the case of western India, and had been accompanied by the rise of a standardized, Sanskritized Marathi written in the Devanagari as opposed to the Modi script. The relationship between classical and vernacular languages and the later use of the "mother tongue" to designate those languages recognized as vernacular further establishes the subtle work of gender ideology in these developments.
44. "Higher Female Education," *Mahratta*, August 24, 1884.
45. Ibid.
46. Letter to the newspaper, *Mahratta*, August 24, 1884.
47. "Female Higher Education," *Mahratta*, August 31, 1884.
48. Baroda had been designated a princely state in 1802 and colonial interference in matters of succession was pressing. The British maintained a Resident in Baroda and the Gaekwad presented the Company and later the Crown with military and monetary compensation See McLeod, *Sovereignty, Power, Control*. The Poona Sarvajanik Sabha, to which the Gaekwad had been an active financial contributor through the 1870s, had grown in stature under the leadership of M. G. Ranade. In fact, membership of the Poona Sarvajanik Sabha overlapped considerably with the native male leaders of the PNHS, as is evident from a reading of the *Quarterly Journal of the Poona Sarvajanik Sabha*.
49. *Report of Proceedings held on the 29th September 1885 in the Town Hall, Hirabaug*.

50. "Vernacular newspapers. Articles in the 'Vaibhav' newspaper reflecting on the manners and morals of European Society." General Department compilation number S71 of 1884.
51. Ibid.
52. Parker, "A Corporation of Superior Prostitutes," 559–633.
53. Denouncing the account in the *Vaibhav* as trash, the letter writers took care to stress that "erroneous impressions may exist between natives and Europeans in regard to their respective habits and tastes, but we can confidently assert that the comparative freedom of English manners is not regarded in educated native society as in any way affecting the purity, and excellence of English domestic and social life any more than the limited freedom in Hindoo society can be confounded with domestic slavery by Europeans." "Vernacular newspapers. Articles in the 'Vaibhav' newspaper reflecting on the manners and morals of European Society." General Department compilation number S71 of 1884. Despite their anguish over having upset European sentiments, it is noteworthy that these writers took advantage of the opportunity to point to prevalent misconceptions among Europeans on the sexual relations of (some) Indians.
54. Speech by the Governor of the Bombay Presidency, *Bombay Gazette*, December 4, 1884.
55. Girls' High School Poona, "Rules for Management of Girls' High School Poona," EDF 36 of 1886, compilation number 2. Recall, too, the article from the Bombay *Samachar* and its allegations of immorality discussed in chapter 2.
56. "Female Highschoolateel Shikshankram" [The curriculum in the female high school], *Kesari*, September 21, 1886 (emphasis in original).
57. Ibid.
58. Stri Shikshan in *Poona Vaibhav* [Glory of Poona], August 24, 1884. The wider controversy over respectability is contained in the General Department Files of the Government of Bombay, under vernacular newspapers: articles in the "Vaibhav" newspaper. General Department (unpublished file), Bombay Presidency, 1884, compilation number s71. According to Rao, by this stage (1900), the school had 230 students, of whom 128 were Brahman, 72 non-Brahman, and 30 Christian, Parsi, or Jewish.
59. I discuss her biography and her father's liberal, reform-minded agenda in detail in chapter 5.
60. *Mahratta*, August 13, 1893. Quoted by Rao, "Women's Education and the Nationalist Response in Western India," 143.
61. "Religious Education in Schools and Colleges," *Mahratta*, July 5, 1903.
62. Quoted in Panse, *Pragati Pathavar*, 45. *Kesari*, September 28, 1886. The reference to the *burkha* could only have been deliberate, intended to stoke the Brahmanical anxieties of its intended audience.
63. Mythological Hindu female figures were increasingly evoked as testimony to

the "golden age" of Vedic Hinduism and the virtues of the self-sacrificing Hindu wife.

64. Panse, *Pragati Pathavar*, 47. Again, the anxiety referenced by Panse echoes fears expressed over the European "Ladies Committee" for the SLSS girls' schools.

65. "Female Highschoolateel Shikshankram," *Kesari*, October 4, 1886.

66. *Kesari* was not the only paper to forge new connections between the nation and sexual difference. For instance, writing on the subject of the high school, the *Poona Vaibhav* of November 28, 1886, argued that Europeans had two objectives in mind by encouraging the kind of girls' education taught at the new school: keeping the native community disengaged from staging political agitations and encouraging the people of other communities to be reduced to their level of morality, and, hence, to prevent themselves from being laughed at. The debate was not restricted to the Hindu or Brahman community or to the late nineteenth century. See Roland, *The Jewish Communities of India*, 44.

67. Narayan Bapuji Kanitkar, *Taruni Shikshan Natika, athva adhunik tarunishikshan va stri svatantra yanche bhavishyakathhan* [A play on the modern education of young girls or a prophecy on modern education and female freedom].

68. Meera Kosambi mentions this play and notes that Kanitkar was the uncle of Kashibai Kanitkar, whose own quest to teach herself English so as to win her husband's approval is documented by Kosambi.

69. Deshpande, *Creative Pasts*, 153 and 252 n. 12.

70. "The Poona Native Girls High School," *Bombay Gazette*, October 21, 1887.

71. *Kanitkar* 2–3 (2nd ed., 1890).

72. Rubin, "Thinking Sex," 15. Rubin pushes further Foucault's history of the disciplinary claims of medicine and psychiatry.

73. Rakhmabai's mother was a remarried widow. Her second marriage was to the surgeon Sakharam Arjun. It was in Dr. Sakharam's home that Rakhmabai had spent her childhood years, and it was Dr. Sakharam's own support for her education, and his later advocacy of her desire to annul her marriage, that prompted some sections of the press to allege his nefarious intentions. In keeping with the anxiety over new, ambiguous colonial laws on inheritance and property (laws that provoked fresh strictures on sexuality from proliferating caste *sabhas*), sections of the native press alleged that Sakharam coveted Rakhmabai's property and wanted to annul her marriage so as to prevent it from passing into the hands of her husband, Dadaji Bhikaji. See Chakravarti, *Rewriting History*.

74. Zirelli, *Signifying Woman*, 13 (emphasis in original). Similar assertions have been made for different parts of the world. See Allman, "Rounding Up Spinsters," specifically for the constellation of political and social changes that served to produce a wider anxiety over "gender chaos."

75. For invaluable background information on the manner in which popular "Parsi" theater sporadically subverted heterosexual normativity, destabilizing the viewer's perception of the actor's gender and thus paving the way for an unsteady awareness of the power of desire, see Kathryn Hansen's "A Different Desire, a Different Femininity: Theatrical Transvestism in the Parsi, Gujarati, and Marathi Theaters, 1850–1940," in *Queering India*, ed. Vanita, 163–80.
76. Haddap, *Bahekleli Taruni*.
77. See also Deshpande's analysis in *Creative Pasts*, 164, which suggests literary similarities between Haddap and the conservative Brahman politics espoused by Vishnushastri Chiplunkar.
78. "The Poona Native Girls High School," *Bombay Gazette*, October 21, 1887, 8.
79. Kanitkar, *Taruni Shikshan Natika*, 13–14.
80. Ibid., 14–15.
81. "Higher Education for Our Girls," *Native Opinion*, September 14, 1884.
82. The *Native Opinion* remained in print from 1864 to 1908 and maintained a somewhat conservative stance; its circulation figures fluctuated between four hundred and six hundred annually. According to Naregal, both the *Native Opinion* and the *Mumbai InduPrakash* exemplified how bilingual newspapers claimed to be the sole spokesmen for native opinions, demonstrating "an intimate knowledge of native opinion and a close familiarity with the forms of modern governance." *Language Politics, Elites, and the Public Sphere*, 222.
83. In her discussion of the affective bonds between colonial and native men, Gandhi has similarly claimed that "both empire and its antagonist, the anticolonial nation, need to be recognised as profoundly heteronormative projects that founded their competing authorities on the categories of sex." "Loving Well," 87–99.
84. The *Mumbai Indu Prakash* was one of M. G. Ranade's ventures. In comparison to the *Native Opinion*, it was markedly pro-reform. It ran from 1862 to 1924 and saw regular contributions from M. G. Ranade and R. G. Bhandarkar, among others. The *Mumbai Indu Prakash* listed its circulation figures as one thousand per issue. See Naregal, *Language Politics, Elites, and the Public Sphere*, 199, 250.
85. *Mumbai Indu Prakash*, September 22, 1884.
86. Ibid.
87. Bhabha, *The Location of Culture*, 87.
88. In her study of the "grammar of colonial desire," Revathi Krishnaswamy has demonstrated that the British discourse on native masculinity asserted that Indian men were effeminate because they were like women. Her work advances Mrinalini Sinha's important study on colonial masculinity. Together these works concur that colonial observations on "Indian" masculinity established that native men were effeminate because they were no different from women. For a wider exploration of ongoing constructions of binaries between

masculinity and femininity, see the works produced in the wake of Sinha and Krishnaswamy, for instance, Teltscher, "Maidenly and Well Nigh Effeminate," 159–70. My interest lies in looking beyond colonial allegations and inscriptions.

89. Here I break with Ashis Nandy's account of the incorporation of the feminine into the masculine as a form of anticolonial, antimodern resistance. While malleable ideas of the "feminine" were certainly harnessed to bolster masculine authority, they were also done to privilege caste authority and difference from "other" Indians.

90. Seth, *Subject Lessons*, 116.

91. Listing the growing numbers of women's presence in educational institutions, he corroborates instead Chatterjee's claim that, by the turn of the century, the woman's question was no longer negotiated with the colonial state; instead "a public consensus had emerged around the desirability of women's education." Seth, *Subject Lessons*, 144.

92. Hall, "Politics, Post-Structuralism and Feminist History," 204–10.

93. Here I recall Derrida's insistence that the production of meaning is ultimately based on an arbitrary relationship between signs. Where structuralism perceived meaning to be fixed through a series of oppositions (for instance, the meaning of "woman" emerges because she is not "man"), poststructuralist reevaluations such as his have argued that meaning was deferred *and* constantly open to re-signification. For more on the production of meaning, see Lorraine, *Gender, Identity, and the Production of Meaning*. See also the essays compiled by Schor and Weed, *The Essential Difference*.

CHAPTER 4: "A NEW GENERATION..."

1. Chandavarkar, *Maharshi Karve*. See also Chandavarkar, *Dhondo Keshav Karve*.

2. In the *Emerging Lesbian*, Sang cites Rofel, who argues that "the local and global are both acts of positioning, perspectives rather than mere locales, used as signifiers of difference" (10).

3. Karve, *Atmavrit va Charitra*. All translations from the original Marathi are mine.

4. Interesting that Dadabhai Naoroji, himself a supporter of the native-administered Students' Literary and Scientific Society school, would send his daughter to the Cathedral Girls' School, which was administered by European missionaries.

5. I am not sure which school he means. It could be the higher classes of the Marathi school run by the Students' Literary and Scientific Society.

6. As I discussed in chapter 3, Agarkar had maintained that any differentiation in the curriculum on the basis of gender would be a retroactive step. In fact, he believed that coeducation would be the most effective means to effect pro-

gressive social change. He made these statements in *Kesari* [Lion] through the 1880s, and then in *Sudharak* [Reformer], which he founded in 1892. Agarkar most significantly clashed with Tilak over the issue of gender differentiation, especially as exemplified in the curriculum of the Poona Native Girls' High School. Raeside, "Agarkar, Apte and the Kanitkars," 156–65.
7. Karve, *Looking Back*.
8. Karve, *Atmavrit va Charitra*, 99.
9. Karve, *Looking Back*, 33.
10. I am reminded most of Mahadev Gopal Ranade, who espoused the remarriage of widows, and yet, when the opportunity arose in his own life, he chose to marry according to traditional norms. See also my discussion on the Ranade marriage in chapter 6.
11. Kosambi, *Crossing Thresholds*, 352–53.
12. Ibid., 111.
13. The Hindu Widow Remarriage Act had been passed in 1856, but in actuality, as Uma Chakravarti has noted, it did not produce any widow remarriages. On the contrary, it served to universalize Brahmanical patriarchy as the basis of all Hindu marriage custom and to delegitimize the Hindu widow's right to inherit her deceased husband's property. Chakravarti, *Rewriting History*, 131.
14. Forbes, *Women in Modern India*, 47.
15. Kosambi, *Crossing Thresholds*, 330.
16. *Mahila ashram* translates as women's home. The connotations are of a refuge or space of sanctity.
17. "The Hindu Women's Home, Poona," *Indian Ladies Magazine* 3, no. 6 (December 1903), 190, ed. Mrs. Satthianadhan.
18. Ibid.
19. Ibid.
20. Forbes, *Women in Modern India*, 51.
21. Quoted in D. D. Karve, *The New Brahmans*, 51.
22. Forbes, *Women in Modern India*, 52.
23. Karve recalls in *Atmavrit va Charitra* that the school had about seventy-five students on its rolls at this point, but it is unclear how many of these students were at the higher English standards.
24. Karve, *Atmavrit va Charitra*, 257.
25. Ibid.
26. Elphinstone, "Minute on Education."
27. For details, see Forbes, *Women in Modern India*, 25–27.
28. Kosambi mentions Telang's speech, after which the two split.
29. There were a number of other women's universities in operation in Japan at that time and the cult of domesticity was essential to their pedagogic mission. For instance, the Tsuda Women's University was founded by Tsuda Umeko,

who was herself sent by the Meiji government to the United States in the late nineteenth century to be trained in the principles of a progressive, national domesticity. Rose, *Tsuda Umeko and Women's Education in Japan*.

30. Naruse's Japan Women's University appears to have been a separate enterprise from the Tsuda Women's University. Another was the Ochanomizu Women's University.
31. Hay, *Asian Ideas of East and West*. The Indian intellectual romance with Japan was not purely peaceful and humanist. As Deshpande mentions, the aftermath of the Russo-Japanese War and the espousal of Japanese martial codes all framed the political ideology of militant male Maharashtrian religious nationalism. *Creative Pasts*, 190.
32. Karve, *Atmavrit va Charitra*, 348–49.
33. Ibid., 349–50.
34. Shreemati Nathabai Damodar Thakersey, *Indian Women's University Calendar* (hereafter SNDT), 1924 (my emphasis).
35. See, for instance, my discussion of Narayan Martand Davne's play in chapter 3, as well as Vishnushastri Chiplunkar's assertion that English be used to regenerate the population.
36. *SNDT Calendar*, 1924.
37. Ibid.
38. *Atmavrit va Charitra*, 365.
39. Ibid.
40. Ibid.
41. A number of historians remember Karve as a radical anti-caste reformer; see for example Sen, "A Father's Duty: State, Patriarchy and Women's Education," 197–236, 208. My interpretation proposes a more complex assessment.
42. Karve maintained that the agenda was to "remove defects in the system which affect both men and women." The curriculum, however, was entirely oriented toward female domestic roles. As he himself said, "The very name suggests . . . studies looking to the needs and circumstances of the generality of women. With this object in view, Domestic Economy and Hygiene are given an important place. . . . Under the head of Domestic Science are included Biology, Anatomy, Human Physiology, and Elements of Psychology with special study of the child mind, which are compulsory. Fine arts, viz. music, painting, needle work and embroidery . . . [are] regular subjects of the examination." Karve, *Looking Back*, 141.
43. Shreemati Nathabai Damoder Thackersay, *Indian Women's University*, lists the syllabus for the university's entrance examination in 1917. The necessary subjects were "English, vernacular, History and hygiene." This record listed, among other English literary titles, Oliver Goldsmith's play *She Stoops to Conquer* and Sir Walter Scott's *Ivanhoe*.

44. "Indian Women's University," *Mahratta*, February 20, 1916. Quoted by Rao, "Women's Education and the Nationalist Response in Western India," 146–47.
45. As Rao's research reveals, the following week Tilak stated, "If our Hindu girls are to spend the most impressionable period of their lives in contact with school work, which never appeals to their Hindutva . . . an unsound educational system which keeps an advanced student a stranger to the basic principles of the Faith . . . the end of education is to produce self respecting and practical men and women imbibed with a pride in the race and religion and the community to which they belong." *Mahratta*, February 27, 1916.
46. For more details on the surprising convergence between Gandhi and Tagore (in the 1930s) on the matter of language, see Seth, *Subject Lessons*, 178–79.
47. Karve, *Atmavrit va Charitra*, 371.
48. SNDT *Eighth Annual Report*, 1924.
49. Karve, *Atmavrit va Charitra*, 372.
50. Ibid., 371.
51. Ibid., 414. The word he uses is *mohini*, which is also the name of the female enticer of Vishnu.
52. Ibid.
53. Ibid., 415.
54. Ibid., 401.
55. The Age of Consent Bill was passed in 1891; it aimed to raise the marriageable age of a woman from ten to twelve years old.
56. *Indian Social Reformer*, July 20, 1920.
57. *Indian Social Reformer*, June 30, 1923. Quoted by Karve, *Atmavrit va Charitra*, 404–5.
58. *Indian Social Reformer*, July 4, 1925. Quoted by Karve, *Atmavrit va Charitra*, 406–7.
59. *Indian Social Reformer*, July 3, 1926. Quoted by Karve, *Atmavrit va Charitra*, 408–9.
60. Criticism of the Indian Women's University was voiced in other quarters as well, although not along the lines declared in the ISR. A state-nominated committee, formed in 1924, on the condition of the Bombay University argued that most people believed a separate university was wasteful and would "lower the standard of higher education for women." According to this committee, instead of creating a separate university for women, Bombay University needed to recognize "the Vernacular as a medium." Karve, *Atmavrit va Charitra*, 413–14.
61. Delamont, *Knowledgeable Women*.
62. Colley and Delamont, *Feminism and the Classroom Teacher*, 100–104.
63. Karve, *Atmavrit va Charitra*, 353.
64. Richardson, "Kenealy, Arabella Madonna (1859–1938)," http://www.oxforddnb.com/view/article/50057, accessed August 18, 2008.

65. Swenson, "The Menopausal Vampire," 27–46.
66. Richardson, "Kenealy."
67. Walford, *The Private Schooling of Girls.*
68. Quoted by Karve, *Atmavrit va Charitra*, 354.
69. At least from the evidence of the speech that he delivered at the Social Conference, it appears that he had already reached conclusions on a separate "feminine" curriculum as early as 1915. But by the time he published his autobiography in 1928, he cited the works of these British and European sexologists, psychologists, and sociologists to corroborate the enduring "scientific" veracity of his earlier claims. In other words, he cited their work out of context, leaning on later published work to authorize earlier ideas.
70. This is not to say that they did not reference it for, as Walford has recorded, subjects such as Greek and Latin could incite debate over gender, and Kenealy entered the debate at least once by complaining that "working-class girls reaching secondary school, where they encountered algebra and Latin, were equally damaged. These schools had engendered the race of stunted, precocious, bold-eyed, cigarette smoking, free living working girls who fill our streets; many tricked out like cocottes, eyes roving after men, impudence upon their tongues." Significantly, however, her reference was to classical Greek and Latin as subjects in the curriculum and not as languages. Walford, *The Private Schooling*, 91.
71. As Niranjana has argued in *Siting Translation*, the primary impetus of the colonial translation endeavor, with its unswerving attention to details of "origin" and "truth," served to reinforce unequal power relations.
72. Karve, *Atmavrit va Charitra*, 425–26.
73. Vaze, *AryaBhushan School Dictionary*, 1928.
74. Karve, *Atmavrit va Charitra*, 427.
75. Ibid., 428.
76. Ibid., 429.
77. Literally, "of one's nation," a political movement of self-reliance, primarily in the realm of textiles. The *swadeshi* movement reached international renown during the partition of Bengal in 1905, whereby large numbers of people were mobilized around the boycott of foreign goods and the consumption of "home-made" products. The leaders of the *swadeshi* movement were also criticized for their violence, Hindu nationalism, and patriarchy. The most strident critique of Hindu nationalist and patriarchal *swadeshi* politics was made by Rabindranath Tagore in his 1911 novel *Ghare Bhaire*. At the time of Karve's writings, the term would have been regenerated by Gandhi's emphasis on non-violence, self-reliance, spinning, and female participation.
78. Karve, *Atmavrit va Charitra*, 433.
79. Ibid., 435.

80. *Shreemati Nathabai Damodar Thackersay Indian Women's University: A Short Account of Its Origin and Growth during 1916–1926*, 4.
81. Ibid.
82. Karve, *Atmavrit va Charitra*, 386.
83. Quoted in Maitrayee Chaudhuri, *The Indian Women's Movement: Reform and Revival*, 145.
84. Karve, *Atmavrit va Charitra*, 443.
85. N. M. Patwardhan, *Charitra (1928 te 1957 paryant)* [Biography: From 1928 to 1957], 1958. Included in Karve, *Atmavrit va Charitra*.
86. Ibid., 489.
87. See Christopher King, *One Language, Two Scripts*. Also Dalmia, *The Nationalisation of Hindu Traditions*, and Gupta, *Sexuality, Community, Obscenity*.
88. I am borrowing from Bourdieu's notion of cultural capital, whereby the deliberately *restricted* circulation of material and symbolic "goods"—including knowledge and culture—were sought after through socially specific codes of desire. Bourdieu, *The Field of Cultural Production*.
89. G. M. Chiplunkar, *The Scientific Basis of Women's Education*.
90. Booth argued that "the entire modern emancipation movement may be looked upon as an attempt on the part of women to adopt themselves to masculine ways and standards." *The Scientific Basis of Women's Education*, ix.
91. Ibid., 90.
92. Ibid., 26.
93. I thank an anonymous reader for making this connection, drawing attention to the widening, global discourse on the "modern girl" at this time in history. For a detailed study of such interconnections, see Weinbaum et al., *The Modern Girl around the World*.
94. Both Seth and Sinha have encapsulated the long life of the Mayo controversy, in which the American journalist Katherine Mayo wrote a scathing exposé of Indian gender relations in 1929 against the backdrop, as Sinha points out, of a wide-scale transformation of global political relations. See Sinha, *Mother India*. While neither Karve nor Chiplunkar seems to have directly entered that fray, the editor of the *Indian Social Reformer*, K. Natrajan, was a vociferous participant. In other words, there were simply a few degrees of separation in the larger public sphere. Seth, *Subject Lessons*, 149.
95. Chiplunkar, *The Scientific Basis of Women's Education*, 31.
96. Ibid., 83.
97. Ibid., 14–15.
98. Ibid., 84–85 (emphasis in original).
99. Ibid., 86.
100. Cited by Chiplunkar, *The Scientific Basis of Women's Education*, 5; Booth, "The Present Day Education of Girls."

101. Chiplunkar, *The Scientific Basis of Women's Education*, 92.
102. By this point the WU would have been renamed the SNDT. The annual meeting of the Senate in 1924 had the Right Honourable Mr. H. A. L. Fisher, once the Minister of Education in England, praise the university for its policies. Fisher congratulated the university for "offering to Indian women . . . the joys of literature and experiencing the exhilaration of ordered thought and accumulating a capital store of interest and of knowledge." It would be in this way that "the spread of culture and enlightenment in the homes of the people the general standard of life in India may be raised.' SNDT, *Ninth Annual Report 1924–25*, 1925.
103. Board of Education, *Report of the Consultative Committee on Differentiation of the Curriculum for Boys and Girls Respectively in Secondary Schools*, 1923.
104. Ibid., 89.
105. Ibid., 101. For a detailed study on the politics of the slippage between language and literature in modern Britain, see Baldick, *The Social Mission of English Criticism, 1848–1932*.
106. Board of Education, *Report of the Consultative Committee*, 123.
107. Ibid.
108. Ibid.
109. Chiplunkar, *The Scientific Basis of Women's Education*, 75.
110. Desai and Bhansali, *A Struggle for Identity Retention*.
111. Chandavarkar, *Maharshi Karve*.
112. The same report does concede an awareness of the widening critique of the differentiated curriculum, one that might compound "an Inferiority Complex in the minds of women in India." SNDT, *Twenty Fifth Annual Report 1940–1941*.
113. Shreemati Nathabai Damodar Thackersay Women's University Bill. *Bombay Government Gazette 1949 Part V. Legislative Assembly Bill no. LX of 1949*, 16 September 1949.
114. Ibid.
115. Ibid.
116. O'Hanlon, "Introduction" to Shinde, *Stri Purush Tulana*, 24–25. For a rich analysis of these reinforcing discourses, albeit from another regional context, see Afsaneh Najmabadi, "Gender and the Secularism of Modernity: How Can a Muslim Woman Be French?"
117. Quoted in SNDT *Convocation Address Speeches*, 1960.

CHAPTER 5: "I SHALL READ PRETTY ENGLISH STORIES"

1. Agashe, *Sadgun Manjari: Eka Hatbhagya Strichya Charitra*. The title may be translated as follows: *Sadgun*: full of the most virtuous qualities. *Manjari*: seeds of the tulsi plant (which is used in Hindu and Brahmanical religious rituals). *Sadgun Manjari*: a portrait, sketch, or biography of an unfortunate woman. All translations from the original Marathi are mine.

2. Avadi's sister also died before she could complete her education.
3. Agashe, *Sadgun Manjari*, 10.
4. It is not my purpose to detach the real Avadi, or the woman-as-agent and empirical subject from her representation in the progressive male imagination. Nor do I merely report from Agashe's work; I am aware that my own commentary reedits his voice. Benefiting here from Spivak's formulation, I emphasize that any urge (Agashe's, the feminist's, the historian's) to hear Avadi's own voice coheres the very truth claims of power-in-the-making. But it is worth recalling Lata Mani's corrective to Spivak's oft-quoted thesis here. Mani asked, "In claiming 'the subaltern cannot speak' does Spivak mean 'cannot' as in 'does not know how to' or 'cannot' in the sense of 'is unable to under the circumstances?'" Mani, *Contentious Traditions*, 159. I take the point, although I emphasize that I am not interested in voice, or agency, and I am far more invested in unraveling what Spivak has called the "subject effect." Spivak, "Subaltern Studies: Deconstructing Historiography."
5. Agashe, *G.A. Agashe Yanche Nivadak Lekh*.
6. Agashe edited a Sanskrit edition of Dandin's *Daśakumāracarita*. For more information on the text itself, see DeCaroli, "An Analysis of Dandin's Daśakumāracarita and Its Implications for Both the Vākāṭaka and Pallava Courts," 672. Agashe's interest in this text is important to the extent that this, too, was a biography. See also Banerji, *A Companion to Sanskrit Literature*.
7. Dhere, *Vismritchitre*, 122.
8. Recent historical research has provided more information on Avadi Bhide, although it has done so with the primary intention of illuminating the social-reform world that her father moved in. Dhere, *Vismritichitre*, 116–39.
9. Metcalf, "Narrating Lives," 474–83. Along similar lines see Roland, *In Search of Self in India and Japan*.
10. Arnold and Blackburn, *Telling Lives in India*, 8.
11. Divekar, "Survey of Material in Marathi on the Economic and Social History of India—I," 81–117, 105.
12. Agashe, *Sadgun Manjari*, 12.
13. Ibid., 30–31.
14. These allegations were terribly potent. In her diary, Avadi recorded receiving death threats in writing, in one case signed by *dharmarakshak*, or keeper of the faith. Ibid., 60.
15. Max Mueller was a nineteenth-century professor of comparative philology and Sanskrit at Oxford University and is credited with using Orientalist scholarship (specifically that produced by William Jones) to cement the "Aryan Theory of Race," or the idea that, based on linguistic roots, Indians shared racial and cultural ancestry with Europeans. See Trautmann, *The Aryans and British India*.

16. Agashe, *Sadgun Manjari*, 6.
17. The play on Shakuntala is attributed to the classical Sanskritic poetic tradition, penned by the Sanskrit-language poet Kalidas from the fourth or fifth century AD. Max Mueller worked assiduously to recuperate Sanskrit literature, in the process serving to locate many of his translations within English Romanticism.
18. O'Hanlon, "Introduction" to Shinde, *Stri Purush Tulana*, 43
19. As O'Hanlon has noted in her "Introduction" to *Stri Purush Tulana*, in many cases the nineteenth-century Marathi word for widow and prostitute was the same.
20. Critiques of patriarchy abound in the nineteenth-century literature from western India. Without exception, those works recognized the dehumanized position of the Brahman widow as naturalizing the wider violence of caste inequities. Both Tarabai Shinde and Pandita Ramabai (the latter was herself a Brahman widow) produced terse criticisms of the social position of the widow, immediately situating widowhood as emblematic of the strengthening grip of an indigenous and caste-mobile patriarchy. A set of essays written in 1910 by young widows of the Widows Home in Poona highlighted the sentiments of the women themselves and made strident criticisms connecting patriarchy to the sexual division of labor: "A widow is worked like a menial.... If she but stops for a few minutes, just to take a breath her mother-in-law throws a volley of abuses.... She does not get her two meals a day.... She is made to work like a coolie..... After her husband's death a widow does not get sufficient food and clothes; if poor she has to work near the fire in the kitchen.... She is overworked like a slave from Africa." Quoted by Chakravarti, *Rewriting History*, 265 n. 35. The essays are unpublished.
21. Agashe, *Sadgun Manjari*, 1–2.
22. Ibid., 3.
23. It is quite possible that in keeping with established custom, Avadi and her husband would not yet have entered into sexual relations. Ibid., 10–11.
24. Ramabai Ranade mentions that this was her first concern when her husband chose to teach her to write. Tanika Sarkar has argued that "(women's) education [was seen as] a double repudiation of the husband . . . both immorality and non-conjugality." And Chakravarti, *Rewriting History*, 209, states that "female education had been viewed as not just redundant (learning being associated in tradition with sacred knowledge, which was a closely guarded preserve) but reprehensible. Its association with widowhood in traditional beliefs is significant as widowhood was the most dreaded state for women. Ramabai Ranade and Kashibai Kanitkar both record this taboo as the reason why they had been kept illiterate in their parental homes." Ranade, *Aamchya Aayushyatil*, 27. Sarkar, "Strishiksha and Its Terrors: Re-reading Nineteenth Century Debates on Reform," 158.

25. Agashe, *Sadgun Manjari*, 12–13.
26. Ramabai Sarasvati, *The High Caste Hindu Woman*. Ramabai provides a deep analysis of the relationship between caste and patriarchy in this text.
27. Anagol states that in 1889 Mary Sorabji was denied promotion to the post of Lady Superintendent of the Female Training College by the Educational Department. Mary Bhor, Anagol explains, was "a second generation Christian, had obtained a teacher training certificate from London [as had Mary Sorabji], and became superintendent of the PNHS in 1905, she wrote a travelogue (my impressions of England, 1900 Poona), and a Marathi novel, *Pushpandarak* 1890," which posed the good and virtuous wife against the "prostitute." Anagol, *The Emergence of Feminism in India*, 89, 234.
28. Discussed in chapter 3.
29. Cornelia Sorabji (1866–1954) was a "second generation Christian" who, as Anagol writes, represented the "colonial subject of the nineteenth century whose 'hybrid' identity was formed through the encounter between Imperial Britain and colonial India." Sorabji gained the degree of bachelor of law from Oxford University but was not permitted to practice law until 1919, with the passage of the Sex Disqualification (removal) Act. Anagol, *Emergence of Feminism in India*, 228–29.
30. Agashe, *Sadgun Manjari*, 17–18.
31. Ellen McDonald, "English Education and Social Reform in Late Nineteenth Century Bombay," 453–70.
32. I borrow this term from Viswanathan, *Masks of Conquest*, 20.
33. Agashe, *Sadgun Manjari*, 18.
34. Spivak, "Three Women's Texts and a Critique of Imperialism."
35. The word he uses for "inner self" is *antaryama*. Agashe, *Sadgun Manjari*, 21.
36. Avadi mentions that her sister-in-law had a diary, and once, coming upon it herself, she read it. In her own diary she then recorded, "If you look at it truthfully then there really was no need for me to do such a thing. But I did see that thing; there was nothing significant there, but I felt really terrible about seeing it." Agashe, *Sadgun Manjari*, 41. Here Agashe injects immediately: "Reading the diary of others is a trivial crime but the repentance it creates in one's mind . . . so fearful of sinning, which the readers should take note of." It is difficult to ascertain whether he believes that the repenting reader is Avadi (hence the vignette establishes her as god-fearing) or whether the repenting reader is himself, in which case opening the slender possibility that he too recorded a degree of remorse at his own reading of Avadi's diary.
37. Agashe, *Sadgun Manjari*, 35.
38. We will never know whether Agashe eventually censored some more intimate observations. He makes it appear that he faithfully reported from its pages, an

act that he thought was urgently necessary in the name of a larger political struggle.
39. Agashe, *Sadgun Manjari*, 35–36.
40. Ibid., 36. The word he uses is *hitguj*.
41. Ibid., 139.
42. Ibid., 44.
43. Ibid., 45.
44. Ibid., 46.
45. Ibid., 47.
46. Ibid., 47–48.
47. Ibid., 22.
48. Ibid., 26 (letter of August 24, 1886, Poona).
49. Ibid., 86.
50. See Grewal, *Home and Harem*.
51. It is unclear whether this was Mary or Cornelia Sorabji, as Avadi wrote to both.
52. Agashe, *Sadgun Manjari*, 29.
53. Ibid., 38.
54. Ibid., 77. Another example, also produced at Chingi's death, was a short poem written by a student, "In Memoriam CHINGU BHIDE": "Chingu, heaven has called thee / Heaven has kept its own. / Into bliss God guides thee / Near his precious throne."
55. Another text that Avadi mentions reading is Dinah Mulock Craik's *John Halifax*. Again, we receive no details on the text itself, although this might indicate the wide popularity of the book (and Agashe's expectations from his audience) at the time. *John Halifax* was first published in 1856 and reprinted successively on both sides of the Atlantic. Enormously successful, the novel celebrated the laboring ethic in the story of a young tradesman's rise to success through incessant hard work, a rise that was supposed to mirror the swelling power of Victorian middle-class values and the concomitant decline of the aristocracy. Foster, *Victorian Women's Fiction*, especially chapter 2 on Craik's "Ambivalent Romanticism." Agashe records the title of the book without mentioning that the author was a woman.
56. Agashe, *Sadgun Manjari*, 102, letter of July 7, 1887, from Avadi to Lady Wedderburn.
57. Ibid., 105–7, letter of September 8, 1887.
58. *Svabhasha* literally translates as "one's own language."
59. The term he uses is *acaran*, literally deportment or conduct. Agashe, *Sadgun Manjari*, 111.
60. Agashe, *Sadgun Manjari*, letter of August 26, 1887, 112.

61. Ibid., 116–17.
62. Ibid., 119–20.
63. Moi, in *Sexual/Textual Politics*, has argued that "woman" in bourgeois society is necessarily produced through "lack," a situation accomplished both through the liberal humanism of modern male authors as well as by some women themselves, 9.
64. The word he uses for inner self is *antaryama*, 21.
65. Brown, *Regulating Aversion*, 16.
66. Again, to turn to Brown, "Liberalism's excessive freighting of the individual subject with self-making, agency, and a relentless responsibility for itself also contributes to the personalization of politically contoured conflicts and inequalities." Ibid., 17.
67. Rao, *The Caste Question*, 17.

CHAPTER 6: "WHY HAD I EVER BEGUN TO LEARN ENGLISH?"

1. Ranade, *Aamchya Aayushyatil Kahee Athavani* [Some memories of our life together], 26–27. All translations from the Marathi originals are mine.
2. In the original Marathi, the pronoun Ramabai uses throughout the text is *svatah*, which translates as oneself, or, as later translators have done, "Himself." This was in keeping with the requirement—one that she had obviously internalized significantly since that first night—that she not name her husband. When she does need to indicate him in the text, she uses the term *svatah*, which is certainly not the same as "he" or "him." See the version translated by Katherine Van Akin Gates as *Himself: An Autobiography of a Hindu Lady*. The title of the text reveals that Gates believes Ramabai to have thoroughly immersed herself in Ranade's identity.
3. Ranade, *Aamchya Aayushyatil*, 27.
4. While I am attempting to write against the centrality of Bengal in the historiography on the nineteenth century (and to orient regional histories away from a presentist assumption on the inevitability of the nation), it is important to appreciate the parallels between Ramabai Ranade's memoirs and Rashundari Devi, as well as the character Bimla in Tagore's 1911 novel, *Ghare Baire, The Home and the World*.
5. Both Judith Walsh and Tanika Sarkar have suggested the possibilities of this occurring simultaneously in nineteenth-century Bengal. Walsh, *Domesticity in Colonial India*; Sarkar, *Hindu Wife, Hindu Nation*.
6. Gandhi, *An Autobiography*.
7. Ranade, *Aamchya Asyushyatil*, 22.
8. Chakravarti, *Rewriting History*, 217.
9. Ranade, *Aamchya Aayushyatil*, 27. While arguing against his father for arranging his second marriage with Ramabai, Ranade invoked the double standards

whereby Durga his widowed sister, was expected to live a life of restraint: "Why am I being urged to marry? If you think it would be good for her to lead a life of restraint then it should apply equally to me." It is fascinating that these lines were reported to Ramabai, after Ranade's death, by Durga herself who claimed to have been eavesdropping outside the door while this rare conversation between male patriarchs took place. Chakravarti, *Rewriting History*, 228 n. 92.

10. Ibid., 228 n. 93.
11. O'Hanlon, "Introduction," 35, quoting Carroll, "Law, Custom and Statutory Social Reform," 379.
12. Chakravarti, *Rewriting History*, 129.
13. Ibid., 124.
14. Ibid., 130.
15. Ibid., 130–31.
16. Ranade, *Aamchya Aayushyatil*, 30
17. Ibid., 38.
18. Sedgwick, *Touching Feeling*.
19. O'Hanlon, "Introduction," 36, quoting *Subodha Patrika*, May 29, 1881, from *Report on Native Newspapers for the Bombay Presidency*, week ending July 9, 1881.
20. *Times of India*, May 17, 1881, quoted in O'Hanlon, "Introduction," 37. Shinde's text, which is the topic of O'Hanlon's analysis, was written at the moment that a young widow tried to kill her "illegitimate" child so as to avert being punished for having had extra-marital sex.
21. Ahmed, "Feminist Futures," 240. Further, Ahmed has asserted (238–39) that emotions are formations that mediate and expose the links between "knowledge / theory and practice / activism."
22. Chakravarti, *Rewriting History*, 265: "As more men went to the cities to study and pursue professions, women's labour was needed to make such moves possible; widows in the family were the most expendable and were therefore much in demand."
23. Ibid., 207. Shifts in family structure and affect have similarly been traced for modern Europe and North America; prominent among those is the work by John D'Emilio, "Capitalism and Gay Identity." D'Emilio examines how the (white) family slowly changed from being an independent unit of production to a group that extracted the affections of its members. Consequently, marriage turned from its emphasis on procreation to the nurturing of children.
24. Despite being aware of the inequities, Ranade in his new role as head of the household no longer interacted with his widowed sister.
25. When it came to his own status as a widower, Ranade bowed to paternal pressure and chose not to marry a widow, sanctioning the double standards around male and female sexuality.

26. Ranade, *Aamchya Aayushyatil*, 41.
27. Ibid., 37.
28. Freud, "Some Psychical Consequences of the Anatomical Distinction between the Sexes," 248–58.
29. Coward, *Patriarchal Precedents: Sexuality and Social Relations*, 266. Quoted by Chow, "Sexuality," 97.
30. Elphinstone, "Minute on Education."
31. Ramabai mentions that she soon completed her study of the second English reader, and that she could read *Aesop's Fables*, tell simple stories, and write sentences in English. Ranade then had her read the New Testament. Over time she would read Marathi newspapers aloud to him and once mentioned that she was reading *Tara* by Meadows Taylor. Ranade later employed an educated Englishwoman—the same Miss Hurford who taught at the PNHS and who played such an active role in Avadibai's life—to continue the education of his wife, although Ramabai often recalled how little interest she had in learning from any other teacher.
32. Ranade, *Aamchya Aayushyatil*, 39.
33. Ibid., 40.
34. Durga's dismissive reference to the office within domestic space, with the bedroom "upstairs," suggests again the multiple shifts being enacted within the home. For a much deeper analysis of the actual shifts in the organization of space and status within the Brahmanical home, see Kosambi, *Crossing Thresholds*, 105–12.
35. Ranade, *Aamchya Aayushyatil*, 40.
36. My analysis here is fortified by Judith Butler's study of individuation, desire, and prohibition, whereby the individuated subject is produced through networks of social prohibition. Butler has argued that "prohibition becomes the displaced site of satisfaction for the 'instinct' or desire that is prohibited, an occasion for the reliving of the instinct under the rubric of the condemning law. . . . Desire is never renounced, but becomes preserved and reasserted in the very structure of the renunciation." Butler, *Excitable Speech*, 98.
37. Ranade, *Aamchya Aayushyatil*, 74.
38. Derrida, *Speech and Phenomena*, 51.
39. Notably, another time that she does this is in the passage quoted earlier on shame, when she states that "that was the first time that I really felt ashamed of myself, I didn't want anyone to see, I wiped my tears and went downstairs." Ranade, *Aamchya Aayushyatil*, 30.
40. This resonates with Sue Thornham's assertion that "we enter culture by learning to say 'I,' in so doing we become a subject—the subject of our own utterances—but we are also subjected: Language is a structure that precedes us and places us; we can operate only according to its rules, and we are

objects as well as subjects in it." Thornham, *Feminist Theory and Cultural Theory*, 80–81.

41. Ramabai's desire, produced through an awareness of lack, evidences Rose's corrective to Lacan's work: "The feminine as a position within language is constituted always as the negative term. It is the phallic term which is the privileged term within language." Rose, *Sexuality in the Field of Vision*, 8.
42. Ranade, *Aamchya Aayushyatil*, 85.
43. Chakravarti, *Rewriting History*, 201.
44. Ranade, *Aamchya Aayushyatil*, 87.
45. Ibid.
46. Ibid., 94. My use of brackets here indicates the difficulty of this translation. As I mentioned, Ramabai never named her husband, nor did she refer to "him" or "his." Marathi facilitated this, as the language allows the gender to remain implicit. When she absolutely had to, she would use the term *svatah*, which literally means "oneself" and which, in one instance, is translated as "himself."
47. Ramabai maintained her investment in these despite moving closer to Tilak's militant Hindu nationalism after her husband's death.
48. Nikambe, *Ratanbai*.
49. Lokuge, "Introduction" to *Ratanbai*, xiii–xiv.
50. Nikambe, *Ratanbai*, 9–10.
51. Ibid., 11, 12.
52. This is a slight but significant divergence from the general composition of English-educated natives in western India, which was largely Chitpavan Brahman.
53. Spencer, *Indian Fiction in English*, 32. Cited in Lokuge, "Introduction," xiv.
54. Lokuge, "Introduction," xl.
55. Ibid., xli.
56. Here I am loosely building on Judith Okely's argument on Simone de Beauvoir's style of "concealed ethnography," whereby Okely argues that a paradoxical strength of *The Second Sex* is the hidden use of herself [Beauvoir] as a "case study . . . hence contradictions and tensions between theory and experience, philosophical neutrality and evident situatedness" emerge. Okely, *Simone de Beauvoir*, 72. In Nikambe's case, the fragility and interdependence of alliances between transnational liberal feminism and the consolidation of the Indian woman via Brahman patriarchy are revealed.
57. Nikambe, *Ratanbai*, 18.
58. Ibid., 43.
59. The novel is replete with details on the caste-specific Saraswat Brahman world. I do not want to make too much of Nikambe's conversion to Christianity. Nikambe herself never signals her conversion in the novel.

60. For the latter festival, we are told that "the lowest caste women" physically take upon themselves "all the abuse, the misery, and unhappiness of the [upper-caste] family." Nikambe, *Ratanbai*, 57.
61. Nikambe, *Ratanbai*, 87, resonating with Ramabai Ranade's bedroom experiences "upstairs."
62. Ibid., 88.
63. Ibid., 59.

CHAPTER 7: DOSEBAI JESSAWALLA AND THE "MARCH OF ADVANCEMENT"

1. She states that her mother "realised in her, to the utmost of her opportunity, her aspirations and ideals in regard to the education of Indian women." Had it not been for her mother, then, Jessawalla acknowledges that Manockjee Cursetjee's daughter might well "have been the first to taste the sweets of English education." Jessawalla, *The Story of My Life*, 37.
2. In Rosemary Hennessey's words, "To read a text symptomatically is to make visible that which hegemonic ideology does not mention, those things which must not be spoken, discursive contestations which are naturalized in the intercourse but which still shape the text's diseased relation to itself. To read symptomatically is to reveal the historicity in the texts of culture and in so doing put on display the exploitative social arrangements that they so often manage." In *Materialist Feminism and the Politics of Discourse*, 92.
3. Jessawalla, *The Story of My Life*, preface, iii.
4. Palsetia, *The Parsis of India, Preservation of Identity in Bombay City*. It is evident, too, from the earlier research of Jim Masselos and Christine Dobbin that battles were waged between groups. Manockjee Cursetjee Shroff (discussed in chapters 2 and 3) was engaged in prolonged battles over inheritance with other Parsis.
5. Burton, *At the Heart of Empire*, 160–64.
6. Ibid., 1.
7. Jessawalla, *The Story of My Life*, iii.
8. Ibid., 16.
9. For a very informative account of the role of the Parsi community (including some of Jessawalla's own relatives) in the opium trade, see especially Farooqui, *Opium City*.
10. Jessawalla, *The Story of My Life*, 22.
11. Though this, too, came at a cost: Dosebai relates in detail how her mother's "confinement" was especially traumatic because her husband's family considered her "estranged" and hence not worthy of the physical support that women of her social class regularly enjoyed at the time of childbirth.
12. Ibid., 24.
13. Ibid.

14. Ibid., 32.
15. Ibid., 33.
16. It was not only the native patriarchs who were invested in devaluing or ignoring her work (while simultaneously emulating its cultural meaning). An article in the *Bombay Courier* of August 23, 1842, mentioned the originality of her efforts, yet credited it entirely to the example of the "enlightened" views earned "by Maneckjee Cursetjee for literary acquirements on his late visit to Europe" which would have "strongly influenced his family to avail themselves still further of the benefits of a liberal education." Quoted by Jessawalla, *The Story of My Life*, 36.
17. Ibid., 34.
18. Ibid., 30–31.
19. Ibid., 31.
20. McDonald, "English Education and Social Reform in Western India," 453–73.
21. Farooqui, *Opium City*.
22. Luhrmann, *The Good Parsi*.
23. Spivak, "Three Women's Texts and a Critique of Imperialism," 243–61, 267.
24. Jessawalla, *The Story of My Life*, 43.
25. Ibid., 44.
26. Ibid., 59.
27. For instance, Inderpal Grewal has discussed how Sylvia Pankhurst's otherwise trenchant critique of British imperialism was instantly compromised with her ideals of "companionate marriage with free choice of partners . . . an ideal she presents as an alternative to the Indian system." As Grewal says, "Notions such as companionate marriage are formed in relation to oriental despotism and the harem, and this form of marriage suggests new ways for women to position themselves in English society within the domestic space." Grewal, *Home and Harem*, 77. Grewal is reading Pankhurst's text, *India and the Earthly Paradise* (1927).
28. Jessawalla, *The Story of My Life*, 70 (my emphasis).
29. Ibid., 71.
30. Hennessey, *Materialist Feminism and the Politics of Discourse*, 88. Hennessey's work helps pry open these transnational hegemonic social formations, illuminating the ease with which certain upwardly mobile groups in colonial India deployed sexuality to embrace and widen the reach of ideologies of power when speaking to a certain transnational audience.
31. Teresa Ebert has attempted to account for the constituent elements of such an individuated sexual longing, arguing that desire is "the repressed and unattainable wish for that which the subject loses upon entry into signification: the separation of the self from its own unconscious, its own body . . . the unrealizable longing for wholeness of self and unity of oneness with another . . .

[which] patriarchal ideology harnesses and constructs in terms of desire for the gendered other, the sexual or genital male." Ebert, "The Romance of Patriarchy," 19–57, 40.
32. Jessawalla, *The Story of My Life*, 57.
33. Ibid., 126.
34. Ibid., 143.
35. Ibid., 144.
36. Ibid., 145.
37. Ibid., 146.
38. Bhabha, "Of Mimicry and Man."
39. Burton, *Dwelling in the Archive*, 98.
40. See also Rajan, "(Con) Figuring Identity," 78–99.
41. Spivak, *A Critique of Postcolonial Reason*.
42. Spivak, "Three Women's Texts and a Critique of Imperialism," 243–61, 253.
43. Grewal, *Home and Harem*, 4.
44. Ibid., 3.
45. Ibid., 178.
46. Jessawalla, *The Story of My Life*, 92.
47. Ibid., 156.
48. Ibid., 185.
49. Her reference here can only be to Sir Henry Lawrence's legendary resistance to the "mutineers" attack on the British residency in 1857; the fact that Lawrence held on as long as he did due to the loyalty of Indian troops is just not important for Jessawalla!
50. Jessawalla, *The Story of My Life*, 220. Her observations mirror the colonial conviction that Indians lived in a state of filth and that only the British had the hygienic perspective to clean and sanitize the crumbling "native" cities.
51. Ibid., 224. On the whole, Jessawalla recalled monuments, fashion, natural beauty, and civic standards in far greater proportion than human interaction. The few memories of personal encounters seemed more enthusiastic in the case of conversations with important (British and European) personages or interactions with people from areas outside Bombay. At least at this stage in her memoirs, Jessawalla did not appear to be relentlessly in search of the visual, what Sara Suleri has called the "picturesque," or even attempting to represent an authentic, or domestic, native life for European consumption. Rather, in keeping with her tireless zeal to establish her unique triumph over native dictates, her travelogue, too, is a personal memorialization, cataloguing shrines and monuments as part of her marvelous, personal triumph over domesticity, tradition, and stasis. Suleri, *The Rhetoric of English India*.
52. Jessawalla, *The Story of My Life*, 246.

53. Ibid.
54. Foucault, "What Is an Author?," 124–27.
55. Jessawalla, *The Story of My Life*, 273.
56. More crucially, Jamsetjee Jeejeebhoy (1783–1859), the first Indian to be knighted by the British Crown, amassed a huge fortune from the opium trade with China. He diversified his interests, was a shareholder in Bombay's first English paper, the *Bombay Courier*, and multiplied his power during the cotton boom of the nineteenth century. He is remembered as an important patron of education and social reform and an active philanthropist in Bombay city. He was knighted in 1843. See Palsetia, *The Parsis of Bombay*.
57. Burton, *At the Heart of Empire*, 6.
58. Jessawalla, *The Story of My Life*, 272.
59. For instance, building upon Francis Hutchins's work on the "illusion of permanence," Sara Suleri has argued that "for the female as colonizer, the picturesque assumes an ideological urgency through which all subcontinental threats could be temporarily converted into watercolours and thereby domesticated into a less threatening system of belonging. . . . The picturesque becomes synonymous with a desire to transfix a dynamic cultural confrontation into a still life, converting a pictorial imperative into a gesture of self-protection . . . and thus is converted from its status as confessedly minor art into a dense tale of colonial incertitude." Suleri, *The Rhetoric of English India*, 74–75.
60. Jessawalla, *The Story of My Life*, 282.
61. Feminist cultural theorist Rosemary Betterton has suggested that "once women are positioned as active and investigative viewing subjects, questioning what is normal in representation, two critical questions arise: the supposed inevitability / neutrality of the dominant male gaze . . . [and] secondly, the issue of pleasure." Betterton, *Looking On*, 11. See also Thornham, *Feminist Theory and Cultural Studies*.
62. Jessawalla, *The Story of My Life*, 277.
63. Ibid., 309.
64. Ibid., 362. She had never traveled to northern Turkey, and even if she had, the reference would have been anachronistic. Her use of the term indicates her reliance on a British Orientalist designation for some members of the Turkish diaspora in India, thus her cultural memory of a shared Indo-Aryan homeland for "Circassians" and members of the Zoroastrian faith.
65. Ibid., 362.
66. Ibid., 380.
67. Ibid., 362.
68. Ibid., 462.

NOTES

69. Ibid., 474.
70. Ibid., 492–94. The article she cites was carried in the *Bombay Courier*, August 19, 1842.
71. *Bombay Courier*, August 19, 1842. This was the paper connected to Sir Jamsetjee Jeejeebhoy.
72. This might explain, too, the complete lack of interest in this work: unlike other nineteenth-century women's texts from British India, this one has barely been commented upon by scholars. One exception is Ramanna, "A Voice from the Nineteenth Century: The Story of Dosebai Cowasjee Jessawalla."
73. Lury, *Consumer Culture*, 154, and Winship, *Inside Women's Magazines*, who argue that cultural capital for women lies in the skills developed through the work of "femininity," skills deliberately negated and invisibilized so as to make femininity appear as transhistorical and natural. See Steedman, *Landscape for a Good Woman*, for a firsthand insight into the cultural work of femininity.

CHAPTER 8: "I AM AN INDIAN. I HAVE NO LANGUAGE"

1. My exploration of "failure" is informed by Judith Butler's assertion on gender and the constitution of meaning, whereby she deploys "failure" as a critical tool in excavating conflicts over *re*-signification. Butler, *Excitable Speech*.
2. Athavale, *Mazi Kahani*, 1.
3. Ibid., 4.
4. *Brahman Balvidhva*: literally, a Brahman child widow. The young age for Brahman girls' marriage required that there be a hiatus between the actual marriage ceremony and the consummation of sexual relations. A *balvidhva* would, therefore, be married, widowed, and a virgin. Parvatibai was not a *balvidhva*, but her sister Baya definitely was.
5. Brahman widows were forced to shave their scalps. This was not only disfiguring and painful, but the act of having their hair sheared signified extreme social ostracism and was both emotionally and physically degrading.
6. Athavale, *Mazi Kahani*, 12.
7. Discussed in chapter 3.
8. Athavale, *Mazi Kahani*, 15.
9. Ellen McDonald has argued that it was the very elements of the English education curriculum that fostered philanthropy among Bombay city's first colonial subjects. McDonald, "English Education and Social Reform in Late Nineteenth Century Bombay."
10. Athavale, *Mazi Kahani*, 107.
11. Ibid., Appendix B. *Kesari*, January 17, 1905.
12. Athavale, *Mazi Kahani*, 38.
13. *Sudharak*: social reformer, usually believed to be "westernized" and English-educated.

14. Ibid., 16.
15. Ibid., 39.
16. Near Gvalia / Gwalior Tank.
17. Ibid., 42.
18. Ibid.
19. Ibid.
20. Because of the outbreak of World War I, she went to the United States via Japan.
21. Ibid., 53.
22. Ibid.
23. See Grewal, *Home and Harem*, for a different, and very compelling, reading of this and other encounters that Athavale experienced in her travels.
24. Athavale, *Mazi Kahani*, 55.
25. Athavale does not mention meeting Indian women while in the United States. The many Indian men who fill her memoirs were evidently in the United States as students or white-collar employees. These were the years marked by exclusionary immigration policies against "Asians"; thus it is possible that most of the Indians she remembers were in the United States on short-term work contracts. The immigration policies of these years would also have contributed to highlighting Athavale's trepidation and dependence on domestic service as a means to secure a living. It is significant that she would have traveled to the United States to raise funds despite harsh immigration controls.
26. Ibid., 61.
27. This reminds me of the interaction between Anna Pandurang and the young Rabindranath Tagore. A fascinating account of their conversations in the English language has been recorded by Mote. *Vishrabdh Sharada. Samaj va Sahitya (1817–1947)*, Vol. 1, 125–67.
28. Ibid., 80.
29. Ibid., 94.
30. Rosalind O'Hanlon has stressed how the performance of normative sexuality served to amplify transregional Brahmanical power: "Both sati and restrictions on remarriage helped to disseminate and reinforce models for female self-abnegation and deference to a much wider audience of Indians than were ever directly affected by either." O'Hanlon, *Comparison between Women and Men*, 29.
31. Karve, *Atmavrit va Charitra*, 342.
32. Athavale, *Mazi Kahani*, 95.
33. Ibid., 69.
34. Scott, "AHR Forum."

BIBLIOGRAPHY

GOVERNMENT ARCHIVES

Bombay Presidency Proceedings. Education Department.
Bombay Presidency Proceedings. General Department.
Bombay Presidency Proceedings, Judicial Department.

CONTEMPORARY OFFICIAL REPORTS

Alexandra Native Girls' English Institution, Poona. Reports for the Years 1863–1933 (some years missing).
Board of Education. *Report of the Consultative Committee on Differentiation of the Curriculum for Boys and Girls Respectively in Secondary Schools.* London: H. M. Stationery Office, 1923.
Bombay Government Gazette. 1949.
Director of Public Instruction, Bombay Presidency. Annual Reports for the Years 1868–1901.
New English School. *Annual Reports of the New English School for Boys Poona.*
Proceedings of a Deputation from the People of Poona Waited by Appointment upon His Excellency the Governor in the Council Hall. Poona, on Saturday the 9th of August, Re a High School for Native Girls. Bombay: Printed at the Bombay Gazette Steam Press, 1884.
Report of the Indian Education Commission (Hunter Commission):
Vol. 1. *Report of the Indian Education Commission. Appointed by the Resolution of the Government of India dated 3rd February 1882.* Calcutta: Superintendent of Government Printing, 1882.
Vol. 2. *Evidence Taken before the Bombay Provincial Committee and Memorials Addressed to the Education Commission.* Calcutta: Superintendent of Government Printing, 1884.
Report of the Maharashtra Female Education Society for the Period Ending 31st March 1889.
Report of the Proceedings of the Bombay Native Education Society, 1825–1840.
Report of Proceedings Held on the 29th September 1885 in the Town Hall, Hirabaug, for

the Distribution of Prizes to the Successful Students of the High School for Native Girls POONA, under the Presidency of H. H. Maharaja Sayaji Rao Gaekavad, of Baroda. Poona: Printed at the Orphanage Press by C. Birch, 1885.

Reports of Native Newspapers for the Bombay Presidency for the Years 1868–1920.

Shreemati Nathabai Damodar Thakersay. Indian Women's University. Calendar 1924.

Shreemati Nathabai Damodar Thakersay. Convocation Address Speeches. 1960. Bombay: SNDT Archives.

Shreemati Nathabai Damodar Thakersay. Annual Reports, 1916–.

Shreemati Nathabai Damodar Thackersay. *Indian Women's University: A Short Account of Its Origin and Growth during 1916–1926.* Poona: AryaBhushan Press, n.d.

Students' Literary and Scientific Society, Bombay. Proceedings and Reports for the Years 1848–1910 (some years missing).

NEWSPAPERS AND MAGAZINES

Bombay Courier
Bombay Gazette
Bombay Samachar
Indian Ladies Magazine
Indian Social Reformer
Kesari
The Mahratta
Mumbai Indu Prakash
Native Opinion
Oriental Christian Spectator
Poona Vaibhav
Sudharak
Sumitra
Times of India

BOOKS AND ARTICLES

Agashe, Ganesh Janard. *G. A. Agashe Yanche Nivadak Lekh.* Pune: n.p., 1958.

———. *Sadgun Manjari: Eka Hatbhagya Strichya Charitra* [One replete with virtuous qualities: A sketch of an unfortunate woman]. Pune: Arya Bhushan, 1890.

Ahmed, Sara. "Feminist Futures." *A Concise Companion to Feminist Theory,* ed. Mary Eagleton. Oxford: Blackwell, 2003.

———. *The Promise of Happiness.* Durham: Duke University Press, 2010.

Ajgaonkar, V. A. "The Problem of the Higher Education of Girls in the Bombay Presidency." M.Phil. thesis. Leeds University, 1939.

Alam, Muzaffar. "The Pursuit of Persian: Language in Mughal Politics." *Modern Asian Studies* 32, no. 2 (1998), 317–49.

Albuquerque, Teresa. *Urbs Prima in India: An Epoch in the History of Bombay 1840–1865*. New Delhi Promilla, 1985.

Alexander, M. Jacqui. *Pedagogies of Crossing: Meditations on Feminism, Spiritual Practice, Memory and the Sacred*. Durham: Duke University Press, 2005.

Allman, Jean, and Victoria Tashjian. *"I Will Not Eat Stone": A Women's History of Colonial Asante*. Portsmouth, N.H.: Heinemann, 1993.

——. "Rounding Up Spinsters: Gender Chaos and Unmarried Women in Colonial Asante." *Journal of African History* 37, no. 2 (1996), 195–214.

Altekar, Dr. A. S. *The Position of Women in Hindu Civilisation from Prehistoric Times to the Present Day*. Vols. I and II. Benaras: Culture Publication House, Benaras Hindu University, 1938.

Ambedkar, B. R. *The Essential Writings of B. R. Ambedkar*, ed. Valerian Rodrigues. New Delhi: Oxford University Press, 2002.

Amin, Sonia Nishat. *The World of Muslim Women in Colonial Bengal, 1876–1936*. New York: Brill, 1996.

Anagol, Padma. *The Emergence of Feminism in India, 1850–1920*. Burlington, Vt.: Ashgate, 2005.

Anderson, Benedict. *Imagined Communities: Reflections on the Origin and Spread of Nationalism*. New York: Verso, 1991.

Appadurai, Arjun, ed. *The Social Life of Things: Commodities in Cultural Perspective*. Cambridge: Cambridge University Press, 1988.

——. "Theory in Anthropology." *Comparative Studies in Society and History* 28, no. 2 (1986), 356–61.

Aravamudan, Srinivas. *Guru English: South Asian Religion in a Cosmopolitan Language*. Durham: Duke University Press, 2006.

Armstrong, Nancy. *Desire and Domestic Fiction: A Political History of the Novel*. New York: Oxford University Press, 1987.

Arnold, David. *Colonizing the Body: State Medicine and Epidemic Disease in Nineteenth Century India*. Berkeley: University of California Press, 1993.

Arnold, David, and Stuart Blackburn. *Telling Lives in India: Biography, Autobiography and Life History*. Bloomington: Indiana University Press, 2004.

Arondekar, Anjali. *For the Record: On Sexuality and the Colonial Archive in India*. Durham: Duke University Press, 2009.

Athavale, Parvati. *Mazi Kahani* [My story]. Hingne [Pune]: Anathbalikashram, 1928.

Bagal, J. C. *Women's Education in Eastern India, the First Phase; Mainly Based on Contemporary Records*. Calcutta: World Press Private, 1956.

Baldick, Chris. *The Social Mission of English Criticism, 1848–1932*. New York: Oxford University Press, 1983.

Banerji, Himani. "Pygmalion Nation: Toward a Critique of Subaltern Studies and the 'Resolution of the Women's Question.'" *Of Property and Propriety: The Role of Gender and Class in Imperialism and Nationalism*, ed. Judith Whitehead, Himani Banerji, and Shahrzad Mojab, 34–84. Toronto: University of Toronto Press, 2001.

Banerji, Sures Chandra. *A Companion to Sanskrit Literature: Spanning a Period of Over Three Thousand Years, Containing Brief Accounts of Authors, Works, Characters, Technical Terms, Geographical Names, Myths, Legends, and Several Appendices*. Delhi: Motilal Banarsidass, 1989.

Barlow, Tani. "Eugenic Woman, Semicolonialism and Colonial Modernity as Problems for Postcolonial Theory." *Postcolonial Studies and Beyond*, ed. Ania Loomba et al., 359–84. Durham: Duke University Press, 2005.

———. *Formations of Colonial Modernity in East Asia*. Durham: Duke University Press, 1997.

———. *The Question of Women in Chinese Feminism*. Durham: Duke University Press, 2004.

Barrett, Michele, ed. *Virginia Woolf: Women and Writing*. New York: Harvest, 1979.

Basu, Aparna. *Essays on the History of Indian Education*. New Delhi: Concept, 1982.

———. *The Growth of Education and Political Development in India, 1898–1920*. New Delhi: Oxford University Press, 1974.

Bayly, C. A. *Indian Society and the Making of the British Empire*. Cambridge: Cambridge University Press, 1988.

Bayly, Susan. *Caste, Society and Politics in India: From the Eighteenth Century to the Modern Age*. Cambridge: Cambridge University Press, 1999.

Benson, J. "The British Debate over the Medium of Instruction in Indian Education." *Journal of Educational Administration and History* 4, no. 2 (1972), 1–12.

Berlant, Lauren. "Cruel Optimism: On Marx, Loss and the Senses." *New Formations* 63, no. 1 (2007), 33–51.

Betterton, Rosemary. *Looking On: Images of Femininity in the Visual Arts and Media*. London: Pandora, 1987.

Bhabha, Homi. "Of Mimicry and Man: The Ambivalence of Colonial Discourse." *The Location of Culture*. New York: Routledge, 1993 (1987).

Bhatt, Chetan. *Hindu Nationalism: Origins, Ideologies and Modern Myths*. New York: Berg, 2001.

Birken, Lawrence. *Consuming Desire: Sexual Science and the Emergence of a Culture of Abundance, 1871–1914*. Ithaca, N.Y.: Cornell University Press, 1988.

Birla, Ritu. *Stages of Capital: Law, Culture, and Market Governance in Late Colonial India*. Durham: Duke University Press, 2008.

Borthwick, Meredith. *The Changing Condition of Women in Bengal 1849–1905.* Princeton, N.J.: Princeton University Press, 1984.

Bourdieu, Pierre. *Distinction: A Social Critique of the Judgment of Taste.* Trans. Richard Nice. Cambridge: Harvard University Press, 1984.

———. *The Field of Cultural Production: Essays on Art and Literature.* New York: Columbia University Press, 1993.

———. *Language and Symbolic Power.* Cambridge: Harvard University Press, 1991.

Braidotti, Rosi. *Nomadic Subjects: Embodiment and Sexual Difference in Contemporary Feminist Theory.* New York: Columbia University Press, 1994.

Brass, Paul. *The Politics of India since Independence.* Cambridge: Cambridge University Press, 1990.

Brown, Wendy. *Regulating Aversion: Tolerance in the Age of Identity and Empire.* Princeton, N.J.: Princeton University Press, 2006.

Burstyn, Joan N. *Victorian Education and the Ideal of Womanhood.* New Brunswick, N.J.: Rutgers University Press, 1984.

Burton, Antoinette. *At the Heart of Empire: Indians and the Colonial Encounter in Late Victorian Britain.* Berkeley: University of California Press, 1998.

———. "From Child Bride to 'Hindoo Lady': Rukhmabai and the Debate on Sexual Respectability in Imperial Britain." *American Historical Review* 103, no. 4 (October 1998), 1119–46.

———, ed. *Gender, Sexuality and Colonial Modernities.* New York: Routledge, 1999.

———. *The Postcolonial Careers of Santa Rama Rao.* Durham: Duke University Press, 2007.

Butler, Judith. *Bodies That Matter: On the Discursive Limits of "Sex."* New York: Routledge, 1993.

———. *Excitable Speech: A Politics of the Performative.* New York: Routledge, 1997.

———. *Gender Trouble: Feminism and the Subversion of Identity.* New York: Routledge, 1999 (1990).

———. *The Psychic Life of Power: Theories in Subjection.* New York: Routledge, 1997.

———. *Subjects of Desire: Hegelian Reflections on Twentieth Century France.* New York: Columbia University Press, 1987.

Cameron, Deborah. *Feminism and Linguistic Theory.* New York: St. Martin's, 1992.

———. *On Language and Sexual Politics.* New York: Routledge, 2006.

Carroll, Lucy. "Law, Custom and Statutory Social Reform." *Indian Economic and Social History Review* 20, no. 4 (1983), 363–88.

Carter, Julian. *The Heart of Whiteness: Normal Sexuality and Race in America, 1880–1940.* Durham: Duke University Press, 2007.

Cashman, Richard. *The Myth of the Lokmanya: Tilak and Mass Politics in Maharashtra.* Berkeley: University of California Press, 1975.

Chakrabarty, Dipesh. "The Difference-Deferral of (a) Colonial Modernity: Public

Debates on Domesticity in British India." *Subaltern Studies* 8, ed. David Arnold and David Hardiman, 50–89. Delhi: Oxford University Press, 1988.

———. *Provincializing Europe: Postcolonial Thought and Historical Difference*. Princeton, N.J.: Princeton University Press, 2000.

Chakravarti, Uma. *Gendering Caste: Through a Feminist Lens*. Calcutta: Stree, 2003.

———. *Rewriting History: The Life and Times of Pandita*. New Delhi: Oxford University Press, 1999.

Chandavarkar, G. L. *Dhondo Keshav Karve*. New Delhi: Publications Divisions, Government of India, 1958.

———. *Maharshi Karve*. Bombay: Popular Book Depot, 1970.

Chandra, Shefali. "Gendering English: Gender, Sexuality and the Language of Desire in Western India 1850–1940." *Gender and History* 19, no. 2 (2007), 284–304.

———. "Whiteness on the Margins of Native Patriarchy: Race, Caste, Sexuality and the Agenda of Transnational Studies." *Feminist Studies* 37, no. 2 (2011), 127–53.

Chatterjee, Partha. *The Nation and Its Fragments: Colonial and Postcolonial Histories*. Princeton, N.J.: Princeton University Press, 1993.

———. "The Nationalist Resolution of the Woman's Question." *Recasting Women: Essays in Indian Colonial History*, ed. Kumkum Sangari and Sudesh Vaid, 233–53. New Delhi: Kali for Women, 1989.

Chatterji, Lola. "Landmarks in Official Educational Policy." *The Lie of the Land: English Literary Studies in India*, ed. Rajeswari Sunder Rajan, 300–308. New Delhi: Oxford University Press, 1992.

Chaudhuri, Maitrayi. *Indian Women's Movement: Reform and Revival*. New Delhi: Radiant Publications, 1993.

Chiplunkar, G. M. *The Scientific Basis of Women's Education*. Poona: Hudlikar, Deccan Gymkhana Colony, 1930.

Chiplunkar, Vishnushastri. "Aamchya Deshachi Stithhi" [The condition / Plight of our nation]. *Nibandhamaleteel Teen Nibandh* [Three essays from the Nibandhmala], ed. Nirmalkuma Phadkule, 79–164. Pune: V. N. Bhandar 1975 [1882].

———. "Itihaas" [History]. *Nibandhamaleteel Teen Nibandh* [Three essays from the Nibandhmala], ed. Nirmalkuma Phadkule, 28–78. Pune: V. N. Bhandar 1975 [1882].

Chopra, Radhika, Caroline Osella, and Filippo Osella. *South Asian Masculinities: Context of Change, Sites of Continuity*. New Delhi: Kali for Women 2004.

Chow, Rey. "Sexuality." *A Concise Companion to Feminist Theory*, ed. Mary Eagleton, 93–110. Oxford: Blackwell, 2003.

Cixous, Hélène. "The Laugh of the Medusa." *Feminist Theory: A Reader*, ed. Wendy Kolmar and Frances Bartkowski. New York: McGraw-Hill, 2005.

Cohen, Cathy. "'Punks, Bulldaggers and Welfare Queens': The Radical Potential of Queer Politics?" *GLQ: A Journal of Lesbian and Gay Studies* 3, no. 4 (1997), 437–65. Reprint, *Black Queer Studies: A Critical Anthology*, ed. E. Patrick Johnson, 21–51. Durham: Duke University Press, 2005.

Colley, Amanda, and Sara Delamont. *Feminism and the Classroom Teacher: Research, Praxis, Pedagogy*. London: Routledge Falmer, 2002.

Collins, Patricia Hill. *Black Sexual Politics: African-Americans, Gender and the New Racism*. New York: Routledge, 2004.

Connell, R. W. *Masculinities*. Cambridge: Polity, 1995.

Coopan, Vilashini. "The Ruins of Empire: The National and Local Politics of America's Return to Rome." *Postcolonial Studies and Beyond*, ed. Ania Loomba et al., 80–100. Durham: Duke University Press, 2005.

Cooper, Frederick. "Africa's Pasts and Africa's Historians." *Canadian Journal of Historical Studies* 32, no. 2 (2000), 298–336.

———. "Postcolonial Studies and the Study of History." *Postcolonial Studies and Beyond*, ed. Ania Loomba et al., 401–22. Durham: Duke University Press, 2005.

Coward, Rosalind. *Patriarchal Precedents: Sexuality and Social Relations*. London: Routledge and Kegan Paul, 1983.

Crook, Nigel, ed. *The Transmission of Knowledge in South Asia: Essays on Education, Religion, History, and Politics*. New York: Oxford University Press, 1996.

Dalmia, Vasudha. *The Nationalisation of Hindu Traditions: Bharatendu Harishchandra and Nineteenth Century Banaras*. Delhi: Oxford University Press, 1999.

David, M. D. "Beginnings of the Renaissance Movement in Maharashtra." *Indica* 18, no. 1 (1981), 1–12.

Davidoff, Leonore, and Catherine Hall. *Family Fortunes: Men and Women of the English Middle Class 1780–1850*. New York: Routledge, 2002.

Davis, Mike. *Late Victorian Holocausts: El Niño Famines and the Making of the Third World*. New York: Verso, 2001.

Davne, Martand Narayan. "Aadhunik Shikshan Vipak Natak" [Play on the modern education]. *Natya Kathamala* 4, nos. 1–5. Pen: Sudhakar Press, 1891.

DeCaroli, Robert. "An Analysis of Dandin's Daśakumāracarita and Its Implications for Both the Vākāṭaka and Pallava Courts." *Journal of the American Oriental Society* 115, no. 4 (October–December 1995), 671–78.

Delamont, Sara. *Knowledgeable Women: Structuralism and the Reproduction of Elites*. New York: Routledge, 1989.

D'Emilio, John. "Capitalism and Gay Identity." *Making Trouble: Essays on Gay History, Politics and the University*, 3–16. New York: Routledge, 1992.

Derrida, Jacques. "Of Grammatology." *A Derrida Reader: Between the Blinds*, ed. Peggy Kamuf, 31–58. New York: Columbia University Press, 1967.

———. *Speech and Phenomena and Other Essays on Husserl's Theory of Signs*. Trans. D. Allison. Evanston, Ill.: Northwestern University Press, 1973.

Desai, Neera, and Kamlini Bhansali. *A Struggle for Identity Retention*. Bombay: SNDT University, n.d.

Deshpande, G. P., ed. *Selected Writings of Jotirao Phule*. Delhi: Leftword Books, 2002.

Deshpande, Kusumvati, and M. V. Rajyadhaksha. *History of Marathi Literature*. Delhi: Sahitya Akademy, 1988.

Deshpande, Madhav M. *Sociolinguistic Attitudes in India: An Historical Reconstruction*. Ann Arbor, Mich.: Karoma, 1979.

Deshpande, Prachi. *Creative Pasts: Historical Memory and Identity in Western India, 1700–1960*. New York: Columbia University Press, 2007.

Dhere, Aruna. *Vismritchitre* [Portraits of the (forgotten) past]. Pune: Shri Vidya Prakashan, 1998.

Divekar, V. D. "Survey of Material in Marathi on the Economic and Social History of India—I." *Indian Economic and Social History Review* 15, no. 1 (1978), 81–117.

Dobbin, Christine. "The Parsi Panchayat in Bombay City in the Nineteenth Century." *Modern Asian Studies* 4, no. 2 (1970), 149–64.

———. *Urban Leadership in Western India: Politics and Community in Bombay City 1840–1885*. Oxford: Oxford University Press, 1972.

Duara, Prasenjit. *Sovereignty and Authenticity: Manchukuo and the East Asian Modern*. Lanham, Md.: Rowman and Littlefield, 2003.

Ebert, Teresa. "The Romance of Patriarchy: Ideology, Subjectivity, and Postmodern Feminist Cultural Theory." *Cultural Critique* 10 (autumn 1988), 19–57.

Elphinstone, Mountstuart. "Minute on Education." Reprint ed. Kolhapur: Shree Maharani Tarabai Teacher's College, 1923 (1823).

Enloe, Cynthia. *Bananas, Beaches and Bases: Making Feminist Sense of International Politics*. Berkeley: University of California Press, 2000.

Farooqui, Amar. *Opium City: The Making of Early Victorian Bombay*. Gurgaon: Three Essays Collective, 2006.

Feldhaus, Anne. *Images of Women in Maharashtrian Society*. Albany: State University of New York Press, 1998.

Fonseca, Jennifer. "An Analysis of the Relationship between the Political System and Education with Particular Reference to Primary and Secondary Education in Bombay, 1901–1960." Ph.D. diss., University of Bombay, 1987.

Forbes, Geraldine. *Positivism in Bengal: A Case Study in the Transmission and Assimilation of an Ideology*. Calcutta: Minerva, 1975.

———. *Women in Modern India*. Cambridge: Cambridge University Press, 1996.

Foster, Shirley. *Victorian Women's Fiction: Marriage, Freedom, and the Individual*. London: Croom Helm, 1985.

Foucault, Michel. *The Archaeology of Knowledge and the Discourse on Language*. New York: Pantheon, 1972.

———. *The History of Sexuality*, Vol. 1. New York: Vintage, 1990.
———. "Nietzsche, Genealogy, History." *The Foucault Reader*, ed. Paul Rabinow. New York: Pantheon, 1984.
———. "What Is an Author?" Trans. Donald F. Bouchard and Sherry Simon. *Language, Counter-Memory, Practice*, ed. Donald F. Bouchard, 124–27. Ithaca, N.Y.: Cornell University Press, 1977.
Freud, Sigmund. "Femininity." Originally delivered as "Some Psychical Consequences of the Anatomical Distinction between the Sexes." *New Introductory Lectures on Psycho-Analysis*, ed. and trans. James Strachey. New York: W. W. Norton, 1965 (1933).
Frykenburg, Robert E. "Modern Education in South India, 1784–1854: Its Roots and Its Role as a Vehicle of Integration under Company Raj." *American Historical Review* 91, no. 1 (1986), 37–65.
Fukazawa, Hiroshi. *The Medieval Deccan: Peasants, Social Systems, and States, Sixteenth to Eighteenth Centuries*. New York: Oxford University Press, 1991.
Ganachari, Arvind. "Imperialist Appropriation and Disciplining the Indian Mind (1857–1917): Whose History?" *Economic and Political Weekly*, February 2, 2008.
———. *Nationalism and Social Reform in a Colonial Situation*. Delhi: Kalpaz, 2005.
Gandhi, Leela. *Affective Communities: Anticolonial Thought, Fin-de-Siècle Radicalism, and the Politics of Friendship*. Durham: Duke University Press, 2006.
Gandhi, M. K. *An Autobiography: The Story of My Experiments with Truth*. Trans. from the Gujarati by M. Desai. Ahmedabad: Navjivan, 1996 [1927].
Ghosh, Anindita. *Power in Print: Popular Publishing and the Politics of Language and Culture in a Colonial Society, 1778–1905*. New Delhi: Oxford University Press, 2006.
Ghosh, S. G. "Bentinck, Macaulay and the Introduction of English Education in India." *History of Education* 24, no. 1 (1995), 17–24.
Gilbert, Sandra, and Susan Gubar. *The Madwoman in the Attic: The Woman Writer and the Nineteenth-Century Literary Imagination*. New Haven: Yale University Press, 1979.
Gopinath, Gayatri. *Impossible Desires: Queer Diasporas and South Asian Public Cultures*. Durham: Duke University Press, 2005.
Gordon, Stewart. *The Marathas 1600–1818*. Cambridge: Cambridge University Press, 1998.
Goswami, Manu. *Producing India: From Colonial Economy to National Space*. Chicago: University of Chicago Press, 2004.
Gramsci, Antonio, Quintin Hoare, and Geoffrey Nowell Smith, eds. *Selections from the Prison Notebooks of Antonio Gramsci*. New York: International, 1971.
Greenough, Paul, and Balmurli Natrajan, eds. *Against Stigma: Studies in Caste, Race and Justice since Durban*. New Delhi: Orient Black Swan, 2009.
Grewal, Inderpal. *Home and Harem: Nation, Empire, Gender and the Culture of Travel*. Durham: Duke University Press, 1996.

Grewal, Inderpal, and Karen Caplan. "Global Identities: Theorizing Transnational Studies of Sexuality." *GLQ: A Journal of Lesbian and Gay Studies* 7, no. 4 (2001), 663–79.

Guha, Ranajit. "Dominance without Hegemony and Its Historiography." *Subaltern Studies 6*, ed. Ranajit Guha. New Delhi: Oxford University Press, 1989.

Gupta, Charu. *Sexuality, Obscenity, Community: Women, Muslims, and the Hindu Public in Colonial India*. New Delhi: Permanent Black, 2001.

Gupta, Dipankar. *Interrogating Caste: Understanding Hierarchy and Difference in Indian Society*. New Delhi: Penguin, 2000.

Haddap, Vithal Vaman. *Bahekleli Taruni Maujchi Khaas Sensational Kadambari* [The corrupted young woman: An entertaining and exceptionally sensational novel]. Mumbai: Mauj Office, December 1924.

Halberstam, Judith. *Female Masculinity*. Durham: Duke University Press, 1998.

Hall, Catherine. *Civilizing Subjects: Metropole and Colony in the English Imagination 1830–1867*. Chicago: University of Chicago Press, 2002.

———. "Politics, Post-Structuralism and Feminist History." *Gender and History* 3, no. 2 (1991), 204–10.

Hall, Kira, and Mary Bucholtz, eds. *Gender Articulated: Language and the Socially Constructed Self*. New York: Routledge, 1995.

Hall, Stuart. "For Allen White: Metaphors of Transformation." *Stuart Hall, Critical Dialogues in Cultural Studies*, ed. D. Morley and K. H. Chen. London: Routledge, 1996.

———. "On Postmodernism and Articulation: An Interview with Stuart Hall." By Lawrence Grossberg. *Journal of Communication Inquiry* 10, no. 2 (1986), 45–60.

———. "The Rediscovery of 'Ideology': Return of the Repressed in Media Studies." *Culture, Society and the Media*, ed. Michael Gurevitch et al. New York: Methuen, 1982.

Hall, Stuart, et al., eds. "Encoding/Decoding." *Culture, Media, Language: Working Papers in Cultural Studies 1972–1979*. Birmingham: Centre for Contemporary Cultural Studies, 1980.

Hasan, Mushirul, ed. *Knowledge, Power and Politics: Educational Institutions in India*. Delhi: Roli, 1998.

Hay, Stephen. *Asian Ideas of East and West: Tagore and His Critics in India, China, Japan*. Cambridge: Harvard University Press, 1970.

Haynes, Douglas. *Rhetoric and Ritual in Colonial India: The Shaping of a Public Culture in Surat City, 1852–1928*. Berkeley: University of California Press, 1991.

Hennessey, Rosemary. *Materialist Feminism and the Politics of Discourse*. New York: Routledge, 1993.

———. *Profit and Pleasure: Sexual Identities in Late Capitalism*. New York: Routledge, 2000.

———. "Queer Theory, Left Politics." *Rethinking Marxism* 7, no. 3 (1994), 85–111.

Hodgson, Dorothy, and Sheryl McCurdy, eds. *"Wicked" Women and the Reconfiguration of Gender in Africa*. New York: Heinemann, 2001.

Hossain, Rokeya Sakhawat. "Sultana's Dream." *Sultana's Dream and Selections from the Secluded Ones*, ed. Roshan Jahan, 1–6. New York: Feminist Press, 1988 (1911).

Irigaray, Luce. *This Sex Which Is Not One*. Trans. Catherine Porter with Carolyn Burke. Ithaca, N.Y.: Cornell University Press, 1985.

Jacob, Wilson Chacko. *Working Out Egypt: Effendi Masculinity and Subject Formation in Colonial Modernity, 1870–1940*. Durham: Duke University Press, 2011.

Jessawalla, Mrs. Dosebai Cowasjee. *The Story of My Life*. Bombay: Times Press, 1911.

John, Mary. *Discrepant Dislocations: Feminism, Theory, and Postcolonial Histories*. Berkeley: University of California Press, 1991.

John, Mary, and Janaki Nair. *A Question of Silence? The Sexual Economies of Modern India*. New Delhi: Kali for Women, 1998.

Johnson, Gordon. "Chitpavan Brahmins and Politics in Western India in the Late Nineteenth and Early Twentieth Centuries." *Elites in South Asia*, ed. Edmund Leach and S. N. Mukherjee, 95–117. Cambridge: Cambridge University Press, 1970.

Joseph, Betty. *Reading the East India Company, 1720–1840: Colonial Currencies of Gender*. Chicago: University of Chicago Press, 2004.

Joshi, Priya. *In Another Country: Colonialism, Culture and the English Novel in India*. New York: Columbia University Press, 2002.

Joshi, S. J. *Anandi Gopal*. Bombay: Majestic, 1996 (1968).

Joshi, Svati, ed. *Rethinking English: Essays in Literature, Language, History*. New Delhi: Trianka, 1991.

Kachru, Braj. *Alchemy of English: The Spread, Functions and Models of Non-Native Englishes*. Urbana: University of Illinois Press, 1990.

Kamuf, Peggy. *A Derrida Reader: Between the Blinds*. New York: Columbia University Press, 1999.

Kanitkar, Narayan Bapuji. *Taruni Shikshan Natika, Athhva Aadhunik Tarunishikshan v Stri Svatantra Yanche Bhavishyakathhan* [The education of women, or a prophecy on modern education and women's freedom]. Pune: Shri Shivaji Press, 1890 (1886).

Kaplan, Cora. *Sea Changes: Essays on Culture and Feminism*. London: Verso, 1986.

Kapur, Ratna. *Erotic Justice: Law and the New Politics of Postcolonialism*. Portland, Ore.: Glass House, 2005.

Karve, Dhondo Keshav. *Atmavrit va Charitra* [Autobiography and biography]. Pune: Hingne Strishikshan Samstha, 1928.

——. *Looking Back: The Autobiography*. Pune: Maharshi Karve Stree-Shikshan Samstha Karvenagar, 1936.

Keer, Dhananjay. *Mahatma Jotirao Phooley: Father of the Indian Social Revolution.* Bombay: Popular Prakashan, 1974.

Kent, Eliza. *Converting Women: Gender and Protestant Christianity in Colonial South India.* Oxford: Oxford University Press, 2004.

King, Christopher. *One Language, Two Scripts: The Hindi Movement in Nineteenth Century North India.* New York: Oxford University Press, 1995.

Kosambi, Meera. *Crossing Thresholds: Feminist Essays in Social History.* New Delhi: Permanent Black, 2007.

Krishnaswamy, N., and Lalitha Krishnaswamy. *Story of English in India.* New Delhi: Foundation Books, 2001.

Krishnaswamy, Revathi. *Effeminism: The Economy of Colonial Desire.* Ann Arbor: University of Michigan Press, 1998.

Kristeva, Julia. "The Semiotic and the Symbolic." *Revolution in Poetic Language.* New York: Columbia University Press, 1984.

Kumar, Krishna. *Political Agenda of Education: A Study of Colonialist and Nationalist Ideas.* New Delhi: Sage, 2005.

Kumar, Nita. *Lessons from Schools.* Delhi: Sage, 2000.

Kumar, Radha. *A History of Doing: An Illustrated History of Movements for Women's Rights and Feminism in India, 1800–1990.* New Delhi: Kali for Women, 1993.

Lacan, Jaques. "The Signification of the Phallus." *The Woman and Language Debate: A Sourcebook,* ed. Camille Roman, Suzanne Juliasz, and Cristanne Miller, 37–44. New Brunswick, N.J.: Rutgers University Press, 1994.

Lacquer, Thomas. *Making Sex: Body and Gender from the Greeks to Freud.* Cambridge: Harvard University Press, 1992.

Lal, Ruby. *Domesticity and Power in the Early Mughal World.* Cambridge: Cambridge University Press, 2005.

Landes, Joan, ed. *Feminism, the Public and the Private.* New York: Oxford University Press, 1998.

Liu, Lydia. "The Female Body and Nationalist Discourse: The Field of Life and Death Revisited." *Scattered Hegemonies: Postmodernity and Transnational Feminist Practices,* ed. Inderpal Grewal and Caren Kaplan, 37–62. Minneapolis: University of Minnesotta Press, 1994.

Lokuge, Chandini, ed. *Ratanbai: A High-Caste Child-Wife.* New Delhi: Oxford University Press, 2004.

Loomba, Ania. *Colonialism / Postcolonialism.* New York: Routledge, 1999.

——. "Dead Women Tell No Tales: Issues of Female Subjectivity, Subaltern Agency and Tradition in Colonial and Postcolonial Writings on Widow Immolation in India." *History Workshop* 36 (1993), 209–27.

Loomba, Ania, Suvir Kaul, Matti Bunzl, Antoinette Burton, and Jed Esty, eds. *Postcolonial Studies and Beyond.* Durham: Duke University Press, 2005.

Lorraine, Tamsin E. *Gender, Identity, and the Production of Meaning.* Boulder: Westview, 1990.

Ludden, David. "Why Area Studies." *Localizing Knowledge in a Globalizing World: Recasting the Area Studies Debate,* ed. Ali Mirsepassi, Amrita Basu, and Frederick Weaver. Syracuse: Syracuse University Press, 2003.

Luhrmann, T. M. *The Good Parsi: The Fate of a Colonial Elite in a Postcolonial Society.* Cambridge: Harvard University Press, 1996.

Lukose, Ritty. *Liberalization's Children: Gender, Youth and Consumer Citizenship in Globalizing India.* Durham: Duke University Press, 2007.

Lury, Celia. *Consumer Culture.* Oxford: Polity, 1996.

Macaulay, T. B. "Minute on Indian Education." *Thomas Babington Macaulay: Selected Writings,* ed. John Clive and Thomas Pinney, 237–51. Chicago: University of Chicago Press, 1972 [1835].

Mali, M. G., ed. *Savitribai Phule, Samagya Vadmya.* Pune: Sahitya ani Sanskriti Mandal, 1988.

Mani, Lata. *Contentious Traditions: The Debate over Sati in Colonial India.* Berkeley: University of California Press, 1998.

Masselos, Jim. *Towards Nationalism: Group Affiliations and the Politics of Public Associations in Nineteenth Century Western India.* Bombay: Popular Prakashan, 1974.

Mayhew, Arthur. *The Education of India: A Study of British Educational Policy in India, 1835–1920, and of Its Bearing on National Life and Problems in India To-Day.* London: Faber and Gwyer, 1926.

McCully, Bruce. *English Education and the Origins of Indian Nationalism.* New York: Columbia University Press, 1940.

McDonald, Ellen E. "English Education and Social Reform in Late Nineteenth Century Bombay: A Case Study in the Transmission of a Cultural Ideal." *Journal of Asian Studies* 25, no. 3 (1966).

McLane, J. R. *Indian Nationalism and the Early Congress.* Princeton, N.J.: Princeton University Press, 1977.

McLeod, John. *Sovereignty, Power, Control: Politics in the State of Western India 1916–1947.* Boston: Brill, 1999.

Mehta, Uday Singh. *Liberalism and Empire: A Study in Nineteenth Century British Liberal Thought.* Chicago: University of Chicago Press, 1999.

Menon, Nivedita. *Recovering Subversion: Feminist Politics beyond the Law.* Urbana: University of Illinois Press, 1999.

Metcalf, Barbara. "Narrating Lives: A Mughal Empress, a French Nabob, a Nationalist Muslim Intellectual." *Journal of Asian Studies* 54, no. 2 (May 1995), 474–83.

Metcalf, Thomas. *Ideologies of the Raj.* Cambridge: Cambridge University Press, 1997.

Mill, James. *The History of British India.* London: Baldwin, Cradock, and Joy, 1817.

Mitchell, Timothy. *Colonising Egypt.* New York: Cambridge University Press, 1988.

Mohanty, Chandra Talpade. "Under Western Eyes: Feminist Scholarship and Colonial Discourses." *Feminist Review* 30 (autumn 1988), 61–88.

Mohanty, Satya. *Literary Theory and the Claims of History: Postmodernism, Objectivity, Multicultural Politics.* Ithaca, N.Y.: Cornell University Press, 1997.

Moi, Toril. *Sexual/Textual Politics: Feminist Literary Theory.* New York: Routledge, 2002.

Moon, Vasant. *Growing Up Untouchable in India: A Dalit Autobiography.* Lanham, Md.: Rowman and Littlefield, 2000.

Mote, H. V. *Vishrabdh Sharada: Samaj va Sahitya (1817–1947) Vol. 1.* Bombay: Popular Prakashan, 1971.

Mukherjee, Meenakshi. *Realism and Reality: The Novel and Society in India.* New York: Oxford University Press, 1985.

Muñoz, José Esteban. *Disidentifications: Queer of Colour and the Performance of Politics.* Minneapolis: University of Minnesota Press, 1999.

Nagarkar, Kiran. *Ravan and Eddie.* New York: Viking, 1995.

Nair, Janaki. "Uncovering the Zenana: Visions of Indian Womanhood in Englishwomen's Writings, 1813–1940." *Journal of Women's History* 2, no. 1 (spring 1990), 8–34.

Najmabadi, Afsaneh. "Gender and Secularism of Modernity: How Can a Muslim Woman Be French?" *Feminist Studies* 32, no. 2 (2006), 127–53.

——. *Women with Moustaches and Men without Beards: Gender and Sexual Anxieties of Iranian Modernity.* Berkeley: University of California Press, 2005.

Nandy, Ashis. *The Intimate Enemy: Loss and Recovery of Self under Colonialism.* New Delhi: Oxford University Press, 1983.

Naregal, Veena. *Language Politics, Elites, and the Public Sphere.* New Delhi: Permanent Black, 2001.

Nicholson, Linda. *Gender and History: The Limits of Social Theory in the Age of the Family.* New York: Columbia University Press, 1986.

——. *Identity before Identity Politics.* Cambridge: Cambridge University Press, 2008.

Nikambe, Shevantiba. *Ratanbai: A Sketch of a Bombay High Caste Hindu Young Wife.* London: Marshall Brothers, 1895.

Niranjana, Tejaswini. *Siting Translation: History, Post-Structuralism, and the Colonial Context.* Berkeley: University of California Press, 1992.

O'Hanlon, Rosalind. *Caste, Conflict and Ideology: Mahatma Jyotirao Phule and Low Caste Protest in Nineteenth Century Western India.* Cambridge: Cambridge University Press, 1985.

——, ed. *A Comparison between Women and Men: Tarabai Shinde and the Critique of Gender Relations in Colonial India.* Madras: Oxford University Press, 1994.

———. "Issues of Masculinity in North Indian History: The Bangash Nawabs of Farrukhabad." *Indian Journal of Gender Studies* 4, no. 1 (1997), 1–19.

———. "Issues of Widowhood in Colonial Western India." *Contesting Power, Resistance and Everyday Social Relations in South Asia*, ed. Douglas Haynes and Gyan Prakash, 62–108. Berkeley: University of California Press, 1992.

Okely, Judith. *Simone de Beauvoir*. New York: Pantheon, 1986.

Omvedt, Gail. *Dalit Visions: The Anticaste Movement and Indian Cultural Identity*. Delhi: Orient Longman, 1994.

O'Rell, Max. *John Bull's Womankind*. London: Field and Tuer; Simpkin, Marshall; Hamilton, Adams, 1884.

Orsini, Francesca, ed. *Love in South Asia: A Cultural History*. Cambridge: Cambridge University Press, 2007.

Palsetia, Jesse, S. *The Parsis of Bombay: Preservation of Identity in Bombay City*. Leiden: Brill, 2001.

Panse, Venubai. *PragatiPathavar: Svarn Mahotsav Smarak Granth. High School for Indian Girls* [The golden jubilee report for the High School for Indian Girls]. Pune: High School for Indian Girls, Huzurpaga, 1934.

Parasher, S. V. *Indian English, Functions and Forms*. New Delhi: Bahri, 1991.

Parchure, C. N., S. Atre, and M. M. Onkar, eds. *Anadi Gopal: New Profiles from Unpublished Sources*. Pune: Bharat Itihas Sankalan Samiti, 1997.

Parker, Kunal. "A Corporation of Superior Prostitutes: Anglo-Indian Legal Conceptions of Temple Dancing Girls, 1800–1914." *Modern Asian Studies* 32, no. 3 (1998), 559–633.

The Parsi Girl of the Period. Bombay: Jam-e-Jamshed Printing Press Company, 1884.

Patwardhan, N. M. *Charitra (1928 te 1957 paryant)* [Biography, from 1928 to 1957]. Published with Karve, *Atmavrit va Charitra* (1928). Pune: Hingne Strishikshan Samstha, 1958.

Perry, Erskine. "On the Geographical Distribution of India, and the Feasibility of Introducing English as a Lingua Franca." *Journal of the Bombay Royal Asiatic Society* 4 (1853).

Phadke, Y. D. *V. K. Chiplconkar*. New Delhi: National Book Trust, 1982.

Phadkule, Nirmalkumar, ed. *Nibandhamaleteel Teen Nibandh* [Three essays from the Nibandhmala]. Pune: V. N. Bhandar 1975 (1882).

Phule, Savitribai Phule. "Ingreji Mawli" [English is our mother, poem # 38]. *Savitribai Phule, Samagra Vanmaya* [Savitribai Phule, Collected Works], ed. M. G. Mali. Pune: Sahitya ani Sanskriti Mandal, 1988.

Pollock, Sheldon. "The Cosmopolitan Vernacular." *Journal of Asian Studies* 57, no. 1, (1988), 6–37.

———. "India in the Vernacular Millennium: Literary Culture and Polity, 1000–1500." "Collective Identities and Political Order," ed. Shmuel Eisenstadt et al. Special issue, *Daedalus* 127, no. 3 (1998), 41–74.

———. "The Sanskrit Cosmopolis, 300–1300: Transculturation, Vernacularization, and the Question of Ideology." *Ideology and Status of Sanskrit: Contributions to the History of the Sanskrit Language*, ed. Jan E. M. Houben, 197–247. New York: Brill, 1996.

Porter, Andrew. "Empires in the Mind." *The Cambridge Illustrated History of the British Empire*, ed. P. J. Marshall. Cambridge: Cambridge University Press, 1997.

Povinelli, Elizabeth. *The Empire of Love: Toward a Theory of Intimacy, Genealogy, and Carnality*. Durham: Duke University Press, 2006.

Prakash, Gyan. *Another Reason: Science and the Imagination of Modern India*. Princeton, N.J.: Princeton University Press, 1999.

Puri, Jyoti. "Concerning 'Kamasutras': Challenging Narratives of History and Sexuality." *Signs* 27, no. 3 (2002), 603–39.

Raeside, I. M. P. "Agarkar, Apte and the Kanitkars." *Writers, Editors and Reformers: Social and Political Transformations of Maharastra, 1830–1930*, ed. N. K. Wagle, 156–65. Delhi: Manohar Press, 1999.

Rajan, Gita. "(Con) Figuring Identity: Cultural Space of the Indo-British Border Intellectual." *Writing New Identities: Gender, Nation, and Immigration in Contemporary Europe*, ed. Gisela Brinker Gabler and Sidonie Smith, 78–99. Minneapolis: University of Minnesota Press, 1996.

Ramanna, Mridula. "The Content of the Curriculum: Bombay's Educational Institutions 1824–1854." *Indica* 32, no. 1 (1995), 1–12.

———. "English Education and Social Change in Bombay City, 1815–1858." Ph.D. diss., Bombay University, 1985.

———. "Indian Financial Support of Western Education: Bombay 1820–1856." *India Past and Present* 4, no. 1 (1987), 105–22.

———. "Social Background of the Education in Bombay City, 1824–1858." *Economic and Political Weekly* 24 (January 1989), 105–22.

———. "A Voice from the Nineteenth Century: The Story of Dosebai Cowasjee Jessawalla." *Journal of the K. R. Cama Oriental Institute* 61 (1997), 1–16.

Ramanujan, A. K., and V. K. Dharwadker, eds. *The Collected Works of A. K. Ramanujan*. New Delhi: Oxford University Press, 1999.

———. *Folk Tales from India*. London: Pantheon, 1994.

Ramaswamy, Sumathi. *Passions of the Tongue: Language Devotion in Tamil India, 1891–1970*. Berkeley: University of California Press, 1997.

Ranade, Pratibha. *Stri Prashnanchi Charcha: Ekonisave Shatak* [The debate over the women's question: The nineteenth century]. Bombay: Popular Prakashan, 1999.

Ranade, Ramabai. *Aamchya Aayushyatil Kahi Aathavani* [Some memories of our life together]. Bombay: Pratibha Pratishthan, 1993 (1910).

———. *Himself: The Autobiography of a Hindu Lady.* Trans. and adapted by Katherine Van Akin Gates. New York: Longmans, 1938.

Rao, Anupuma. *The Caste Question: Dalits and the Politics of Modern India.* New Delhi: Permanent Black, 2010.

———, ed., *Gender and Caste.* New Delhi: Kali for Women, 2003.

Rao, Paramila. "Women's Education and the Nationalist Response in Western India." *Indian Journal of Gender Studies* 15, no. 1 (2008), 141–48.

Rege, Sharmila. *Writing Caste, Writing Gender: Narrating Dalit Women's Testimonies.* New Delhi: Zubaan, 2006.

Reiner, I. M., and N. M. Goldberg. *Tilak and the Struggle for Indian Freedom.* New Delhi: People's Publishing House, 1966.

Rice, J. *A Lecture on the Importance and Necessity of Rendering the English Language a Peculiar Branch of Female Education; and on the Mode of Instruction by Which It May Be Made Subservient to the Purposes of Improving the Understanding, and of Inculcating the Precepts of Religion and Virtue: As It Was Delivered at Hickford's Great Room in Brewer Street, May 4, 1772.* London: G. Kearsly, 1773.

Richardson, Angelique. "Kennealy, Arabella Madonna (1859–1938)." *Oxford Dictionary of National Biography.* Oxford: Oxford University Press, 2004.

Richey, J. A., ed. *Selections from Educational Records: Part II.* Calcutta: Superintendent of Government Printing, 1922.

Robinson, Ronald. "Non-European Foundations of European Imperialism: Sketch for a Theory of Collaboration." *Studies in the Theory of Imperialism*, ed. Roger Owen and R. B. Sutcliffe, 117–40. Oxford: Oxford University Press, 1972.

Rofel, Lisa. "Qualities of Desire: Imagining Gay Identities in China." *GLQ: A Journal of Lesbian and Gay Studies* 5, no. 4 (1999), 451–74.

Roland, Alan. *In Search of Self in India and Japan: Toward a Cross-Cultural Psychology.* Princeton, N.J.: Princeton University Press, 1988.

Roland, Joan. *The Jewish Communities of India: Identity in a Colonial Era.* New Brunswick, N.J.: Transaction, 1998 (1988).

Roman, Camille, Suzanne Juliasz, and Cristanne Miller, eds. *The Woman and Language Debate: A Sourcebook.* New Brunswick, N.J.: Rutgers University Press, 1994.

Rose, Barbara. *Tsuda Umeko and Women's Education in Japan.* New Haven: Yale University Press, 1992.

Rose, Jacqueline. *Sexuality in the Field of Vision.* London: Verso, 1986.

Rose, Nicolas. *Inventing Our Selves: Psychology, Power and Personhood.* Cambridge: Cambridge University Press, 1998.

Roy, Parama. *Indian Traffic: Identities in Question in Colonial and Postcolonial India.* Berkeley: University of California Press, 1998.

Rubin, Gayle. "Thinking Sex: Notes for a Radical Theory of the Politics of Sexuality." *The Lesbian and Gay Studies Reader*, ed. Henry Abelove et al., 3–44. New York: Routledge, 1993.

———. "The Traffic in Women: Notes on the 'Political Economy' of Sex." *Toward an Anthropology of Women*, ed. Rayna Reiter. New York: Monthly Review Press, 1975.

Runge, Laura. *Gender and Language in British Literary Criticism, 1660–1790*. Cambridge: Cambridge University Press, 1997.

Sadana, Rashmi. "Two Tales of a City: The Place of English and the Limits of Postcolonial Critique." *Interventions: International Journal of Postcolonial Critique* 11, no. 1 (March 2009), 1–15.

Said, Edward. *Orientalism*. New York: Vintage, 1978.

Salih, Sara. "On Judith Butler and Performativity." *Sexualities and Communication in Everyday Life: A Reader*, ed. Karen Lovaas and Mercilee M. Jenkins. Thousand Oaks: Sage, 2006.

Sang, Tze-Lan D. *The Emerging Lesbian: Female Same Sex Desire in Modern China*. Chicago: University of Chicago Press, 2003.

Sangari, Kumkum. *Politics of the Possible: Essays on Gender, History, Narrative, Colonial English*. New Delhi: Tulika, 1999.

———. "Relating Histories: Literature, Literacy and Gender in Early Nineteenth Century Calcutta and England." *Rethinking English: Essays in Literature, Language, History*, ed. Svati Joshi, 32–123. New Delhi: Trianka, 1991.

Sangari, Kumkum, and Sudesh Vaid, eds. *Recasting Women: Essays in Colonial History*. New Delhi: Kali for Women, 1989.

Saraswati, Ramabai. *The High Caste Hindu Woman*. 2nd ed. Philadelphia: Press of the J. B. Rodgers Printing Co., 1887.

———. *Stri Dharma Niti* [Morals for women]. Kedgaon: Ramabai Mukti Mission, 1883.

Sardesai, G. S. *A New History of the Marathas 1606–1707*. Bombay: Phoenix, 1946.

Sarkar, Mahua. *Visible Histories, Disappearing Women: Producing Muslim Womanhood in Late Colonial Bengal*. Durham: Duke University Press, 2008.

Sarkar, Sumit, and Tanika Sarkar. *Women and Social Reform in India: A Reader*. New Delhi: Permanent Black, 2008.

Sarkar, Tanika. *Hindu Wife, Hindu Nation: Community, Religion, and Cultural Nationalism*. Delhi: Permanent Black, 2001.

———. "Strishiksha and Its Terrors: Re-Reading Nineteenth Century Debates on Reform." *Literature and Gender*, ed. Supriya Chaudhuri and Sajni Mukherji, 153–84. New Delhi: Orient Longman, 2002.

Schor, Naomi, and Elizabeth Weed. *The Essential Difference*. Bloomington: Indiana University Press, 1994.

Scott, Joan. "AHR Forum: Unanswered Questions." *American Historical Review* 113, no. 5 (2008), 1422–29.

———. *Gender and the Politics of History.* New York: Columbia University Press, 1998.

———. *Politics of the Veil.* Princeton, N.J.: Princeton University Press, 2007.

Seal, Anil. *The Emergence of Indian Nationalism: Competition and Collaboration in the Later Nineteenth Century.* Cambridge: Cambridge University Press, 1968.

———. "Imperialism and Nationalism in India." *Modern Asian Studies* 7, no. 3 (1973), 321–47.

Sedgwick, Eve K. *Between Men: English Literature and Male Homosocial Desire.* New York: Columbia University Press, 1985.

———. *Touching, Feeling: Affect, Pedagogy, Performativity.* Durham: Duke University Press, 2003.

Sen, Samita. "A Father's Duty: State, Patriarchy and Women's Education." *Education and the Disprivileged: Nineteenth and Twentieth Century India*, ed. Sabyasachi Bhattacharya, 197–236. Delhi: Sangam, 2002.

Seth, Sanjay. *Subject Lessons: The Western Education of Colonial India.* Durham: Duke University Press, 2007.

Sharp, H. *Sections from Educational Records, Part One (1781–1839).* Calcutta: Superintendent of Government Printing, 1960 (1920).

Shinde, Tarabai. *Stri Purush Tulana, Athhava striya va purush yaat saahasi kaun he spasht karoon daakhvinya karita ha nibandh* [A comparison between women and men. Or, an essay to demonstrate who is more wicked]. Pune: Stri Shivaji Press, 1882.

Shohat, Ella. *Taboo Memories, Diasporic Voices.* Durham: Duke University Press, 2006.

Shroff, Manockjee Cursetjee. *A Few Passing Ideas for the Benefit of India and Indians.* London: Emily Faithfull, 1862.

Singh, Jyotsna. *Colonial Narratives / Cultural Dialogues: "Discoveries" of India in the Language of Colonialism.* New York: Routledge, 1996.

Sinha, Mrinalini. *Colonial Masculinity: The "Manly Englishman" and the "Effeminate Bengali" in the Late Nineteenth Century.* Manchester: Manchester University Press, 1995.

———. "Giving Masculinity a History: Some Contributions from the Historiography of Colonial India." *Gender and History* 11, no. 3 (1999), 445–60.

———. *Spectres of Mother India: The Global Restructuring of an Empire.* Durham: Duke University Press, 2006.

Slacks, Jennifer Daryl. "The Theory and Method of Articulation in Cultural Studies." *Stuart Hall: Critical Dialogues in Cultural Studies*, ed. David Morley and Kuan-Hsing Chen. New York: Routledge, 1996.

Slate, Nico. "Translating Race and Caste." *Journal of Historical Sociology* 24, no. 1 (2001), 62–79.

Spencer, Dorothy. *Indian Fiction in English: An Annotated Bibliography.* Philadelphia: University of Pennsylvania Press, 1960.

Spivak, Gayatri. "The Burden of English." *Orientalism and the Postcolonial Predicament,* ed. Carol Breckenridge and Peter van der Veer. Philadelphia: University of Pennsylvania Press, 1993.

———. "Can the Subaltern Speak?" *Marxism and the Interpretation of Culture,* ed. Lawrence Grossberg and Cary Nelson. Urbana: University of Illinois Press, 1988.

———. *A Critique of Postcolonial Reason: Toward a History of the Vanishing Present.* Durham: Duke University Press, 1999.

———. "The New Subaltern: A Silent Interview." *Mapping Subaltern Studies and the Postcolonial.* Ed. Vinayak Chaturvedi, 324–40. London: Verso, 2000.

———. "Subaltern Studies: Deconstructing Historiography." *Selected Subaltern Studies,* ed. Ranajit Guha and Gayatri Spivak, 3–32. New York: Oxford University Press, 1988.

———. "Three Women's Texts and a Critique of Imperialism." *Critical Inquiry* 12, no. 1 (1985), 243–61.

Spodek, Howard. "Pluralist Politics in British India: The Cambridge Cluster of Historians of Modern India." *American Historical Review* 84, no. 3 (1979), 688–707.

Stallybrass, Peter, and Allon White, *The Politics and Poetics of Transgression.* New York: Routledge, 1986.

Steedman, Carolyn. *Landscape for a Good Woman.* New Brunswick, N.J.: Rutgers University Press, 1987.

Strobel, Margaret. *European Women and the Second British Empire.* Bloomington: Indiana University Press, 1991.

———. "Women's History, Gender History and European Colonialism." *Colonialism and the Modern World,* ed. Gregory Blue, Martin Bunton, and Ralph Croizier, 51–70. New York: M. E. Sharpe, 2002.

Suleri, Sara. *The Rhetoric of English India.* Chicago: University of Chicago Press, 1992.

Sunder Rajan, Rajeswari. *The Lie of the Land: English Literary Studies in India.* New Delhi: Oxford University Press, 1992.

———. *Real and Imagined Women: Gender, Culture and Postcolonialism.* New York: Routledge, 1993.

Swenson, Kristine. "The Menopausal Vampire: Arabella Kenealy and the Boundaries of True Womanhood." *Women's Writing* 10, no. 1 (2003), 27–46.

Teltscher, Kate. " 'Maidenly and Well Nigh Effeminate': Constructions of Hindu

Masculinity and Religion in Seventeenth Century English Texts." *Postcolonial Studies* 3, no. 2 (2000), 159–70.

Tharu, Susie, and K. Lalita, eds. *Women Writing in India: 600 B.C. to the Present* (vols. 1 and 2). New Delhi: Oxford University Press, 1993.

Thornham, Sue. *Feminist Theory and Cultural Studies: Stories of Unsettled Relations*. London: Hodder Arnold, 2000.

Tikekar, Aroon. *The Cloister's Pale: A Biography of the University of Bombay*. Bombay: Somaiya Publications, 1984.

Toor, Saadia. "The Erotics and Politics of Sexuality: Gender Studies Comes of Age." *The Book Review* 26, no. 10 (2002), 12.

Trautmann, Thomas. *The Aryans and British India*. Berkeley: University of California Press, 1998.

Trevelyan, Charles. *On the Education of the People of India*. London: Longman, Orme and Longmans, 1838.

Trivedi, Harish. *Colonial Transactions: English Literature and India*. Manchester: Manchester University Press, 1995.

Tucker, Richard. *Ranade and the Roots of Indian Nationalism*. Chicago: University of Chicago Press, 1972.

Vanita, Ruth. *Queering India: Same Sex Love and Eroticism in Indian Society and Culture*. New York: Routledge, 2002.

Vanita, Ruth, and Saleem Kidwai, eds. *Same Sex Love in India: Readings from Literature and History*. New York: St. Martin's, 2000.

Vaze, Sridhar Ganesh. *The Arya Bhushan School Dictionary*. Pune: Aryabhushan, 1928.

Viswanathan, Gauri. "The Beginnings of English Literary Study in British India." *The Postcolonial Studies Reader*, ed. Bill Ashcroft et al., 376–80. New York: Routledge, 1995.

———. *Masks of Conquest: Literary Study and British Rule in India*. New York: Columbia University Press, 1989.

Visweswaran, Kamala. *Fictions of Feminist Ethnography*. Minneapolis: University of Minnesota Press, 1994.

———. *Un/Common Cultures: Racism and the Rearticulation of Cultural Difference*. Durham: Duke University Press, 2010.

Volosinov, V. N. *Marxism and the Philosophy of Language*. Trans. Ladislav Matejka and I. R. Tetunik. New York: Seminar, 1973.

Walford, Geoffrey. *The Private Schooling of Girls: Past and Present*. New York: Routledge, 1993.

Walsh, Judith. *Domesticity in Colonial India: What Women Learned When Men Gave Them Advice*. Lanham, Md.: Rowman and Littlefield, 2004.

Weber, Max. "Objectivity in Social Science and Social Policy." *The Methodology of* the Social Sciences: Max Weber, ed. Edward Shils and Henry Finch. New York: Free Press, 1949.

Weinbaum, Eve, et al. *The Modern Girl around the World: Consumption, Modernity, Globalization.* Durham: Duke University Press, 2009.

Winship, Janice. *Inside Women's Magazines.* London: Pandora, 1987.

Young, Richard Fox. *Resistant Hinduism: Sanskrit Sources and Anti-Christian Apologetics in Early Nineteenth Century India.* Vienna: Institut für Indologie der Universität Wien, 1981.

Zelliot, Eleanor. *From Untouchable to Dalit: Essays on the Ambedkar Movement.* New Delhi: Manohar, 1992.

——. Introduction. *Growing Up Untouchable in India: A Dalit Autobiography*, by Vasant Moon. Lanham, Md.: Rowman and Littlefield, 2000.

Zirelli, Linda. *Signifying Woman: Culture and Chaos in Rousseau, Burke, and Mill.* Ithaca, N.Y.: Cornell University Press, 1994.

INDEX

Agarkar, Gopal, 60, 61, 65, 72, 177
Agashe, Ganesh Janard: audience of, 119–20; background of, 118; *Sadgun Manjari*, 117–32; on subject's diary, 117, 124–26
Age of Consent Bill, 97
Ahmed, Sara, 142
Ahmedabad Female School, 50–51
Alam, Muzaffar, 14
Alexandra Native Girls' English Institution, 35–36, 41–42, 86, 161, 166
Ambedkar, Bhimrao, 22, 97
AMS (Arya Mahila Samaj), 57–58
Anderson, Benedict, 12–13
Anglicists, 10, 15
Anglicization: being English vs., 13; condemnation of, 71; debate on, 11; of education policy, 9; Hindu power and, 68; indigeneity and, 14, 18, 35; Marathi and, 16, 59; policy of, 15, 38, 42, 69; vernacular curriculum vs., 105
Anglo-Vernacular standard III, 52
Arnold, David, 118–19
Aryabhushan Press, 59, 60
Arya Mahila Samaj (AMS), 57–58
Athavale, Parvatibai, 20; autobiography of, 176; background, 176; caste of, 182, 189; domestic work, 182–84; education of, 176–77; on female sexuality, 187; influence of Chiplunkar on, 176–78, 187, 189; Karve and, 177–81; on learning English, 175, 178–83, 185–86, 188–90; on national service, 178–79; speech by, 185, 188; travels, 181–86
Atmavrit (Karve), 101

Bahekleli Taruni (Haddap), 77
Bannerjee, Himani, 205 n. 122
Barlow, Tani, 24
Bayly, Susan, 18
Bentinck, William, 9
Bethune, J. E. D., 32–33, 35
Betterton, Rosemary, 241 n. 61
Bhabha, Homi, 13, 79, 167
Bhandarkar, R. G., 16, 40, 64–65, 88
Bhide, Avadibai: background, 117–22; biography of, 122–32; diary of, 117, 124–26; English education of, 117, 122–23, 128–29; on ideal woman, 132; on Marathi literature, 129–30; on traveling abroad, 181–82; widowhood, 122, 123, 133, 134
Bhide, Rao Bahadur Vishnu Moreshwar, 117, 118, 122
Bilingualism, 13, 14, 30, 41, 47, 59–61, 152, 155
Biographical writings, 118–20
Blackburn, Stuart, 118–19
Bombay Education Society, 40

Bombay Native Education Society, 40
Bombay Normal School, 50–54
Bombay Samachar (newspaper), 50
Bombay University, 98; Elphinstone School and, 40; English education and, 10; indigenous studies and, 103; Marathi language study in, 16, 89; women in, 93, 111
Booth, Meyrick, 99–101, 107
Brahmans: caste anxiety, 74; Chitpavan sub-caste, 15, 16, 40; English and, 16, 23, 40; on female sexuality, 87; language and, 13–14, 16; Marathi and, 16; marriage and, 19; new colonial, 30, 59; power and gender, 24, 55, 61, 97; sexuality and intellectual class, 22
Brown, Wendy, 133–34
Burton, Antoinette, 158, 167, 170
Butler, Judith, 197 n. 15, 204 n. 109, 209 n. 37, 236 n. 36

Carpenter, Mary, 49–51, 126
Carter, Julian, 206 n. 126
Cashman, Richard, 15
Caste and class: anxiety, 74; chastity and, 8, 18, 31, 54, 119; conjugality and, 6, 44, 48–55, 72, 74; English education and, 7, 9–10, 13, 15, 42, 52, 164; English language and, 6, 138; gender and, 20; indigenous interests, 13; liberalism and, 11, 136, 179, 187; Marathi and, 15; marriage and, 18–19; patriarchy, 11, 18, 20, 21, 23, 66, 74, 121, 151, 203–4 n. 105, 224 n. 13; power and, 25–27; ritual and, 8, 9, 22–23, 25, 70, 84, 118, 133–36, 138, 149, 151, 153–54, 158; satire on, 3; secularization of, 8, 9, 81, 118, 134–36; sexuality and, 4, 11, 18, 22, 25, 31, 66, 121; social progress and, 10; standards of, 5; virtuous woman and, 9, 23, 76, 125, 134–36, 171–81; vocabulary of gender and, 6
Chabuk (newspaper), 42–44, 47, 48, 54
Chakravarti, Uma, 18, 31, 135, 142, 143
Chastity and caste, 8, 18, 31, 54, 119
Chatterjee, Partha, 24–26, 106
Chiplunkar, G. M., 106–8, 176–78, 187, 189
Chiplunkar, Krishnashastri, 59
Chiplunkar, Vishnushastri: background, 59; on English, 61–63, 78–79; on Marathi, 15, 60, 61, 120; on masculinity, 78–79; writings, 60–62, 83
Chitpavan caste, 15, 16, 40
Chitrashala Press, 59
Christianity, 127–28, 151, 183
Class. *See* Caste and class
Colonialism: education policy, 9–13; indigeneity vs., 24; modernity and, 23–27; nationalism and, 24–27, 37, 106; power and language of, 4; sexuality and, 26; social mobility and, 71
Conjugality: caste, class, and, 6, 44, 48–55, 72, 74; English and, 71, 146–47, 165, 175; equality and, 46; expectation of, 18; hetero-, 164; naturalization of, 98–99, 173–74; prohibitions on, 146; as social progress, 10, 68; turn toward, 8; women's employment and, 107
Cosmopolitanism: English and, 9; Indian, 157–60; vernacular vs., 96; Western education and, 163
Coward, Rosalind, 144
Cultural and linquistic ventriloquism, 63, 65, 147, 150
Curriculum: anglicized vs. vernacular, 103; debate on, 64–68, 71–74; feminist, 100
Cursetjee Shroff, Manockjee, 32–37, 61, 92, 159

Dakshina Fund, 29, 30, 59
Dalit, 21, 134, 203 n. 99
Davne, Martand Narayan, 78
Deccan College, 14, 15, 30, 59
Depoliticization, 133–34
Derrida, Jacques, 197 n. 16, 208 n. 21
Deshpande, Prachi, 30, 60, 74
Desire: colonial, 26, 80, 222 n. 88; education and, 39, 127; English and, 6, 9, 53, 58, 75, 96, 129, 138, 140, 146, 151–55, 174; female, 144; forms of, 4, 81; gender and, 25, 27, 34, 132, 147; individuated, 52, 136; of native patriarchy, 152; sexual, 8, 76–77, 82, 83, 113, 135, 155, 158, 165, 174; of transnational reading public, 152; of white supremacy, 80
Dharmashastras, 72–73
Disidentification, 21
Divekar, V. D., 119
Domesticity: English education and, 63, 64; mother tongue and, 68, 81; scientific knowledge of, 105; women and, 45, 63, 75, 95, 113
Drama in Four Acts, Directed against the Modern High-Class System of Female Education, A (Kanitkar), 74

East India Company, 14, 29, 198 n. 24
Education. *See* English education; Women
Elphinstone, John, 10
Elphinstone, Mountstuart: background, 206 n. 6; education policies, 30; on English, 40, 55, 82, 90, 144; governorship of, 29–30; on Sanskrit, 14–15, 29
Elphinstone School, 40–42, 86
English education: in Bombay, 6–7; caste and, 7, 9–10, 13, 15, 42, 52, 164; as civilizing, 10; colonialist policy, 9–13; domesticity and, 63, 64; gender and, 77, 126–32; imperialism and, 12; as international language, 105; liberal social reform and, 40–41, 46; mistrust of, 45; prohibition against, 153; prostitution and, 75, 77, 78; sexual difference and, 31–32; sociability and, 36; social position and, 35, 40; threat of, 51; vernacular and, 33, 34, 71; of women, 30–39, 48, 57, 102, 105–13

English language: bilingualism and, 13; caste and, 6, 138; Christianity and, 127–28, 151; as civilizing, 69; colonial education and, 9; colonial government and, 199 n. 34; conjugality and, 71, 146–47, 165, 175; dangers of, 7–8, 66, 92–93; domestication of, 4, 10, 27, 84, 113, 117, 118, 129, 135, 158–59, 165, 174, 189–90; domesticity and, 64, 73; elevation of, 16; femininity and, 58, 78; gender and, 58, 77–78, 82; as Indian language, 5–9; liberal cosmopolitanism and, 9; Marathi and, 16–17, 60, 66–67, 77; morality and, 54; motherhood and, 90–94; mother tongue vs., 102–3; mystique of, 3; power of, 4, 6, 8, 43, 165; reproduction and, 103, 113, 149, 188; sexual danger and, 40–48; sexuality and, 3–4, 11, 20, 22–23, 44, 58, 61–62, 77, 95–105; social relations and, 113; study of, in urban centers, 6–7; tigress metaphor, 61–62 *See also* Indian English language
Eugenics, 99–101

Female Normal Schools, 31, 49–54, 64, 73
Femininity and language, 58, 64, 78
Fergusson, James, 119

Festivals, 16
Forbes, Geraldine, 88
Frere, Bartle, 36, 46–48, 51
Freud, Sigmund, 144

Gaekwad of Baroda, 69
Gandhi, Behramji Khursedji, 41
Gandhi, Mohandas Karamchand, 95–96, 138–39, 183
"Gardener and the Maid, The" (Sorabji), 127–28
G. B. L. (writer), 66–67, 68–69
Gender: Brahmanical power and, 55, 61; cultural codes and, 209 n. 37; desire and, 25, 27, 34; English and, 58, 77–78, 82, 126–32; familial relations and, 43–44; identity and shame, 141; language and, 13–17, 34–35; linguistic decline and, 16; literature and, 105–13; mimicry of English and, 61; nationalism and, 21; native history of English and, 11; performativity of, 37–38, 52; power and, 6, 8, 61, 80–82, 144; reform, 37; signification and, 22; studies, defined, 199 n. 33; subjectivity, 144
Gordon, Stewart, 14
Grant, Alexander, 51
Grewal, Inderpal, 168–69, 239 n. 27
Gujarati language, 34, 42–44, 50–52, 64, 68
Gupta, Charu, 25

Haddap, Vithal Vaaman, 77
Hennessey, Rosemary, 23, 238 n. 2, 239 n. 30
Heterosexuality: nationalism and, 26; as normative, 23; transnational reading public and, 138, 152
High Caste Hindu Woman (Ramabai), 123

Hindi language, 105
Hindu, The (newspaper), 97
Hindus: caste power, 68; castes and education, 15, 72; control over print resources, 55; masculinity, 25–26; mimicry of rulers, 61; modernity and, 5; Muslims vs., 74; Parsis and, 158; patriotism, 60; unique knowledge of, 107; women and English language, 9
Hindustan, 94, 96, 119, 177
Hurford, Miss, 120, 123, 131, 217 n. 30, 218 n. 32, 236 n. 31

"Ideal Woman, The" (Bhide), 132
INC (Indian National Congress), 72
Indian English language: desire and, 58; exclusivity of, 8; forces behind, 27; Indian womanhood and, 155; indigenization and, 12; mobile Indian subject and, 157; native identity and, 59; sexual power and, 13; social prohibition and, 155; women and, 5–9
Indian National Congress (INC), 72
Indian Social Reformer (ISR), 97–99
Indian Women's University (IWU), 83, 93, 95, 97–98; language policies of, 84; support for, 102–5
Indigeneity: anglicization and, 14, 18, 35; caste and, 13; colonialism vs., 24; Indian English language and, 12; nationalism and, 24; studies, 103; transnationalism and, 101
Individuation, 8, 134–36, 164, 214 n. 100, 236 n. 36
ISR (*Indian Social Reformer*), 97, 98–99
IWU (Indian Women's University), 83, 93, 95, 97–98; language policies of, 84; support for, 102–5
Iyer, G. Subramaniam, 97

Jeejeebhoy, Jamsetjee, 32, 241 n. 56
Jehangir, Cowasjee, 10
Jessawalla, Dosebai Cowasjee: autobiography of, 157; biculturalism of, 157–58; cosmopolitanism of, 163, 169, 174; English education of, 157–59, 161–62; individualism of, 163, 165, 166, 168, 170; mother of, 159–63; observations of, 171, 173, 174; subjectivity of, 163, 165, 168, 170; on tradition, 166, 170; travels, 169–73
Jewish education, 163–64
Joshi, Anandibai, 183

Kanitkar, Narayan B., 74, 77
Kapur, Ratna, 26
Karve, Dhondo Keshev, 85–90; on access for women, 85; Athavale and, 177–81; background, 83–87; criticism of, 95, 97–98, 104; on English as compulsory, 95–96, 103–4; Japanese influence on, 90–91, 103; marriage of, 87, 175–76; memoirs of, 83, 85, 91, 96, 101, 105; on mother tongue, 84, 94, 102, 105; reform by, 88–89; on reproduction, 93, 94, 108, 113; on sexual difference, 91–92; on women's education, 89–90, 92–94, 101–2, 105–6, 177
Kenealy, Arabella, 100–101
Kesari (newspaper), 60, 61, 65, 66, 71, 73–74
Knowledge, access to, 21
Kosambi, Dharmanand, 182
Kosambi, Meera, 19

Language: cultural mores and, 51; domesticity and, 64, 72; feminization of, 34; gender and 13–17, 34–35, 61; identity and, 33; sexuality and, 8, 16, 34, 59; sexualizing, 102; social context and, 5; symbolic value of, 34; translations, 101–2. *See also* Mother tongue
Liberal humanism, 27, 234 n. 63
Liberalism: caste and, 11, 136, 179, 187; colonial modernity and, 23–27; debates on, 7; education and, 46; language of, 30; reexamination of, 25; sexuality and, 32; Whiggish, 10
Linguistic ventriloquism, 63, 65, 147, 150
Literature by women, 68–69
Lokuge, Chandini, 151–52

Macaulay, Thomas Babington, 9–10, 12–13, 21, 79–80
Mahilashram, 88
Mahratta (newspaper), 60, 65, 66
Malabari, Behramji, 158
Mandlik, Saheb Vishwanath, 47–48
Marathi language: as academic subject, 15, 89; bilingualism and, 13, 30; biography in, 119; Brahmans and, 13–14; Dakshina Fund and, 29; English and, 16–17, 60, 66–67, 77; as iconic regional language, 15; instruction in, 51, 55, 64, 88, 90; literary style of, 61, 120; marginalization of, 23; nationalism and, 14, 15, 59, 120. Parsis and, 13–14; prominence of, 14; sexuality and, 32
Marriage: caste and, 18–19; companionate, 32, 46, 69, 107, 138, 148, 158, 164, 173, 175, 187, 239 n. 27; consummation of, 122, 138–39, 242 n. 4; education and, 43; remarriage, 139–40; state investment in, 38
Marshall Brothers publishing house, 150
Masculinity: of Hindus, 25–26; native, conception of, 55, 58, 62, 78–80; power and language, 144
Masks of Conquest (Viswanathan), 11–12

Masselos, Jim, 37, 44
Mayhew, Arthur, 10
Mayo, Katherine, 108, 189
Mazi Kahani (Athavale), 176
McDonald, Ellen, 40, 123
Meheribai (Jessawalla's mother), 159–63
Metcalf, Barbara, 118
Mimicry, 61, 77–80
"Minute on Education" (Elphinstone), 10
"Minute on Education" (Macaulay), 9–10, 12–13, 79–80
Modernity: colonial, 23–27; English language and, 5; of Indian tradition, 7; life histories and, 118–19; sexuality and, 23, 91; spirituality vs., 64–65; vernacular language and, 34, 60–61
Moral education, 42
Moropant, 130–32
Motherhood, 75, 81, 82, 90–94, 98, 105, 107
Mother tongue: domesticity and, 68, 81; education and, 47, 93–95, 97, 103, 108–9, 111–12; English vs., 102–3; reproduction and, 101; sexuality and, 16, 81, 84, 101; Tamil as, 34; use of term, 48, 68, 219 n. 43
Mueller, Max, 120
Mumbai Indu Prakash (newspaper), 79
Mumbai Vartman, 42–44, 47, 48, 54
Muñoz, José, 203 n. 98
Muslims: education and, 15; Hindu civilization and, 11; Hindus vs., 74

Nagarkar, Kiran, 3–4
Najmabadi, Afsaneh, 23
Naoroji, Dadabhai, 41
Naregal, Veena, 13–15, 30, 59, 60, 201 n. 56
Naruse, Mr., 91, 99
Natarajan, Kamakashi, 97

Nationalism: anticolonial, 18, 89, 101; Brahmanical, 136; colonialism and, 24–27, 37, 106; cultural, 37, 60, 74, 143; female emancipation and, 24, 185; gender and, 21, 24, 25, 180; hetero-, 26, 80, 186; Hindu, 15–16, 22, 24, 62, 72, 121, 177; Marathi linguistic, 14, 15, 59, 120; sexuality and, 7, 68, 154, 187; subjectivity and, 167
National service, 178–79
National Social Conference, 91–93, 178
Native, use of term, 195 n. 2
New English School for Boys, 11, 60, 89, 180
Nibandhmala (magazine), 59, 61
Nightingale, Florence, 126
Nikambe, Shevantibai, 149–55
Nineteenth Century and After (Booth), 99
Normal Schools, 31, 49–54, 64, 73
Northcot, Stafford, 49

O'Hanlon, Rosalind, 18–21, 31, 121, 142, 243 n. 30
Omvedt, Gail, 21

Palsetia, Jesse, 158
Panchayat, Parsi, 37
Panse, Venubai, 73
Parker, Kunal, 70
Parliamentary Act (1813), 198 n. 24
Parsi Chabuk, 42–44, 47, 48, 54
Parsis: English and, 16, 40; Hindus and, 158; language and, 13–14; patriarchy of, 160; women and modernity, 5
Patriarchy: caste, 11, 18, 20, 21, 23, 66, 74, 121, 151, 203–4 n. 105, 224 n. 13; diasporic, 189; hetero-, 155; native, 152, 162, 189; power of, 23, 121, 147, 155
Performativity, 37–38, 52, 175, 188, 197 n. 15

Perry, Erskine, 15, 42–43
Persian language, 14–16; marginalization of, 29, 33
Peshwa court, 14, 21–22, 29, 33
Phule, Jotiba, 15, 20–21, 59, 60, 97
Phule, Savitribai, 21–22
PNHS (Poona Native Girls' High School), 57, 70, 89, 117, 147, 177; curriculum debate at, 64–68, 71–74
Poona: elite gathering in, 57–58, 63; English studies in, 5–7; Marathi and, 14
Poona Native Girls' High School (PNHS), 57, 70, 89, 117, 147, 177; curriculum debate at, 64–68, 71–74
Poona Sanskrit College, 14, 15, 30, 59
Poona Vaibhav (newspaper), 70
Postcolonial critique, 9–13
Povinelli, Elizabeth, 214 n. 100
Power: education and, 43; of English, 4, 6, 8, 43, 165; gender and, 55, 61, 80–82, 144; Hindu caste, 68; language and, 4, 6, 19; patriarchal, 23, 121, 147, 155; queer critique of, 5; in sexuality, 22, 62; women and, 18
Prohibition: language and, 4, 138–49, 155; social, 146, 155, 236 n. 36
Prohibitions: on conjugal exclusivity, 146; on mother tongue, 102; standards of, 5; on teaching girls and women, 48, 97, 137, 155
Prostitution, 19, 70–71, 75, 77, 78, 121, 189

Queer studies: critique of power, 5; on normative sexuality, 23

Rakhmabai, Dr., 19, 43, 75–76, 128, 161, 211 n. 58, 221 n. 73
Ramabai, Pandita, 19–20, 57, 87–88
Ramaswamy, Sumathi, 34
Ramohan Roy, Raja, 49

Ranade, Mahadev Govind, 40, 57, 79, 88, 123; on English, 155; as judge, 215 n. 3; on liberal social reform, 90; marriage of, 137–41, 143, 145–49; on remarriage of widows, 224 n. 10
Ranade, Ramabai: autobiography of, 138, 155; Durga and, 142–43; education of, 137, 140–41, 143–48; English and, 143–48; marriage of, 137–41, 143, 145–49, 155; shame of, 141–43
Rao, Anupama, 134
Rao, Paramila, 72–73, 118
Rao, T. Madhava, 142
Rast Goftar (newspaper), 53
Ratanbai (Nikambe), 154–55; storyline, 150–51; themes, 151–53, 165
Ravan and Eddie (Nagarkar), 3–4
Report of Native Newspapers (RNN), 52
Reproduction: English and, 103, 113, 149, 183; Karve on, 93, 94, 108, 113; mother tongue and, 101; sexual difference and, 100, 108
Ritual: caste and, 8, 9, 22–23, 25, 70, 84, 118, 133–36, 138, 149, 151, 153–54, 158; sexuality and, 18, 21, 27, 55, 58, 81, 97, 102
RNN (*Report of Native Newspapers*), 52
Rubin, Gayle, 76

Sabha, Sarvajanik, 71
Sadana, Rashmi, 12
Sadgun Manjari (Agashe): background, 117–21; as biographical writing 122–26; on English and gender, 126–32
Sangari, Kumkum, 20
Sangeet Aadhunik Shikshan Vipaak Natika (Davne), 78
Sanskrit language: elevation of, 16, 120; forbidden to women, 19; marginalization of, 30, 33, 40; patronage of, 14

Savitri Akhyana (Moropant), 130–32
Scientific Basis of Women's Education (Chiplunkar), 106–7
Secularization of caste, 8, 9, 81, 118, 134–36
Sedgwick, Eve, 141
Seth, Sanjay, 13, 81, 177
Sexual-citational grafting, 8, 17, 34, 37, 308 n. 21
Sexuality: anxiety over, 26; caste and, 4, 11, 18, 22, 25, 31, 66, 121; danger and, 40–48; discourses on, 98–99; English and, 3–4, 11, 20, 22–23, 40–48, 58, 61–62, 77, 95–105; female, 11, 18, 55, 62, 68, 74, 87, 121, 133, 142; intellectual class and, 22; language and, 8, 16, 34; liberalism and, 32; Marathi and, 16; modernity and, 23, 91; morality and, 76; nationalism and, 7, 68, 154, 187; out-of-wedlock, 74; performance of, 243 n. 30; power of English and, 4, 6, 8; restrictions on, 133; ritualization of, 18, 21, 27, 55, 58, 81, 97, 102; secularization and, 135; study of history and, 206 n. 126
Sexual politics, 4
Shame, 141–42
Shankerseth, Jagonath, 44
Sharada Sadan, 87–88
Shinde, Tarabai, 19, 121
Shreemati Nathibai Damodar Thakersay Indian Women's University (SNDT), 83, 93, 95, 97–98; language policies of, 84; support for, 102–5
Signification, 21–22
SLSS (Students' Literary and Scientific Society), 31, 41–42, 44, 48–49
SNDT (Shreemati Nathibai Damodar Thakersay Indian Women's University), 83, 93, 95, 97–98; language policies of, 84; support for, 102–4, 105
Social mobility and English, 3
Sorabji, Cornelia, 123, 127, 129, 167, 232 n. 29
Sorabji, Jane, 127–28
Sorabji, Mary, 123, 127, 232 n. 27
Spirituality: modernity vs., 64–65; of women, 24, 25, 31
Spivak, Gayatri, 163, 167, 200 n. 42
Story of My Life, The (Jessawalla), 157; domestication of English in, 158–59
Stri Dharma Niti (Ramabai), 20
Stri Purush Tulana (Shinde), 121
"Stri Shikshan" (article), 70–71
Students' Literary and Scientific Society (SLSS), 31, 41–42, 44, 48–49
Subjectivity: colonialism and, 167; consumerism and, 164; English and, 58, 145; formation of, 8, 236–37 n. 40; gender, 144
Sudharak (newspaper), 65
Sumitra (magazine), 44–45
Sunkersett, Jagonath, 44
Suryadoya, The (newspaper), 50

Tagore, Rabindranath, 90–91, 186
Tamil language, 42
Taruni Shikshan Natika (Kanitkar), 74–77, 135, 136
Teacher-training schools, 49
Temple, Richard, 37–39
Thakersay, Vithaldas, 104
Tigress metaphor, 61–62
Tilak, Bal Gangadhar, 16, 60, 72–74, 95, 177
Times of India (newspaper), 47
Trevelyan, T. E., 10

Universalism, 25, 46, 48
Untouchables, 22

Vernacularists, 10
Vernacular languages. *See* Mother tongue
Viswanathan, Gauri, 11–13
Voting rights, 72, 118

Wadya, Hormusji, 97–98
Wagle, Bal Mangesh, 48
Wedderburn, Lady, 128
Wedderburn, William, 119
Westernization, 35, 78, 93, 178, 180
White supremacy, 80
Widowhood, 18, 19, 21, 22, 118, 121, 139–40, 231 n. 20, 231 n. 24, 242 n. 5
Widow Remarriage Act (1856), 139
Will-O'-The-Wisp (writer), 65, 68
Women: advent of, 23–24; Brahman, 22; domesticity and, 45, 63, 75, 95, 113; education of, 10–11, 39, 46, 57, 105–13, 143; emancipation of, 24, 71, 185; employment and conjugality, 107; English education of, 30–39, 48, 57, 102, 105–13; English language and, 5–10; forbidden languages to, 19; idealized, 27, 118; Indian compared to European, 39; literature by, 68–69; Marathi education of, 30; mimicry and, 77–80; modernity and, 5; obedience of, 18; prohibition on teaching of, 48, 97, 137, 153; significatory power of, 81, 82; social power and, 18, 81; spirituality of, 24, 25, 31; symbolism of, 81; in university, 93, 111; as viewing subjects, 241 n. 61; virtuous, 9, 23, 76, 125, 134–36, 171–81; voting rights of, 72. *See also* Gender; Sexuality
Women, Muslims and the Public Sphere (Gupta), 25
Wood's Despatch, 30, 35, 208–9 n. 30

Zirelli, Linda, 76

SHEFALI CHANDRA is an assistant professor in the Department of History, the International and Area Studies Program, and the Women, Gender and Sexuality Studies Program at Washington University in St. Louis.

LIBRARY OF CONGRESS CATALOGING-IN-PUBLICATION DATA
Chandra, Shefali
The sexual life of English : languages of caste and desire in colonial India / Shefali Chandra.
p. cm.   Includes bibliographical references and index.
ISBN 978-0-8223-5260-0 (cloth : alk. paper)
ISBN 978-0-8223-5227-3 (pbk. : alk. paper)
1. English language—Social aspects—India.
2. English language—India—History. 3. Women—Education—India—History. 4. English language—Study and teaching—India—History. 5. Language and sex—India.
6. India—Languages—Social aspects.
I. Title.   PE3502.I6C44 2012
420.9′54—dc23   2011035894

www.ingramcontent.com/pod-product-compliance
Lightning Source LLC
Chambersburg PA
CBHW070756230426
43665CB00017B/2377